In the House of the Law

In the House of the Law

Gender and Islamic Law in
Ottoman Syria and Palestine

Judith E. Tucker

UNIVERSITY OF CALIFORNIA PRESS

Berkeley   Los Angeles   London

University of California Press
Berkeley and Los Angeles, California

University of California Press, Ltd.
London, England

First Paperback Printing 2000

Library of Congress Cataloging-in-Publication Data

Tucker, Judith E.
    In the house of the law : gender and Islamic law in
Ottoman Syria and Palestine / Judith E. Tucker.
      p. cm.
    Includes bibliographical references and index.
    ISBN 978-0-520-22474-2 (pbk. : alk. paper)
  1. Women—Legal status, laws, etc.—Syria—History.
  2. Women—Legal status, laws, etc.—Palestine—History.
  3. Women—Legal status, laws, etc. (Islamic law)
  4. Turkey—History—Ottoman Empire, 1288–1918.
  5. Women—Syria—Social conditions. 6. Women—
Palestine—Social conditions. I. Title.
KMC145.W64T83 1998
305.42′095691—dc21   97-27168
                                        CIP

Chapter 2 of this book was previously published in a
different form as "Muftis and Matrimony: Islamic Law and
Gender in Ottoman Syria and Palestine," *Islamic Law and
Society*, 1, 3, 65–300 © Brill Publishers.

Printed in the United States of America

13   12

9 8 7 6

The paper used in this publication is both acid-free and
totally chlorine-free (TCF). It meets the minimum
requirements of ANSI/NISO Z39.48-1992 (R 1997)
(*Permanence of Paper*). ∞

For Sharif

CONTENTS

ACKNOWLEDGMENTS

The work on this book took place over a number of years, and had the help of many friends, colleagues, family members, and others.

I did much of the research in Nablus, the West Bank, and Amman, Jordan. I want to thank the late Shaykh Saad al-din al-ʿAlami for facilitating my use of the records of the Islamic court in Nablus, as well as the former *qadi* (judge) and his staff at the court. In Nablus, too, I am grateful to the families of Dr. Najib al-Nabulsi and Yasir Ubayd (Abu Nimr) for their hospitality. In Amman, I worked with records from the Damascus and Jerusalem courts housed in the Research and Documentation Center at the University of Jordan. I would like to acknowledge the work of Dr. Adnan Bakhit, the former director of the Center, and Dr. Nufan Raja al-Hamoud, its current director, in the task of collecting valuable materials for the study of Bilad al-Sham, and to thank them for their gracious reception of researchers like me. My husband's family in Amman, particularly Maryam Miqdadi, Said al-Musa, and Bahiyya and Subhiyya al-Musa, provided the warmth, fellowship, and fun that are so much the hallmarks of their household.

The writing of this book was given a great lift during a later nine-month stay in Jerusalem at the Centre for Research on Women, where Dr. Suha Hindiyyah and Fadwa Labadi provided an environment that encouraged me to think hard about issues of feminism across cultures. The women faculty members of the Women's Studies Program at Birzeit University in the West Bank formed another important group whose research and activities inspired by example; I would like to thank all of them for their friendship and advice: Ilham Abu-Ghazaleh, Lamis Abu-Nahleh, Rita Giacaman, Islah Jad, Penny Johnson, Eileen Kuttab, and Lisa Taraki. Other close friends in the area, including Mary McKone, Lee O'Brien, Susan Rockwell, and Anita Vitullo, were equally important for conversations, suggestions, and good times.

As has been true with all my work, I owe a great debt to the late Albert Hourani, whose early encouragement, intellectual curiosity, and generosity with the gift of his time and interest can never be repaid or forgotten.

Concrete assistance with this book came from many other quarters. Early in my work, Basim Musallam made the suggestion that I look into the *fatwas* literature as a source for social history, a suggestion that eventually bore much fruit. A number of people read and commented on specific chapters; these included Bruce Dunne, Zouhair Ghazzal, Baber Johansen, Aharon Layish, Annelies Moors, Leslie Peirce, and Steve Tamari. A number of others have helped over the years by discussing this material and lending their insights and interpretations; a by no means complete list must include Beshara Doumani, Mary Ann Fay, Ellen Fleischmann, Mary Hegland, Marlee Meriwether, and Peg Strobel. I want to thank Leila Ahmad and Brinkley Messick in particular for taking the time to do thorough readings of the entire manuscript and for many helpful comments that enabled me to make what were, I hope, improvements.

I also received invaluable assistance of all kinds from Liz Kepferle, and expert help with the final preparation of the manuscript from Sara Scalenghe.

Lynne Withey of the University of California Press lent guidance from an early stage, and Julie Brand proved a very helpful editor. I owe special thanks to William Carver, whose keen editorial eye and invaluable suggestions helped me to tighten both text and arguments.

I am grateful for the financial support I received as I worked on this project. Research and writing were funded, in part, by the Georgetown University Faculty Summer Research program, by a National Endowment for the Humanities summer grant, by the Fulbright-Hays Faculty Research Abroad program, and by the Fulbright Senior Scholar program.

For Karmah and Layth Elmusa, this project involved periods of travel and schooling in England and Palestine. I thank them for the flexibility they showed in adapting to life with strikes and curfews, and for the enormous pleasure of their company.

This book is dedicated to my husband, Sharif Elmusa, who was so essential to its completion. I wrote the book during a period of our life in which the bearing and raising of children figured very prominently. Sharif not only did his part in the household with great good cheer but also read versions of the manuscript with his customary care and asked questions that invariably made me rethink my assumptions. For his help and companionship, I cannot thank him enough.

J. E. T.
February 1997

The Eastern Mediterranean, ca. 1774

CHAPTER I

The Law, the Courts, and the Muftis

QUESTION: Two men were married to two virgins and each consummated the marriage. Then one claimed after consummation that he had found his bride already deflowered, and he sent her back to her family. Then he abducted her sister by making a night raid on her [the sister's] husband's house in the village, aided by a group of peasants. Now he wants to annul the marriage, but his wife claims that it was indeed he who deflowered her. Can he annul the marriage? If he accuses her of *zina'* [illicit intercourse] and she is found [somehow] to have been previously deflowered, should she be sentenced for *zina'*, and then killed, or suffer *hadd* punishment [the punishment prescribed by the Qur'an] or *ta'zir* [discretionary punishment], or is her testimony to be accepted?

ANSWER: The man's claim that "I found her deflowered" is of no consequence, because even if he really had found her deflowered he still must pay the entire *mahr* [dower] as legal opinion stipulates, and he does not have the option of annulling the marriage. And in any case, being deflowered does not necessarily mean that illicit intercourse has taken place, for virginity can be lost by jumping, or through menstruation, or with age, and so forth. The wife is guilty of nothing, and the one who did to her what has been mentioned above disobeys God, may He be exalted. The testimony of the woman is valid, such is the situation, and the dower in its entirety is required. . . . He [the husband] must bring his wife's sister back to the place from which he abducted her, and he should be imprisoned until he does so. And God knows best.[1]

Muslim legal thinkers in the seventeenth- and eighteenth-century Arab world were actively engaged in the discussion of women's place in their society. As this *fatwa*, or legal opinion, offered by Khayr al-Din al-Ramli, an eminent seventeenth-century jurist, suggests, they were able and willing to take on questions that spoke directly to the basic issues of women's rights in any society: it was the exercise of male power, the power to coerce and control the female, that Khayr al-Din sought to define and limit here. In the many fatwas offered and in the Islamic courts of the period, Muslim thinkers drew on a broad range of resources—their inherited legal tradition, their observations of their own society, their own ability to reason and judge—to address the questions of male power and female protections, of the law and gendered social roles, and of the existence, ultimately, of an Islamic gender system and its relevance to their own local society.

My decision to explore the ways in which this group of Muslim thinkers and Islamic institutions constructed gender in a particular time and place was influenced by how frequently today we see tradition and authenticity invoked as supports for a restrictive interpretation of women's rights and social roles. Fatima Mernissi, the prominent Moroccan feminist, has called for the revisiting of Islamic history, so that the definition of the authentic and the traditional would not be left solely in the hands of those with an antifeminist agenda. Her own work on the rereading of sacred Islamic texts, the Qur'an and the *hadith* (the traditions of the Prophet Muhammad), joins a battle of interpretation that is being waged with the concerns and needs of contemporary Muslim women in mind.

The return to the past, the return to tradition that men are demanding, is a means of putting things "back in order." An order that no longer satisfies everybody, especially not the women who have never accepted it. The "return" to the veil invites women who have left "their" place (the "their" refers to the place that was designated for them) to leave their newly conquered territories. And it is implied that this place in which society wants to confine them again is to be marginal, and above all subordinate, in accordance with the ideal Islam, that of Muhammad—the Prophet who, on the contrary, preached in A.D. 610 a message so revolutionary that the aristocracy forced him into exile.

The journey back in time then is essential, not because the pilgrimage to Mecca is a duty, but because analysis of the past, no longer as myth or sanctuary, becomes necessary and vital.[2]

Mernissi's study of the Qur'anic commentators, *hadith* collectors, and biographers of the early Islamic period juxtaposes the Prophet Muhammad's revolutionary message of social equality among all people to the conservative and regressive interpretations of that message as perpetrated by some powerful male members of the early Muslim community. In brief, Muhammad's revelation, as well as his daily words and deeds, pointed the way toward women's rights and gender democracy, but much of what he won for women was quickly modified, distorted, or completely lost as the political leaders and scholars of the first few centuries of Islam shaped tradition through various processes of selective and self-serving interpretation.

In returning to the sacred texts of the Qur'an and *hadith*, Mernissi sought to engage the Islamic tradition in its most central and authoritative form. An Islamic view of gender did not congeal into a fixed and hardened form, however, in those early years. On the contrary, a variety of interpretive texts—Qur'anic commentaries, *hadith* collections, biographies, and legal writings of all kinds—formed a growing and changing corpus of authoritative material that could be read and referenced by Muslim thinkers. As political structures, economic rhythms, and social arrangements changed over time, Muslim thinkers reflected on the relevance of various texts for their own times even while they added to the authoritative corpus with interpretive works of their own. Part of the task of reclaiming tradition, then, should include careful study of that tradition as it was shaped and molded throughout Islamic history. It is the long history of Islamic thought and of the lives people lived in harmony or tension with this thought that constitutes the Islamic heritage; and it is this history that furnishes a touchstone for understanding the whole process of creation of tradition and offers the possibility of re-membering and redeeming a past as neither "myth nor sanctuary."

LAW AND SOCIETY

In the following pages I explore the ways in which the intellectuals and the general population of a particular society and culture—in this case the urban milieu of Syria and Palestine in the seventeenth and eigh-teenth centuries—posed questions about gender and devised answers that suited their sense of their inherited tradition as well as their imme-diate needs. As they discussed and elaborated the *shari'a* (Islamic law) and took their business to the Islamic courts, they imbued legal texts with a meaning taken from their own lives. The study of the ways in which a Muslim community constructed a legal discourse on gender in a relatively "normal" period, at least one free of the social turmoil pro-duced by war, conquest, or rapid economic transformation, allows us to glimpse how one Muslim society understood the law and the gender sys-tem it ordained, and how it re-created tradition, without reference to outside pressures.

I do not mean to suggest that the law and the courts played a privi-leged role in the construction of gender in this society. Gender relations and roles were inscribed in local customs, oral tradition, and various writings both sacred and profane, only a small portion of which have been closely examined by modern scholars.[3] My decision to focus on the law was partly a practical one: there is a particularly rich body of sources for the study of legal discourse in the form of period fatwas (collections of judicial responsa) as well as the records of the Islamic courts themselves. None of this material is transparent, of course, as I discuss below with respect to problems of approach and method, but it is abundant and readily available. In addition, my undertaking of what is essentially a legal study also reflects my sense of the locus of current debates on women and gender. Much of the discussion of women and men, their natures and capacities, in countries where the majority of the population is Muslim today, is being framed in terms of how Islam genders society through the precepts of the shariʿa. And it is the shariʿa, in one form or another, that is the official law governing gender relations in the vast majority of these countries.

Although many of the current discussions of Muslim women's rights and power and of their appropriate place in society and their relations with men are anchored in an understanding of the nature of Islamic law, there is wide disagreement about how to approach this law. Practicing Muslims view the shariʿa as divine in origin, based on Qurʾanic revelation and the traditions of the Prophet Muhammad. The existence of the law makes it possible for them to lead a good Muslim life: it provides guidance by setting forth the rights and responsibilities of family members and by prescribing the kind of individual behavior that is acceptable or laudable, as opposed to undesirable or expressly forbidden, in the context of a Muslim society.

Even among Muslims, however, there is a disagreement about what the shariʿa is and how we are to draw upon it for guidance. Conservative thinkers embrace and justify gender difference as it is inscribed in some parts of the shariʿa; their resistance to change and interpretation rests on the notion that we should not tamper with the tenets of the shariʿa that have been transmitted to us. The various regulations about marriage and divorce, child custody, and family obligations—all highly gendered—are to be scrupulously observed. As Barbara Stowasser points out, a twentieth-century conservative like Shaykh al-Shaʿarawi of Egypt may feel the need to defend aspects of the shariʿa against criticism coming from the West by using information gleaned from the natural, social, or pseudosciences, but he will remain utterly opposed to any adjustment of the law to accommodate modern needs.[4] The shariʿa is God's law for all time; the Muslim jurist preserves and transmits that law but does not interpret it. This conservative position is predicated on the idea that the law originated in the Qur'an and the *sunna* (the sayings and doings of the Prophet), underwent a brief period of growth and development through interpretation by the founders of the various legal schools, and then settled into an ideal and enduring form. The shariʿa, then, passed down through the Islamic centuries, is complete and sufficient as a guide for gender relations in the modern world.

Conservatives in Islam cannot but feel somewhat beleaguered: they constantly confront two competing positions in Islamic circles that, in their own very different ways, treat the law as far less rigid. On the one hand, there is the position of the Islamic reformists who, since the days of the nineteenth-century thinkers al-Afghani, Muhammad ʿAbduh, and Muhammad Rashid Rida, have subscribed to the idea that qualified Muslim jurists can and should undertake to interpret the law so as to make it a relevant and useful guide for life in the modern world. The reformer returns to the Qur'anic text as the basis for the law and argues for a reading that emphasizes the equality rather than the complementarity of the sexes. In general, he locates the statements of the Qur'an about gender in sociohistorical context: those statements describe how best to deal with gender issues, given the conditions of the time. Fazlur Rahman, a reformer or modernist liberal (as he terms it) in his own right, discusses the reformer and his agenda in sympathetic terms:

> In the field of the general rights of spouses, while the Qur'an proclaims that husband and wife have reciprocal rights and obligations, it adds that "men are but one degree superior to women" (II,228) because the man is the breadwinner and responsible for the sustenance of the wife (IV,34). From this, two diverging lines of argument have resulted. The conservative holds that this statement of the Qur'an is normative, that the woman, although she can possess and even earn wealth, is not required to spend on the household, which

must be solely the concern of the male, and that, therefore, the male enjoys a certain superiority. The modernist liberal, on the other hand, argues that the Qur'anic statement is descriptive, that, with the inevitable change in society, women can and ought to become economically independent and contribute to the household, and hence the spouses must come to enjoy absolute equality.[5]

In such ways the reform or liberal position claims the juristic right to interpretation (*ijtihad*) when it is necessary to preserve the true intention of the text, as opposed to its surface utterances, which are bound by the temporality, as opposed to the universality, of the Qur'anic message. This is the argument that indeed has buttressed many of the attempted and actual reforms of the shari'a in the realm of personal status in the twentieth century.

On the other hand, there are the Islamists, the second of the two groups opposing the conservative view, who also call for a return to Qur'anic principles, but without the reformist agenda. To return truly to the Qur'an and the *sunna* is to strip away the accretions and false practices produced by centuries of corruption and misrule, to reclaim the pure Islamic message. It is the original message about gender, as divined from various Qur'anic verses and the practices of the early Muslim community, that must serve as a guide for life in all times and places. Islamists deny the legitimacy of the reformist agenda: there is no need to adjust the shari'a to modern life, for the shari'a has eternal relevance.

But this shari'a is the law as gleaned from the original sources; in other words, Islamists are forced to engage in a good deal of interpretation if they are to construct a shari'a without the benefit of assistance from centuries of legal thought and practice. They undertake such interpretation solely to reach the true meaning of the sacred texts, however, not to cater to transient human needs and impulses. Such an approach guided the members of Iran's Assembly of Experts, convened in 1979 to fashion a constitution for the new Islamic Republic. "On matters relating to marriage, divorce, and polygyny, he [Ayatollah Safi] said, the jurists and the men in the assembly would base their decisions on the rulings of the Qur'an. They would do so even if these rulings upset women or were disliked by some men. And since the Constitution would reflect God's commandments, the members would decide these issues in the same way, whether or not there was a single woman in the assembly, and explain their decisions to the people."[6] Here we have a clear statement of an Islamist methodology: God's rules for marriage are to be found in the Qur'an and then applied to Muslim society, regardless of sociohistorical context. The Islamist clerics give themselves and other devout Muslims an active role in the construction of a modern shari'a, but it is not a role justified by the demands of modernization or the pressures of the West.

In addition to codifying shari'a family law, Islamization programs in Iran, Pakistan, and Sudan have included the introduction of laws that not only criminalize extramarital sex but also prescribe severe punishment for contraventions. Because the nature and punishment of these *hadd* (pl. *hudud*) crimes, as well as the evidence needed to convict, are defined in the Qur'an, the activation of these laws appears to fall well within the Islamists' mandate. Supporters of Islamization argue that the institution of severe punishments (from lashing to stoning, depending on the status of the perpetrators) for both partners in any form of extramarital sexual intercourse does not discriminate against women—for punishment is equally harsh. Indeed, at least one scholar insists that the record in Pakistan shows that the "*hudud* ordinances," despite objections raised by human rights organizations, have not had an adverse impact on women, largely because so few cases result in punishment, and because men are more likely to be found guilty than are women.[7] But in the context of the Islamist program of instituting the shari'a in order to redraw Muslim society, the activation of *hudud* laws lies in the context of a legal system that allows men but not women to seek sexual variety through multiple spouses and ease of divorce: it is the sexual *control* of women that is largely at issue here. It has also been noted that in some cases, such as Sudan and Iran, the Islamization of criminal law has tended to relax the rules of evidence and expand the application of *hudud* punishments well beyond that envisioned by the classical formulations of the shariʿa, thus resulting in novel forms of repression.[8]

Not all Islamists agree that codification of the shariʿa is necessary to, or even desirable for, the realization of an Islamic society. Although Islamists who have moved into positions of political power have not hesitated to legislate in the name of the shariʿa, a serious argument can be made that codification and legislation actually contravene the law. Some Islamists who do not hold state power, like those in Egypt, oppose codification of the shariʿa on the grounds that the law exists as a reference and guide for judges, not as an instrument of state control.[9] Muslim jurists or others with sufficient knowledge and probity must preserve the ability to apply the shariʿa in specific circumstances as they know best: the law is God's law, not to be harnessed to the needs and interests of the state.

Although today's Muslim legal scholars may differ in orientation and approach, most efforts toward the elaboration of an Islamic gender system are being undertaken principally by the pens and voices of Islamist interpreters. The Islamist vision of an Islamic gender system not only lays great emphasis on male/female difference in social life, but also posits Islamic law on gender as unitary, unchanging, and sacrosanct, a law whose roots in the early Islamic period serve to define and structure gender difference for all time. In reaching back to the early sources in order to construct a version of the shariʿa for the present, to be embodied in civil codes that govern male-female relations in the family and penal codes that criminalize illicit sexual activity, Islamist thinkers display little or no systematic interest in the intervening centuries of Islamic history and thought.

My purpose here, then, is to raise some questions about the history of Islamic legal discourse on gender, and to challenge, I hope, what seems to be an ahistorical and incomplete vision of what Islam has to say about, and do with, gender. I follow in Fatima Mernissi's footsteps, but focus on a different time and place. My concern here is not with the vision, intentions, and life of the Prophet Muhammad and his early followers, but rather with a Muslim community that, some thousand years later, spoke, wrote, and lived an Islamic tradition. I approach this material as a historian, a feminist, and a non-Muslim. I look at gender in two distinct ways.[10] First, gender is a *symbolic construction* produced, in this instance, by the Muslim thinkers who developed a consciously Islamic legal discourse on gender over the great breadth of time and space of Islamic history. I do not mean to suggest that this discourse was produced in isolation from a lived social world. On the contrary, the Muslim intellectuals who elaborated legal positions on the rights, power, and social responsibilities of men as men and women as women inhabited, and responded to, the society of which they formed a part. Their construction of gender as symbol cannot be isolated from the second aspect of gender—gender conceived of as a *social relationship*.

Gender as a social relationship is the product of the historical development of human experience, a relationship that changes, evolves, and adapts in rhythm with a changing society. We are fortunate to be able to draw, not only on the ruminations of prominent jurists (the *muftis*), but also on the minutes of actual proceedings of the Islamic courts in order to understand how legal thought developed in relation to the strategies that individuals pursued in court. Women and men pressed claims or defended interests on the basis of gender, and the court judges (*qadis*) and jurisconsults (*muftis*) molded their judgments and opinions in response to these laypeople's arguments and activities. Study of the court records, then, helps us to recognize the dynamics of interaction between scholarly legal discourse and the lived experience of the many Muslims, and non-Muslims as well, who brought their own expectations and understandings of gender and family to the Islamic courts. The courts witnessed the interaction between gender as symbol and gender as social relationship on a concrete level. Islamic legal discourse evolved in rhythm and reciprocity with the development of gendered social relations on the ground. Any study of the law must be a historical study, in the sense that social context—the ways in which the law was elaborated in response to concrete social, economic, and political conditions—is of paramount importance.

LAW AS HISTORY

Until rather recently, Ottoman Syria and Palestine in the eighteenth century would not have been targeted as fertile ground for inquiry into the development of Islamic law: received wisdom has long held that jurists in this period applied the law in a mechanical fashion, in accordance with the idea that the "gate of *ijtihad*" had been closed, and that jurists therefore had no license to interpret the law in response to changing situations. The authoritative pioneers of Western scholarship on Islamic law, Joseph Schacht and J. N. D. Anderson, concurred that the late ninth century marked the end of the development of Islamic legal doctrine.[11] From that point forward, Muslim jurists worked with stable sacred texts and settled doctrine: their task was one of explaining and applying the law, not of interpreting it. The jurists no longer expended effort on mastering and interpreting God's law through the exertion of their mental powers of analysis: the main mental activity for jurists was not *ijtihad* (interpretation) but rather *taqlid*, the acceptance and application of the doctrines of established schools and jurists. Islamic jurisprudence (*fiqh*) had thus become a theoretical construct without history; the *usul al-fiqh*, the sources and methodology of the law, had become a form of arcane and mummified knowledge that had little or nothing to do with the social experiences of Muslims over the ensuing centuries. Actual legal practice, by contrast, continued to be shaped by all sorts of other influences, including local custom, political expedience, and the whims of local officials. The study of Islamic law was the study of cultural artifact, whereas the study of actual legal practice was the study of the vagaries of political and economic life.[12] Islamic law, the thinking went, would have nothing to tell us about the social history of a Muslim community.

Recent scholarship focusing on Islamic law and society, however, has sharply questioned such conclusions. First, the entire concept of the "closing of the gates of *ijtihad*" has been thoroughly undermined. Wael Hallaq, in his "Was the Gate of Ijtihad Closed?" demonstrated that *ijtihad* was clearly a widely accepted practice throughout the Islamic centuries, though not necessarily so termed. Although the use of *ijtihad* was at times controversial, there was never a consensus that the law was no longer open to interpretation. Indeed, as Rudolph Peters argues elsewhere, a living tradition of *ijtihad* was pressed into the service of the Islamic movements of the eighteenth and nineteenth centuries. Muslim thinkers like Shah Wali Allah (d. 1762) and al-Sanusi (d. 1859) criticized blind adherence to any one legal school and viewed *ijtihad* not just as a permissible practice but as a responsibility of Muslims.[13] There is nothing particularly innovative, then, in the use Islamists and Reformers make of *ijtihad*. More important, the license some Muslim jurists exercised in interpreting the law opens the door to the possibility that legal doctrine was not in fact frozen, but rather was evolving in rhythm with social and political developments over the centuries.

A closer look at the actual mechanisms by which the law evolved suggests that it was not primarily changes in the texts of *usul al-fiqh* that allowed for doctrinal development, but rather innovation in other legal genres. Prior to the modern (and contested) codification of the shari'a, no one text or definitive set of texts embodied the whole of Islamic law. Like bodies of law elsewhere, Islamic law has had a long and vast textual life: through the medium of a number of different types of texts, Muslim thinkers have attempted to understand and implement God's law. Brinkley Messick, in his study of text and law in Yemen, points to the possibility of change and fluidity in a scholarly tradition based on a plurality of authoritative texts:

> Authoritative texts are as fundamental to the history of shari'a scholarship as they are to the history of other intellectual disciplines. Such a text was "relied upon" in a place and time: the knowledgeable consulted it, specialists based findings upon it, scholars elaborated its points in commentaries, teachers clarified its subtleties, students committed its passages to heart. . . . The

fates of such texts were diverse, ranging from an enduring general prominence or more limited respect among the cognoscenti to a purely ephemeral authority and the all-but-forgotten status of the superseded.[14]

A Muslim jurist of, say, the early eighteenth century would be well acquainted with (and would have committed to memory large parts of) a number of authoritative texts—including the Qur'an, the *hadith* reports, works of *furu' al-fiqh* (the substantive Islamic law that was elaborated in a variety of texts, including the *mutun* or textbooks that summarized the doctrine of his own legal school) and the *shuruh* (commentaries on legal doctrine in relation to specific situations or problems)—as well as the collections of fatwas (the responsa or answers to specific legal queries) that had been delivered by previous jurists of his school and by others who enjoyed a reputation for learning and uprightness.

Some types of legal texts accommodated change and growth in legal doctrine, while others were fairly impermeable. Scholars accepted the Qur'an and the *hadith* reports as authoritative texts, not subject to any revision in substance or interpretation. And despite the persistence of the claim to *ijtihad*, there is little evidence to suggest that the *mutun* underwent any significant substantive development after the tenth and eleventh centuries. Indeed, according to Baber Johansen, Western scholars who based their theory of the steady-state character of Islamic law on their readings of *mutun* were not mistaken in their claims of continuity and conservatism. When we come to the *shuruh* texts, however, we begin to see some room for maneuver: in the process of commenting on the *mutun*, the jurists even within a given school of law demonstrate the possibility of multiple legal opinions about a particular doctrine. The commentaries offer different legal opinions concerning the interpretation of doctrine, thereby suggesting that schools of law can harbor more than one opinion on a given point. It is the fatwa collections, however, that are, for Johansen, the locus of doctrinal change.[15]

In a fatwa, the mufti (jurisconsult) responds to a question concerning the application of law to a specific problem confronting a member of his community. In devising his answer, the mufti may review the relevant material from *mutun* and *shuruh* literature as well as citing fatwas from renowned muftis of his own legal school. He weighs and sifts these opinions in light of the details of the actual case before him and reaches a decision that may constitute a restatement of prior opinion or actually entail a shift in the interpretation of legal doctrine. In either case, there is little doubt that the mufti knew himself to be engaged in an enterprise of considerable mental effort in which he called upon not only his knowledge of the texts of his tradition but also his ability to deal with many internal contradictions in the tradition and interpret the meaning of these texts in the specific historical context before him. The resulting fatwa was not a binding legal judgment but rather a considered opinion, of an informational nature, that had no necessary outcome but might, of course, have a significant impact in a particular case and, moreover, on the law over time.[16]

Muftis did not proceed in their deliberations in an entirely random fashion. They were guided in their work by manuals that outlined both the qualifications a mufti should bring to the work of issuing fatwas and the procedures he should employ. An examination of manuals (*adab al-mufti*) of the Hanafi legal school from the fifteenth, sixteenth, and seventeenth centuries should leave us in no doubt that muftis were expected to have the training and knowledge necessary to take on a challenging task.[17] Although the manuals differ in details, they all include the requirement that a mufti be in control of the received texts, including the Qur'an, the *hadith*, the biographies of the companions of the Prophet, the key histories, and the texts essential to a mastery of the theory and principles of the law in general and of his own legal school in particular. In some cases, a mufti is also expected to know Arabic grammar, arithmetic, and the customs of the people of his community. The mufti acquires such knowledge to the end of developing his capacity for *ijtihad*, and although some authors of the manuals doubt whether individuals fully capable of interpreting the law can be found, there is no question that such is the mandate of the mufti. The mufti should be guided in the process of interpretation, according to the manuals, by his clear recognition of a hierarchy of textual sources. When he evaluates legal texts, for example, the Hanafi mufti should privilege the writings of the eponymous founder of that school, Abu Hanifa (d. 767). The works of his disciples, Abu Yusuf, Muhammad b. Hasan, Zufur b. Hudhayl, and Hasan b. Ziyad, enjoy derivative authority and should be weighed in that order. When the mufti comes to make a decision, he draws on his knowledge of the texts and his capacity for interpretation; if he must choose between two equally valid positions, he should choose the one that is more convenient for his petitioner.

As scholars begin to pay more attention to the muftis and their fatwas, we are learning to appreciate the role the fatwa has played in the evolution of legal doctrine. In Hallaq's examination of a murder case in twelfth-century Cordoba, jurists applied the existing legal doctrine of the Maliki school and allowed the victim's brother and sons to demand the execution of the murderer as their right of retaliation. The victim's children were still in their legal minority, however, and therefore could not exercise their right to choose between retaliation and the payment of blood-money. Several Maliki jurisconsults and the Maliki judge in the case concurred that the doctrine pertaining to this case, elaborated by none other than Malik b. Aras himself, supported the position that the victim's agnates could act unilaterally as long as the children were still minors. At this juncture, a leading Maliki jurist of the time, Ibn Rushd, chose to issue a fatwa in which he acknowledged the existing legal doctrine but argued that the application of the doctrine in this case violated the principles of Islamic law: the jurists had failed to take into account the fact that the murderer was drunk at the time of the crime, the need to protect the rights of the minor children, and the Islamic preference for pardon over execution. Above all, he insisted in his fatwa on his responsibility as a legal thinker to exercise his mental powers:

> [Those seekers of knowledge] did not understand what lay behind
> my opinion, and they thought that the jurisconsult must not

abandon the authoritative doctrine applicable to the case. But what they thought is incorrect, for the jurisconsult must not follow a doctrine, nor issue legal opinions according to it, unless he knows that it is sound. . . . The doctrine contrary to which I have issued a legal opinion runs counter to the fundamental principles of Islamic jurisprudence. . . . Accordingly, sound reasoning requires one to abandon the [traditional] doctrine in favor of that which is more appropriate, especially in view of the fact that the killer was intoxicated when he committed the crime.[18]

Not only did Ibn Rushd take a legal position that flew in the face of a long-established legal doctrine, but his fatwa was subsequently incorporated into the corpus of Maliki jurisprudence, where it achieved the status of equally acceptable doctrine, all of which supports Hallaq's argument that growth and change in Islamic law came largely through the activities of the muftis.[19]

Collections of fatwas from seventeenth- and eighteenth-century Syria and Palestine illustrate a range of style that demonstrates a divergence of views concerning what constituted the proper role of the mufti and the fatwa in that period, as well as differences in the background and training of the muftis themselves. Khayr al-Din al-Ramli, a mufti in Ramla in the seventeenth century, Hamid b. ʿAli al-ʿImadi, a mufti in Damascus in the eighteenth century, and ʿAbd al-Fattah al-Tamimi, a mufti in Jerusalem in the eighteenth century, all followed the Hanafi *madhhab*, the official Sunni school under the Ottoman Empire. In delivering their fatwas, however, they took distinctly different approaches to questions of textual authority and their mandate as interpreters of the law. Khayr al-Din, as we shall see, might refer directly to the Qurʾan and the writings of Abu Hanifa, the founder of his school, as well as to collections of fatwas he considered authoritative. He also felt it appropriate, however, to draw on his knowledge of local custom and human nature in order to fashion legal decisions that were well suited to the specific contexts of the cases at hand. Expansive and discursive in style, Khayr al-Din's fatwas display the way in which he exercised his mental powers. al-'Imadi wrote closer to the texts: when he reasoned, he was careful to cite authoritative fatwas, including those of Khayr al-Din, and he rarely went outside the accepted legal sources to justify his decisions. Like Khayr al-Din, however, he often reviewed a number of different options culled from the sources before he settled on the best choice in a given situation. al-Tamimi, by contrast, delivered his opinions in a terse shorthand style, devoid of textual reference or juristic reasoning. His fatwas consist of a brief statement of the question posed and an even briefer delivery of the response: for him, seemingly, there was only one authoritative answer to any given question.

These three muftis, then, went about their business in rather different ways. We encounter here a whole spectrum of understanding of the fatwa and the mufti. The amount of specific detail about the case at hand, the display of juristic reasoning, and the citation of authoritative text vary markedly from one authored set of fatwas to another. We can assume that all three muftis were familiar with the fatwa collections of their predecessors and that all therefore worked from similar models, but their perceptions of their own roles as muftis diverged significantly: Khayr al-Din practiced *ijtihad* openly and without apology; al-'Imadi was somewhat more circumspect and careful to cite textual precedent; and al-Tamimi gave the impression that rote application of preexisting rules comprised the sum total of his duties. Are we dealing here with individual preferences, with discrepancies in training, with contextual variations? We cannot be sure. Legal schools and mufti manuals notwithstanding, however, there was more than one way to deliver a fatwa in seventeenth- and eighteenth-century Syria and Palestine.

Some of these fatwas were occasioned by legal cases brought before a qadi (judge) in an Islamic court. In the Ottoman period in Syria and Palestine, all major cities and towns housed an Islamic court or tribunal (*mahkama*) presided over by a qadi appointed by the Ottoman government. The voluminous records of court transactions, the *sijill*s, testify to the many uses local residents made of the court. The court functioned as a registry office: the buying, selling, and endowing of real estate, the establishment of business partnerships, the certification of loans, the partition of estates—all these as well as other transactions for which it might be useful to have official recognition—were faithfully recorded in court.[20] In most cases, the recording of such transactions was a straightforward exercise requiring little more from the qadi than his presence. Residents came to the court most often not to litigate as such, but to create a record that might be useful in the future in laying claim to a piece of property or in collecting on a debt.

A minority of cases, however, did involve what we would identify as litigation: claims of nonpayment of debt, accusations of theft or injury, and demands for support or custody were some of the issues that were brought for judgment, not solely for purposes of registration. When a contested issue came to the court, the qadi would be called upon to exercise an active judicial role by examining evidence, calling witnesses, questioning litigants, and deciding which points of law were applicable to the case. Zouhair Ghazzal has presented such a contested case in detail, one in which a Beirut qadi in 1844 examined a claim of illegal appropriation of a *waqf* (religious endowment).[21] The qadi not only worked his way through the problem in the usual fashion by calling witnesses, demanding oaths, and such, but he also explained the legal texts and precedents on which he based his final judgment. Such explanation was far from the norm in court records: usually the qadi issued his judgment without informing us what texts he had consulted and what reasoning process he had employed. That the Beirut qadi felt it necessary to supply the background to his judgment suggests, according to Ghazzal, that such cases did not arise very often.

The qadis were no more forthcoming in the other types of cases they examined, namely those that had to do with family matters and the relations between men and women that most concern us in this study. Residents of the local community came to court to register marriages, to dispute marriage arrangements, to negotiate some types of divorce, to argue about child custody, to claim support from various family members, and to protest sexual assault. Although there were far fewer of these types of cases than of those involving business and property exchange, they were, with the exception of the recording of ordinary marriage contracts, much more contentious in tone. Most of these cases feature a litigant who felt strongly entitled, aggrieved, or both. The voice of lived experience comes through these cases more vividly than it does in most property cases. Although the narrative of the events that led up to the court appearance was no doubt shaped by the court scribe, many of the details of these "as told to" stories are clearly based on a litigant's verbal testimony and capture not just the sequence of events but also the anger, chagrin, or bewilderment that the victim experienced. In addition, all of the cases dealing with family matters were strongly gendered, in the sense that women and men made their claims or defended their actions with explicit reference to their rights or obligations as gendered individuals. The qadi, however, is just as shadowy a figure here as he is in property cases. He delivers a judgment at the end of the day, but we are rarely informed about the relevant texts and reasoning.

Ghazzal, on the basis of his work on the Beirut case and others, warns us that the records of actual court cases cannot be read in isolation as simple exercises in judicial reasoning or reflections of social reality. Court documents were drafted by qadis and scribes with certain ends in mind. In the quarrel about *waqf* property, for example, the case is ultimately decided not on the basis of substantive legal reasoning but on the authority of a powerful local official. Legal cover may have been sought for the outcome, but an examination of legal argument alone would not enable us to understand this case. It is in the way in which this case was embedded in local society, in the way in which it furthered the interests of powerful individuals, that it finds its logic and meaning. Almost all court records present us with similar problems of interpretation. We are rarely privy to the social context of the case, to prior disputes or agreements between litigants, or to judicial collusion with local powerholders. Nor can we be sure of the actual outcome of the case: was a particular judgment upheld and implemented? A case is not complete in itself. Still, the cases in which marital problems, child-custody struggles, or sexual assaults are brought before the qadi in search of recourse are one of the few windows we have on how people of the time perceived their rights, and what they expected from their social relationships. The *sijill*s are that most rare form of historical document, one that records the ideas and strategies of the common person, albeit filtered through the lens of judicial and scribal authority.

What was the relationship between the system of Islamic courts and the mufti and his fatwas? Were the innovations and doctrinal developments of the fatwa occasioned or furthered in some way by judicial practice in the courts? Were qadis fully cognizant of the ways in which the muftis of their era were interpreting the law? Thanks to the work of Haim Gerber, we have some ideas about the role of the mufti in the core regions of the Ottoman Empire.[22] In Istanbul, Ankara, Bursa, and Kayseri, the mufti and his fatwa were an integral part of court proceedings. In Bursa, for example, fatwas issued by the grand mufti of Istanbul were often brought to court in support of the position of a litigant. This semi-official statement of how the law was to be applied in an actual human situation contributed much to the qadi's deliberations: Gerber suggests that, indeed, the mufti supplied the critical link between legal thought and court practice. In this role, we find two distinct facets to the mufti's activities. First, as Ottoman officials, the muftis of the core regions tended to issue fatwas that supported official Ottoman edicts and standardized certain points of law at the expense of the qadis' discretionary leeway. Second, the muftis took a "pragmatic and liberal" approach insofar as they were ready to accommodate various social and economic changes of the time. Muftis functioned, then, not only as the link between legal thought and practice, but also as an interface between the state and the courts, so as to ensure that court decisions were compatible with official interpretations of the law. In both aspects of their work, the muftis were an integral part of the life of the court.

The relationship between the mufti and the court in Ottoman Syria and Palestine does not seem to have been precisely what it was in the core regions. There were pivotal differences in the background, training, and official standing of the muftis in the outlying regions that could not but modify the role they played, as contrasted with the role of the muftis in the core. The muftis in southern Syria and Palestine were mostly local men, many of whom had been educated in Cairo, Mecca, or Damascus; and with the exception of the mufti of Damascus, they did not form part of the ranks of Ottoman officialdom. The office of mufti also might remain within a particular family for a period of time: in Damascus, first the 'Imadi family and then the Muradi family controlled the position of Hanafi mufti from the latter part of the seventeenth century right through the first half of the nineteenth century.[23] Many of the muftis shared neither language nor educational background with the qadis, some of whom were Turkish-speaking Ottoman officials often arrived from outside to head the local courts for a year or two.[24] Not surprisingly, there is little evidence to suggest that the mufti and qadi worked hand-in-glove. Although a litigant occasionally appeared in court with a fatwa delivered by the local mufti in support of his or her case, this practice was by no means the standard procedure that it appeared to be in the core regions. Many of the muftis' fatwas do not seem to be connected to a particular court case at all, but rather have the look of responses to individual requests for a legal opinion, or even reflections on specific local situations they came to know of. Unlike their core-region counterparts, most Syrian and Palestinian muftis served the court system only as a secondary endeavor; their primary mission was that of delivering legal advice to the local community of which they were a part. So many of their fatwas were delivered without reference to a pending court case that we can only assume that they sometimes acted as legal guides and arbiters for people who wished, for one reason or another, to avoid the court altogether. Such an impression is reinforced, in the case of the muftis I studied, by the richness of their fatwas, in terms of the kinds of subjects and situations covered, in comparison to the *sijill*s. They delivered opinions on the legality of various local customs, for example, that it is difficult to find mention of in the court records.

I do not mean to suggest, however, that the muftis operated at cross-purposes with the courts; on the contrary, the doctrines that the muftis espoused seem to be faithfully followed in court. There is no apparent disjuncture between the approach of the muftis and that of the qadis, but the Syrian and Palestinian muftis seem to have maintained a direct line to their communities and a willingness to take on legal problems raised outside of the court venue.

The court material I use in this study comes from the extant records of the Islamic courts of Damascus, Nablus, and Jerusalem in the eighteenth century. Damascus and Jerusalem were chosen as the home territories of Hamid b. ʿAli al-ʿImadi and ʿAbd al-Fattah al-Tamimi, respectively. The Nablus records, in the absence of records from Ramla, provide material from a Palestinian highland town that shares, with Ramla, the characteristics of a market town serving an agricultural hinterland. Although the vast majority of cases in these records deal with property relations of some kind, mostly sales of real estate and *waqf* business, residents of all three towns also came to court for a variety of other purposes, many of which impinged upon the question of gender relations central to this study. I have used a limited number of cases, selected from a reading of six complete court registers (*sijills*) from the three towns, in order to be able to understand what kinds of issues the urban population brought to court, and how the judges applied legal doctrine. In their deliberations and judgments, both the muftis and the courts of the period shared a specific historical context, the contours of which necessarily frame this study.

THE SETTING

The muftis and courts of Damascus, Jerusalem, Nablus, and Ramla were all located in geographic proximity in a region linked by complex administrative, economic, and cultural ties. Under the Ottoman Empire, the area of southern Syria and Palestine was part of the province of Damascus, and all of the inhabitants of these towns were ruled by the governor seated in Damascus.[25] The authority of other powerful officials— the *mutasallim* or governor's deputy, the *qadi al-qudah* or chief judge, and the official Hanafi mufti—also extended, at least in theory, throughout the province. The governor made an annual tour of the provincial territory, the main object of which was to collect tax revenues, earmarked for the support of the pilgrimage to Mecca, from the various officeholders in the province's districts (*sanjaqs*), which included the districts of Ajlun and Lajjun, Nablus, Jaffa, Gaza and Ramla, and Jerusalem.[26] Aside from this annual assertion of governance and exaction of taxes, day-to-day administration in the province was delegated to a number of local deputy governors and local qadis and muftis, some appointed from Damascus and others who owed their positions to local nomination. The ability of the governor and other officials in Damascus to project their power throughout the province was limited no doubt by a number of factors, not the least of which was the governor's responsibility for the pilgrimage caravan, which took him out of the province for four months out of every year.[27] The other top officials were kept busy as well, with their responsibilities in the city, and had no tradition of annual tours of the province like that of the governor. At the same time, many of the courts of the provincial towns were staffed by Damascus-born officials, and notable families from provincial towns often intermarried with their Damascene counterparts.[28] Despite the limited nature of centralized government at the time, the towns of Damascus, Jerusalem, Nablus, and Ramla formed part of the same administrative unit, were subject to rule by the same provincial officials, and shared a provincial elite.

The economic integration of the region was very much a product of flourishing regional trade networks, some of which centered around Damascus. Cotton from the Ramla area and olive oil and ash (alkali) from Nablus were among the raw materials feeding Damascus manufactories. In the seventeenth and eighteenth centuries, the center of commercial activity continued to shift from northern to southern Syria, as a result of a number of developments: war with Iran encouraged trade caravans to use the Baghdad-Damascus route rather than the Isfahan-Aleppo route; the growth of the Red Sea port of Jiddah privileged Damascus; and the pilgrimage caravan expanded, with Damascus as the primary locus for the assembly of its pilgrims. All of these factors contributed to an upsurge in commercial activity throughout the region. Damascus, however, was not the hub of all economic activity. Jerusalem, Ramla, and Nablus were centers of production in their own right: all three towns boasted soap industries and traded oil among themselves. In the course of the seventeenth and eighteenth centuries, all three also began to orient their trade more toward the Palestinian coast, where the port of Sayda was expanding rapidly to accommodate an upsurge in trade with Europe. In general, the picture we have of economic activity in the region is one, particularly in the eighteenth century, of substantial growth of both industry and trade, a multiplicity of economic linkages among the urban and rural areas, and a growing external orientation, both toward other parts of the Empire and toward Europe.[29]

Administrative, economic, and social linkages are much in evidence in the fatwas and the court records: Damascenes do business in Nablus; married women in Ramla have brothers in Jerusalem acting as their legal agents; women from Jerusalem marry in Damascus. A network of social relations based on family ties, business dealings, and shared culture lent coherence to the region of southern Syria and Palestine. The local jurists, though some served as official or quasi-official servants of the Ottoman Empire, were typical of the region's intellectuals in their strong regional orientation. They were Arabic speakers who were born in Syria or Palestine to families of local prominence, they were educated there or in contiguous Arab lands, and they usually settled down in or near their towns of birth. Along with others of their class, they formed a local elite who served the Empire more as representatives of their local community than as members of Ottoman officialdom. Their activities as local judges and muftis could not but further regional cohesion.

The region was not, however, undifferentiated territory. Net distinctions between the urban areas and the countryside were certainly drawn, as we shall see, by the muftis themselves, who were townsmen all. The cities and towns were the seat of all that really mattered, so far as the jurists were concerned: the courts, schools, and great mosques and tombs that made intellectual and religious life possible were almost all located in urban areas. But as ʿAbd al-Nour points out, the line between city and countryside could be rather indistinct. Cities and towns did not differ from villages in legal status or organization, and fairly constant rural-urban immigration mixed villagers into the city populations. Overall population increase in the seventeenth and eighteenth centuries co-incided with rates of urbanization, estimated at 25 to 30 percent, that were extremely high relative to those of other early modern societies.[30] This level of mobility and urban-rural contact helps explain the absence of strong prejudice: although the jurists may occasionally lament the lax practices of their rural neighbors, there is little evidence of generalized disparagement of rural people and their ways.

This is not to deny the presence of a certain urban chauvinism and strong feelings of particularistic identity among city dwellers. Although most urban areas were very mixed in their functions and housed a range of administrative, commercial, and manufacturing activities, we can eas-ily sense the elements of a distinctive identity in most cities and towns. Of the four urban areas that concern us here, Damascus was by far the largest, with a population of perhaps 90,000 people by the end of the eighteenth century. As a provincial capital, the city housed the Ottoman officials and troops whose job it was to administer the region for the Em-pire. The governor, his deputy (*mutasallim*), and the chief judge (*qadi al-qudah*) originally were members of the Ottoman official elite who had been sent to the province for brief terms. The fourth most important of-ficial, the mufti, was, as we have seen, usually a local man, as was the qadi's assistant (*naʾib*) and many of the other provincial judges. At the end of the seventeenth century and into the eighteenth century, members of the Damascene *ʿulama*' (educated elite) asserted their power through a number of protests against the governor's injustice and unfair exactions. After a brief period of exile as punishment, they returned to the city with enhanced respect among the population, ready to play a key role in the governance of Damascus for much of the eighteenth century. The main powerholders in the city for most of the century, however, were members of the ʿAzm family, a local family whose ability to gain influence in Istanbul and maintain order in Syria enabled them to establish a virtual monopoly over the governorship in Damascus and other critical posts as well. The city was thus not only a seat of imperial power: it was also an arena in which local notables gained a prominence that enabled them to play influential roles throughout the region.[31]

Damascus was also an economic power in the area. It was surrounded by agricultural villages that furnished raw materials for its many workshops, especially those producing textiles, and provided markets for finished Damascene goods. The city was an important entrepôt for all kinds of Empire trade—silk, cotton, oil, and glass moved through the city as part of a flourishing east-west trade. In this period, most Damascene trade was with other provinces of the Empire; two mountain ranges formed a barrier between the city and the Mediterranean coast, thus discouraging any reorientation toward Europe.[32]

Perhaps no event was as consequential for the Damascene economy as the *hajj*, the annual pilgrimage to Mecca. All pilgrims from the north and east of the Empire (and beyond) gathered in the city for the annual caravan, which was organized under the protection of the Empire. Pilgrims from the Balkans and Anatolia, from the areas of Baghdad, Aleppo, and even Iran converged on Damascus to join the caravan. The numbers fluctuated from year to year, but anywhere from 20,000 to 60,000 people might arrive in the city for a given pilgrimage. Many brought goods to trade, and all of them spent at least some time in Damascus, where they would purchase supplies for the trip. Indeed, in a pilgrimage timetable supplied by an eighteenth-century pilgrim from Istanbul, the entire Istanbul-Mecca round-trip via Damascus required 238 days, 43 of which were spent in Damascus itself.[33] Karl Barbir identified four different trading activities associated with the pilgrimage that benefited Damascus and its environs: goods were shipped with the caravan in either direction; supplies were sold to pilgrims in Damascus and along the route; merchants accompanied the caravan and sold supplies to pilgrims along the way; and the governor of Damascus carried merchandise to Mecca to sell for his own profit.[34]

The far smaller town of Nablus was the second most important center of commerce and production in southern Syria and Palestine. As a *sanjaq* seat, Nablus housed an administration made up largely of members of leading local families who were notorious for their penchant for autonomous action. As in Damascus, the local notables never appeared to entertain the notion of mounting an actual challenge to Ottoman rule, but their relations with Istanbul involved more foot-dragging than was the norm. From their bases in the town of Nablus or in outlying village redoubts, the al-Nimrs, Tuqans, 'Abd al-Hadis, Jarrars, Jayyusis, and others acquired power at various times through their ability to employ family solidarity and patronage for influence or even armed struggle when necessary. Indeed, the political narratives of the period read as Byzantine accounts of conflicts and alliances among family groups that competed to acquire, preserve, and increase their power, whether that be economic, in the form of landholdings through control of *timar*s (land grants) and *iltizam*s (tax-farms), or administrative, in the form of major offices, including governorships.

Nablus, too, was well situated for the purposes of regional trade. Its merchants plied the routes from Nablus to Cairo or Damascus, exporting soap, cotton, olive oil, and textiles. A group of merchant families in Nablus, trading primarily in soap and grains, prospered, and the ranks of a social group were further swelled by tradesmen and artisans, whose markets were more purely regional. As was the case with other towns in the region, the rural hinterland figured prominently in the town's development: the surrounding villages provided most of the resources that enabled Nablus to prosper, especially in the course of the eighteenth century, and to achieve an economic dominance in the region second only to that of Damascus.[35]

The city of Jerusalem was not primarily a merchant town, and its location had certain obvious disadvantages: it lay neither on the Cairo-Damascus trade route nor on a major Meccan pilgrimage route. It was, however, the main urban center of the *sanjaq* of Jerusalem and served as a market town for some 220 surrounding villages, as well as the town of Hebron and neighboring bedouin tribes. As the seat of Ottoman district administration and as an important center for local commerce, Jerusalem played an economic and political role in the province. It was also a center of soap and handicraft production.

There is evidence to suggest that Jerusalem's hinterland was more difficult to govern than was that, say, of Nablus; proximity to desert lands and a high level of bedouin activity circumscribed the city's ability to draw on local resources.[36] Its religious significance as a holy city in Islam lent it distinction, however, and its mosques and shrines attracted pilgrims. Many of the religious sites as well as social services—fountains, soup kitchens, and so on—in the city were endowed by *waqfs* established in villages throughout Palestine, and members of the Ottoman ruling elite, including Sultan Sulayman's beloved and powerful wife, Hurrem, had taken a personal interest in the city's development.[37] Although it remained modest in size during this period, Jerusalem did boast a number of institutions, such as mosques, shrines, and schools, that not only attracted visitors but also made it a center of cultural and religious life for the province.

Of the four urban areas under consideration, Ramla was by far the smallest. It was the administrative seat of a subdistrict (*nahiya*) in the Ramla and Gaza district. Its distinctive features had much to do with its location in the coastal plain. Early on, Ramla emerged as a center for handicraft production, particularly spinning and soap-making.[38] As a market town in a cotton-growing area, Ramla attracted the attention of European merchants, some of whom set up shop there. France appointed a vice-consul in Ramla in the eighteenth century, underscoring French commercial interests in the area. Europeans may have also been drawn to the town by the presence of a sizable indigenous Christian community, perhaps one-third of the total population.[39] The exercise of power and moral authority at the local level appeared to be the prerogative, however, of a Muslim elite. When the inhabitants of Ramla staged a revolt in 1767 to protest the tax demands of the governor of Damascus, it was the qadi and mufti of the town who took the leadership roles.[40] Still, Ramla, despite its small size, boasted—compared with its neighbors in the region—a sizable cosmopolitan population and a high level of commercialization of agriculture and handicrafts.

The province of Damascus was also home to a number of bedouin tribes, whose presence impinged in varying degrees on the urban environment. The long-standing tensions as well as modes of cooperation between the nomadic bedouins and the settled peoples of the region were brought into focus at the time of the annual pilgrimage. The trip from Damascus to Mecca was a caravan journey of some 35 days through a generally inhospitable landscape, and a successful pilgrimage depended on the cooperation of bedouin tribes who were hired to provide camels and protection and to act as guides for the caravan. As Muslims and Arabic-speakers themselves, the bedouins had much in common with the pilgrims they shepherded. Usually all went well, and the pilgrims returned without incident. Upon occasion, however, the caravan would be attacked and looted by a bedouin tribe in response to the withholding of payment or perhaps the failure to be hired at all on that particular trip. At any rate, the protection of the caravan against bedouin assault remained a preoccupation of the commander of the pilgrimage throughout the seventeenth and eighteenth centuries.[41] In the context of the pilgrimage and other vital trade in the region, the bedouin provided services critical to the economy; at the same time, they were viewed by the settled peoples as a distinct and volatile element whose adherence to law and obedience to authority could not be presumed.

The muftis and courts we study here occupied this terrain, one of considerable political, economic, and cultural cohesion. In recent years scholars have sharply revised the views previously held on the general state of affairs in southern Syria and Palestine in the seventeenth and eighteenth centuries. The picture of a bleak landscape marked by population decline, economic misery, and political decay and corruption, all punctuated by bedouin defilements, has given way to a more balanced view that takes into account substantial population growth, considerable vitality in the agricultural and commercial sectors, and the presence of a local elite whose drive to assert their own authority often worked to the advantage of local institutions and political and economic stability.[42] Throughout this time and place, muftis and qadis were intimately involved in most aspects of life, as officials with notarial functions, as arbiters of disputes, as representatives of state power, and as members of a vital local elite. Their judicial functions brought them into close contact with a broad segment of the population they served; their concerns cannot but reflect the kinds of situations they were called upon to ponder and to judge. Indeed, the work of a particular mufti often seems to bear the stamp of the town in which he operated. al-'Imadi's fatwas, for example, exude a sensitivity to the social distinctions of complex urban life; class distinctions figure largely in his discussions of gender. Khayr al-Din's opinions, by contrast, evince a much greater attention to the problems of rural life and peasant practice. 'Abd al-Fattah al-Tamimi's work, produced in a center of orthodoxy, tends the most, of the three, to champion the straight and narrow approach to legal interpretation.

All three muftis, however, lived and worked in communities marked by clear social distinctions. Their opinions, and the court cases of the period, clearly distinguish among the three principal urban classes of the time: a small, elite upper class composed of a few families enjoying economic position and political dominance through the long-term monopoly of official government positions and land grants; a larger "middle" class of merchants, *'ulama'*, and prosperous craftsmen engaged in trade, production, and services; and a lower class composed of the bulk of the working population of the town. As we shall see, many of the muftis' discussions of gender were informed by a developed sense of social distinction, of the ways in which social position and power were shaped by class difference as well as by gender difference. For all of these scholars, however, the elaboration of the social relationships born of marriage and divorce, the rights and responsibilities of parenthood, and the gendering of space and sexuality took place within the context of a shared cultural tradition and were embedded in the political, economic, and social conditions of Ottoman Syria and Palestine.

THE MUFTIS

The life of the Shaykh Khayr al-Din (in full, Khayr al-Din b. Ahmad b. Nur al-Din 'Ali b. Zayn al-Din b. 'Abd al-Wahhab al-Ayubi al-'Alimi al-Faruqi al-Ramli) began in the Palestinian town of Ramla in 993 H./1585 A.D. The third son of a family of local prominence and documented lineage, Khayr al-Din took up Qur'anic studies as a boy in Ramla and progressed to legal studies, focused on the *fiqh* of the Shafi'i school. At the age of fourteen, he traveled to Egypt to join his two older brothers, who were studying at al-Azhar (the premier institution of Islamic learning in the region). After his return to Ramla at age 20, he began a long and productive career as a mufti that ended only with his death at age 88 in 1081 H./1671 A.D. This seemingly uneventful life yielded a collection of finely argued fatwas that were to serve as a model and authoritative reference for jurists for generations to come.

In eulogizing this life, Khayr al-Din's biographer, al-Muhibbi, tells us much about how the age viewed a mufti, his qualifications, and his mission.[43] His education was broad: he studied Qur'an and *hadith*, *fiqh*, linguistics, grammar, rhetoric, and prosody. He was also well versed in the doctrines of more than one legal school (*madhhab*). Khayr al-Din's intimate knowledge of legal doctrine across *madhhab*s and his eclectic approach to legal reasoning are illustrated (by al-Muhibbi) in typical anecdotal fashion. He had studied with a Shafi'i shaykh in Ramla and continued to adhere to the Shafi'i school at al-Azhar. One of his brothers, however, encouraged him to pursue Hanafi legal studies, possibly because of the greater possibilities and prestige afforded by the "official" school of the Empire. Troubled by the thought of forsaking the Shafi'i school, he sought guidance at the tomb of the Imam al-Shafi'i himself in Cairo. As Khayr al-Din slept by the tomb, he dreamed that the imam came to assure him that all the schools shared the right path, and he awoke ready to devote himself to the study of Hanafi law. His intimate acquaintance with both Shafi'i and Hanafi doctrine was to inform his work throughout his tenure and no doubt underlay his toleration of a variety of legal approaches.

Khayr al-Din began to issue fatwas while still a young man in Cairo, and after his return to Ramla he taught, presumably in the field of legal studies, and continued to issue fatwas to those who requested them. But he did not hold an official post as a mufti. On the contrary, his biographer, al-Muhibbi, is careful to note that Khayr al-Din received neither a state stipend nor income from a *waqf* in return for his services. His position as mufti evolved as he responded to legal questions posed by members of his community, and the "excellence of his answers" encouraged others to seek him out. Eventually, his reputation spread as far as Damascus and even among the bedouin, who accepted his judgments with uncharacteristic docility. His had become an authority that took precedence over that of the officially appointed qadi: a fatwa from Khayr al-Din could override a local court decision. Such was the career path: it was not just years of diligent study that equipped a man to be a mufti; he must also prove himself through practice and win the acclamation of the local population. The Empire had no discernible role here, and, indeed, a mufti of sufficient reputation enjoyed an authority that appointed officials could not contest. The striking contrast between the picture drawn by Khayr al-Din's biographer and the standard practices of the core regions of the Empire, where muftis were the obedient servants of the state, working within the confines of the court system, suggests that both the muftis and the courts operated rather differently out in the provinces.

The absence of official position and therefore of salary meant that Khayr al-Din was, by necessity, a man of parts. He was a farmer who became very much involved in the commercialized agriculture of the Ramla area, tending vineyards and acquiring land for olive, fig, and various other fruit trees. He also owned significant urban real estate. The income from these activities allowed him to pursue his avocation as a mufti. His immersion in worldly affairs helped, no doubt, in many of his deliberations, for he had firsthand knowledge of the agricultural and business practices of the day, which were often brought before him. al-Muhibbi viewed these kinds of activities in a thoroughly positive light. Khayr al-Din also drew on these experiences and the impressive holdings of his personal library to write treatises on various subjects, as well as poetry.

In keeping with the biographical tradition of the day, we are told very little about Khayr al-Din's family life. He had at least one son, and must therefore have been a husband and father. Otherwise, we are not privy to information that could help us with his family context. The personal traits that al-Muhibbi ascribes to him—kindness, generosity, and humility—imply a certain sensitivity and ability to empathize; as we shall see, these qualities did imbue his fatwas with a spirit of toleration and flexibility. al-Muhibbi sums up the impact of Khayr al-Din's career with his usual hyperbole: "Ramla in his era was the most just of all places and an illustrious model of [Islamic] lawfulness."[44]

Hamid al-'Imadi's life diverged from that of Khayr al-Din in significant ways.[45] Hamid b. 'Ali b. Ibrahim b. 'Abd al-Rahim b. 'Imad al-Din b. Muhibb al-Din, known as Hamid al-'Imadi, pursued a career as an official mufti in eighteenth-century Damascus. From the beginning, his was an education in preparation for official life. Born in 1103 H./1692 A.D. in Damascus, the son of the Hanafi mufti of Damascus before him, al-'Imadi studied with a wide array of scholars of considerable reputation and official connections. He could do so by remaining in Damascus until the age of 25, taking advantage of the presence of local scholars of standing like 'Abd al-Ghani al-Nabulsi, the well-known sufi, as well as the muftis of the Hanbali and Shafi'i *madhhab*s, and the accessibility of visiting scholars from as far away as Egypt and India. Like those of Khayr al-Din, his legal studies were not focused on Hanafi doctrine alone but entailed serious study of the *fiqh* of other legal schools. At the age of 25, al-'Imadi made the journey to Mecca, a pilgrimage cum study tour that allowed him to study with scholars from Mecca and Medina. He also had the opportunity of meeting and studying with the highest-ranking judge of the Empire, the *qadi 'askar*. After his return to Damascus, al-'Imadi received an official appointment as the Hanafi mufti in 1137 H./1724–25 A.D., in which capacity he taught and delivered fatwas, two volumes of which have come down to us.

His education, like that of Khayr al-Din, exposed him to a range of teachers and approaches that equipped him to pursue an eclectic strategy in his juristic activities. He was not, however, a mufti by popular acclamation. He owed his position to official appointment, and he could lose it by falling into official disfavor. His biographer, Muhammad Khalil Muradi, relates that one of al-'Imadi's nephews intrigued against him in Istanbul and managed to have him dismissed in order to take his place as mufti. During the ten-month period in which al-'Imadi lacked an official position, the "people" continued to think of him as a mufti, and it was he, not his nephew, upon whom they called for legal guidance: he remained their *mutarjim* (interpreter). The conclusion we can draw here is an interesting one: Istanbul could appoint someone as mufti for the province of Damascus, but appointment alone did not guarantee legitimacy. As the scion of a learned family of jurists and muftis, and as a man who had earned a reputation as "educated, moral, mannered, and knowledgeable," al-'Imadi's appointment as mufti met with general acceptance. His dismissal did not erase the innate qualities of mufti-ness—the training, experience, and judiciousness—that had made him a capable mufti in the eyes of the population. He continued to be a mufti, a person capable of delivering meaningful judicial opinions, despite the ill-advised actions of Istanbul.

Having spent most of his life in official posts as a teacher and jurist, al-'Imadi did not appear to pursue the same range of economic activities as did Khayr al-Din, though he did invest in real estate, as was the norm among the notable families of the city. He also cultivated a number of intellectual interests: he wrote treatises about subjects as diverse as the problems posed by opium and tobacco, he composed poetry, and he researched and wrote biographies. We know as little about his personal life as we do about Khayr al-Din's. At his death he was survived only by two sons, and we may thus presume that his wife and any daughters he might have fathered predeceased him.

The life of ʿAbd al-Fattah b. Darwish al-Tamimi offers a third variation on the career of mufti. In this case, of a rather obscure jurist whose fatwas had no ascertainable impact on those who came after him, his biographer provides us with very little information indeed.[46] ʿAbd al-Fattah hailed from a Nablus family with connections to the judiciary. His father had been a preacher (*khatib*) in the Ibrahimi mosque in Hebron and served as *naʿib* (assistant) to the qadi in Nablus, as well as qadi in his own right in Jerusalem. ʿAbd al-Fattah studied in Jerusalem with the Hanafi mufti there, one Shaykh al-Sayyid ʿAbd al-Rahim al-Lutfi, and eventually settled down in the city, married the shaykh's daughter, and worked as the shaykh's assistant. It was in his capacity as the mufti's deputy that he began to issue his own fatwas, a number of which were collected and passed down in manuscript form. He also pursued a career as a judge: he held the post of qadi for periods of time in Ramla, Gaza, and Nablus before his death in 1138 H./1725–26 A.D. We have no indication that ʿAbd al-Fattah enjoyed as much variety in his teachers and lessons or the opportunities for travel as had the other muftis whose careers we have examined. And indeed, his fatwas have a rote quality and a narrowness of vision that reflect his more limited experience.

To become a mufti in seventeenth- or eighteenth-century Syria or Palestine was, above all, to achieve a certain eminence as an interpreter of the law. Although the Hanafi mufti in Damascus was an official of the Empire, even his authority was based in large measure upon his ability to establish himself as someone who had a proper background, admirable personal qualities, and a good track record of legal interpretation. The other, locally based muftis owed their positions almost entirely to a general recognition of their abilities. They were expected by their biographers to act not as representatives of the Empire—effectiveness as a state servant is never mentioned as a positive quality in a mufti—but rather as purveyors of justice and enlightenment to their communities. Their knowledge of the law and their ability to engage in active, relevant interpretation were the attributes that made them worthy of the mufti's mantle.

The muftis interacted with the local Islamic courts. They were asked to deliver opinions about court cases either before or after the fact. A plaintiff could seek a fatwa from a mufti in order to be able to produce it in court in support of his or her position. A disgruntled party might, in the wake of a qadi's unfavorable judgment, request a fatwa in preparation for raising the issue once more. A fatwa was neither required nor excluded by court procedure, but the fact that fatwas were introduced into court rather infrequently, and that the local mufti appeared to issue most of his opinions in response to questions that did not arise out of current litigation, suggests that the relation between the court and the mufti was not always a close one.

The muftis did issue opinions on situations that were likely to come to court, however, and we will be interested in the extent to which their interpretation of legal doctrine touching on matters of gender was honored in the ways in which judges decided their cases. It was also often the mufti, and almost never the qadi, who discussed issues of doctrine and legal principle in a way that allows us to read their opinions as a discourse on gender. It was the interplay between the muftis' discussion of gender at a symbolic level and the working out of gender as a social relationship in the specifics of the fatwa and the courts that shaped a definable "Islamic" vision of a gendered social order in that time and place.

CHAPTER 2

With Her Consent

Marriage

QUESTION: A virgin in her legal majority and of sound mind was abducted by her brother and married off to an unsuitable man. Does her father have the right to annul the marriage contract on the basis of the [husband's] unsuitability?

ANSWER: Yes, if the father asks for that, then the judge should separate the spouses whether or not the marriage was consummated, so long as she has not borne children, and is not pregnant, and did not receive the *mahr* [dower] before the marriage. . . . This is the case if her brother has married her off with her consent. But if she was given in marriage without her consent, she can reject [the marriage], and there is no need for the father [to ask for] separation [and raise] opposition, for he is not [in this case] a commissioned agent. [But] if she authorizes him to represent her, then he has the right to request from the judge an annulment [*faskh*] of the marriage and a separation, and the judge should separate them. According to al-Hasan, there is no need for [all] this because the contract is not valid in the first place. And God knows best.[1]

It was, in large part, through such discussions of marriage that the Muslim jurists of seventeenth- and eighteenth-century Syria and Palestine elaborated their vision of the relationship between gender and social power in their community. In the many fatwas that dealt with marriage arrangements, marriage contracts, and the rights and responsibilities of husbands and wives, the muftis constructed a legal discourse in which the gendered relationship created by marriage occupied pride of place. Their discussions of marriage are illustrative of the complexities of the legal approach to gender in this period, an approach that focused on gender difference and male social power yet proved flexible and responsive to changing social conditions. Indeed, if we look at the records of the Islamic courts, we see a number of ways in which this discourse could prepare the ground for the pursuit of personal strategies, particularly women's strategies, that might improve one's personal situation. The opinions delivered by the muftis defined marital relations in a strongly gendered fashion, one constitutive of gender difference in the society as a whole, and the courts provided a forum in which this construct of gender difference interacted with gender as social relationship. The legal discourse on marriage formed a backdrop against which wives and husbands brought complaints or made claims against one another; in so doing, they in turn contributed to the ongoing elaboration of an Islamic tradition that took account of social reality by commissioning jurisconsults to deliver opinions, buttressed by legal argument, in response to actual situations arising in the courts.

In Islamic law, marriage is a contractual relationship. A woman and a man are united by their agreement to a marriage contract, whether oral or written, in which the names and lineages of the bride and groom are given, an amount of *mahr* (an indirect dowry paid by the groom to the bride) is stated, and witnesses to the couple's freely given consent are named. It was theoretically possible, in Hanafi jurisprudence, to add conditions to the marriage contract specifying that the wife would receive an automatic divorce should her husband commit certain acts, such as taking a second wife or acquiring a concubine. Although Khayr al-Din, for example, clearly recognized the validity of such conditions, they were rarely specified in the written marriage contracts of the period.[2] Some of these contracts were entered in the records of the Islamic court. This was a common practice in eighteenth-century Jerusalem, but less often the case in Damascus or Nablus, where we find only the occasional marriage contract.[3] A typical contract drawn up for the offspring of two comfortable merchant families in eighteenth-century Nablus contained all the required information and various embellishments as well:

> The groom, the youth of right conduct, Salih al-Din, son of the merchant 'Umar Ya'ish.
>
> The bride, the pride of the guarded women, the *sayyida* Khadija, daughter of the pride of the nobles, the *sayyid* Hashim al-Hanbali, the virgin, in her majority, whose dower is 100 *dhahab bunduqi*, a kaftan, a silk cloth, a rug, a belt, 20 *ratl*s of wool, 20 *ratl*s of cotton, 10 dresses, and a black female slave to serve her. She receives now 60 *dhahab bunduqi*, the above-mentioned items, and the slave by the acknowledgment of her agent for the contract, and the rest is deferred until one of them dies.
>
> Her brother, the *sayyid* Hasan, son of the *sayyid* Hashim, is her agent, and his agency is witnessed by her cousin, the *sayyid* Muhammad, son of Muhi-al-Din al-Hanbali, and by her brother the *sayyid* Salih, legal witnesses.
>
> And the agent of the groom is the merchant Muhi-al-Din Ya'ish, whose agency was witnessed by the pride of the nobles, the *sayyid* Sa'ad al-Din al-Hanbali, and the aforementioned *sayyid* Muhammad.
>
> End of Rabi' I 1138 H. (1725 A.D.)[4]

Such contracts appeared to be standard and widely understood: the muftis addressed the form of the contract only when it contained apparent irregularities (as, for example, the absence of a *mahr*) or when the issue of coercion arose. Most of the court cases and fatwas dealing with marriage focus instead on various aspects of the relationship implicit in the contract.

The muftis tended to ground their discussion of marriage on their understanding of the purpose of this union in the context of their local

Muslim society. That this was a strongly gendered society in which the male and the female were neatly differentiated, not only biologically but also socially, politically, and economically, was an unquestioned assumption embedded in much of their reasoning. Their view of marriage rested, in fundamental ways, on gender difference, on gender in binary opposition: marriage was not a symmetrical relationship. One has little sense, however, that this differentiation was easily reducible in their eyes to male dominance and female submission. As the jurists struggled to define and regulate the institution of marriage, they always reflected a deep concern for the ways in which marriage could not only elaborate and organize gender difference but also strengthen and unify their gendered society: marriage was a highly gendered institution, yet one in which the perceived tensions bred by gender difference might be softened and rendered less fractious. As *'ulama'*, the muftis were charged with the protection of the moral standards of their community, but also, at least in theory, with the physical safety and unity of the group as a whole. Their discussions of marriage must be read in the light of some unspoken yet fundamental assumptions about the social purposes of marriage.

THE PURPOSES OF MARRIAGE

Marriage was a key to social harmony. All three of the muftis whose fatwas we study here focused on the institution of marriage as a basic social building block, a bulwark against social discord and disorganization. Many of the issues they chose to focus on underscored a view of marriage as a social necessity, as the desirable state of being for all members of the community, almost without exception. It is in this context that we can understand the stress they placed on the special responsibility the *wali* (guardian) of a minor bore for arranging a marriage. Every minor had a *wali*, usually his or her father or grandfather. If the father and grandfather were both absent or deceased, other paternal relatives might assume the *wilaya* (guardianship). The guardian of an orphan had, according to al-ʿImadi, a responsibility to arrange a marriage for his charge even before the child reached puberty.[5] Not only minors, but other legal incompetents, including the insane, could be married off by their guardians.[6] Indeed, al-'Imadi took the position that should a *wali* balk at what appeared to be a sound offer of marriage made to his minor charge, the qadi (judge) should step in to oversee the marriage arrangements.[7]

A stand-in *wali* was entrusted with furthering the well-being of his or her charge and protecting the child's interests in the absence of the natural protector, the father or grandfather. That these interests should include the arrangement of an early marriage is a position clearly adopted by al-'Imadi, who was even willing, if necessary, to override the rights of the official *wali* in order not to miss the opportunity to make a good match. The interest of the community in making sure all its members were married extended even to the mentally or physically ill, because all adults, regardless of their situation, benefit from being in the married state.

This strongly promarital position did not mean that any and every marriage was acceptable in the eyes of the muftis. On the contrary, these men were very conscious of the rules of *kafa'a,* the legal concept of the suitability of the match in terms of lineage, legal status, social class, and moral standards, and they chose to enforce them. If a marriage were to reinforce social harmony, it was important to avoid the instability attendant upon mesalliance. All three of our muftis applied the rules of *kafa'a* in fairly predictable ways. A *sharifa* (a member of the status group of descendants of the Prophet) should marry only within her lineage.[8] A woman of free origins should not be permitted to marry a slave.[9] Compatibility of class was somewhat less tangible, but a girl from "people of learning and religious piety" should not be married to an "illiterate profligate,"[10] and a girl of good background should not be married to a man who is "sinful, poor, or employed in a vile profession."[11] Clearly, the interests of the community would not be served by marriages that appeared to be inherently unstable because of the disparate backgrounds of the bride and groom.

Indeed, the absence of compatibility was enough to render a marriage invalid if that marriage were contracted by a woman or her *wakil* (authorized agent) without her father's or grandfather's approval. The muftis did agree that the law allowed the father of a minor girl to marry her off to whomever he pleased, and thus override the demands of *kafa'a*, but on this matter even the father's judgment might be questioned. Khayr al-Din argued that if a father known for his "poor judgment and his inability to see the consequences [of his actions]" married his daughter to an unsuitable person, the qadi might step in and proclaim the marriage legally defective.[12]

A firm promarital position, based on the understanding that marriage was the natural and desirable state for all Muslim adults, was thus tempered in juristic reasoning by the demands of social harmony. A marriage was central to social relations, and it must reinforce social ties within the community and promote harmony and stability. Problematic unions that united ill-suited couples were to be avoided. Indeed, the community interest in good marriage arrangements, as perceived and protected by the Muslim judge, could take precedence over the right of the father to marry off his minor daughter. A father could not, in the jurists' view, exercise his power over his daughter in a wholly arbitrary and despotic fashion.

Marriage was also defined as a relationship of material support, and the provision of that support was strongly gendered. The marriage contract, provided the marriage had been consummated, initiated certain responsibilities: a husband was responsible for providing for his wife and any children born of the union. A man was solely responsible for his wife's *nafaqa* (support), regardless of the wife's own resources. Once the marriage contract was signed *and* the marriage was consummated, the husband had to begin to provide *nafaqa* in the form of "nourishment, clothing, and shelter"; should a man fail to do so, he could be jailed until he did.[13] The muftis also agreed that the Islamic courts should play an active role in ensuring the delivery of this support. Should a husband go away on a trip or disappear without leaving sufficient support, the qadi was authorized to discover any of the husband's assets that might be attached: if the husband were the beneficiary of any *waqf* revenues or had any outstanding debts owed to him, the qadi could assign these monies to his wife.[14]

Support had also to be provided at a level appropriate to the wife's social background: she had to be maintained in the style to which she was accustomed. The muftis devoted time to defining what was appropriate for members of their communities. Khayr al-Din established a "customary" standard of living for a poor woman of the Ramla vicinity: a diet of barley bread and corn oil, and a clothing allowance of two gowns (one winter and one summer), two shirts, two head scarves, and one cloak.[15] al-'Imadi, operating in a city of more pronounced social nuance, distinguished the diets of three social classes. The rich woman ate wheaten bread and meat for lunch and should have an ample supper. The woman of the "middle" stratum could expect a lunch of bread of unspecified grain and animal fat. The poor woman must make do with bread and cheese. The attention to detail in the discussions of *nafaqa* reinforces the legal position that the husband was not simply being exhorted to support his wife, but was in fact legally required to provide her with the full amount of material support she could expect as a woman of her particular class.

The gravity of this responsibility was further underscored by the precise definition of its scope. All agreed that a husband owed this support from the moment of the consummation of the marriage until such time as the marriage was terminated by divorce or death. In the case of divorce, the former husband must continue to support his wife until the end of her waiting period, when she would be legally free to remarry. In the case of a wife's death, the responsibilities of the husband might actually extend into the grave. Khayr al-Din drew a clear parallel between *nafaqa* and burial costs: just as the clothing and housing of a wife is his responsibility during her lifetime, so is her shroud and her grave his responsibility after her death.[16] Marriage, then, stood at the center of a gendered system of nurture. The man was clearly assigned the responsibility of providing food, shelter, and other necessities of life for his wife and children (the wife's responsibilities, as we shall see, lay elsewhere). The muftis took these gendered arrangements for family provision very seriously, for marriage was the institution that undergirded the most basic social tie of the community, and they took considerable pains to define and standardize the material responsibilities it entailed.[17]

In addition to its importance in achieving social harmony and the arrangement of material provision, marriage was also critical, in the legal discourse, for the control and satisfaction of sexual drives. Marriage was a sexual relationship, and the consummation of the marriage was essential to establishing the groom's responsibilities for *nafaqa:* the full legal consequences of a marriage could not be realized until sexual intercourse had taken place. Legal discourse distinguished between the signing of the marriage contract, at which time the groom must pay the *mahr,* and the moment of first sexual intercourse, which activated the full obligations of marital support. A marriage could be contracted before either party was ready for sexual intercourse, but a marriage could of course not be consummated until both bride and groom were physically mature. The muftis did not equate such maturity with puberty (the marker of legal majority), however: a girl might be mature enough for sexual intercourse before she began to menstruate. Her readiness for intimacy was signaled in large part by her appearance, by whether or not she had become an "object of desire," "fleshy" (*samina*), or "buxom" (*dakhma*), physical attributes that signified that she could now "endure intercourse."[18] Until such time, the marriage, although legally contracted, clearly lacked an essential element.

The muftis all agreed that marriage existed to channel and fulfill the sexual drives of both men and women, and the refusal or inability of one of the partners to have sexual intercourse could invalidate a marriage. A woman could refuse to have intercourse with her husband if he had failed to pay the stipulated *mahr,* but once the accounts were settled, she had to be available as a sexual partner.[19] If she persisted in refusing him, he would be absolved of any responsibility for *nafaqa* or, according to what appears to be a minority opinion of al-Tamimi (neither of the other two muftis mention it as permissible), he could rape her.[20] The woman who through physical or mental disability was incapable of intercourse but did not consciously refuse her husband was to be treated differently. If, according to al-'Imadi, a woman became mentally or physically ill, or so obese as to make intercourse impossible, she should still receive *nafaqa*.[21] A man was entitled to the sexual companionship of his wife, and his obligations were directly tied to her availability for sexual intercourse, but should she be disabled, she should not be punished for her disability; *nafaqa* should continue.

Just as a man could expect and require sexual activity from a marriage partner, so could a woman. Once a wife had moved to her husband's domicile, was considered ready for sexual intercourse, and did not refuse any of her husband's advances, she should receive *nafaqa*, and if her husband was still a minor, was ill, or was otherwise incapable of intercourse, he had still to pay her the full *nafaqa*.[22] If he were to prove incapable of intercourse over the long term, then she could seek legal remedies. al-Tamimi responded to a woman whose marriage had been "consummated" and yet she had not been deflowered ("did not flow"). After she had waited for a period of one year for the matter to resolve itself, she could raise the problem with a qadi and request a divorce.[23] al-'Imadi agreed that in order to have her marriage annulled for impotence, a woman must testify to the judge that she was still a virgin after a full year of living with her husband (not counting days of sickness or separation).[24] The sexual rights of husband and wife were not exactly symmetrical: whereas a man's marital obligations could be relaxed in light of his wife's refusal to sleep with him, the jurists did not entertain the notion that a woman could forthwith modify her marital behavior in response to her husband's nonperformance. Still, after a year had passed, she could seek to have her marriage terminated on the grounds of her husband's sexual failings.

The muftis' discussions of sex and marriage are remarkably free of references to procreation. If the siring and bearing of children figured prominently in the jurists' sense of the purpose of marriage, they were curiously silent about it. The discussion of sexuality takes place entirely within the context of sexual desire, and of the need to satisfy this desire within the institution of marriage. Indeed, in all their discussions the jurists limit themselves to marriage as a contractual relationship between two people who, as we shall see, acquire both rights and responsibilities as a result. Marriage institutes arrangements of shared nurture and rights of sexual companionship; no larger purpose is made explicit. But the consistent valuing of marriage for all members of the community, the emphasis on matches that respect social barriers, the close attention to the material details of the arrangement, and the recognition that marriage channels powerful sexual drives all point to an institution that serves the needs not just of two individuals but of a community. The achievement of social harmony and stability rested on the achievement of successful matrimonial unions through careful attention to gender difference.

It is small wonder, then, that the muftis and the courts spent so much time and energy considering marriage arrangements and the behavior required of husbands and wives. As an elaborate and detailed legal discourse on these arrangements and behaviors continued to develop, marriage came to hold the key to a vision of a distinctly gendered society.

ARRANGING A MARRIAGE

How should a marriage begin? In addressing the question of what the law prescribed and permitted in marriage arrangements, the muftis seemed to draw on two potentially contradictory principles. First, a family enjoyed rights and responsibilities in the arrangement of its children's marriages. Second, an individual, whether male or female, once he or she reached legal majority, had the right to choose his or her spouse.

For children in their minority, the matter was rather straightforward. The muftis all agreed that the marriage guardian (*wali*) could arrange a marriage for the girl or boy under his guardianship. The consent of the child was not required, logically enough, because the minor was not yet legally competent. As long as the *wali* was the father or paternal grandfather, he could arrange whatever marriage he wished without regard for the suitability of the match, although, as we have seen in some extreme cases, the judge might intervene to protect the interests of the minor.[25] In general, however, the rights of the patriarch appeared to hold sway.

If, however, the *wilaya* or guardianship had devolved to another relative, in the absence of the father or grandfather, the *wali's* rights were more restricted. This stand-in *wali* could marry his or her charge only to a person who was suitable, in the legal sense of *kafa'a*, and the marriage contract would have to specify a "fair" *mahr*. In a case where a fatherless girl in her minority was married by her paternal uncle to his own son without a proper *mahr* in a "criminally fraudulent manner," al-'Imadi declared the marriage illegal and therefore annulled.[26]

Further, if a minor girl were married off by someone other than her father or grandfather, she had the option, upon reaching her legal majority, of refusing the marriage. Such a refusal, which had to be given at the time she first reached puberty, immediately ended the marriage.[27] Despite the clarity of the muftis on this issue, the girl's ability to exercise this right could be thwarted in various ways, as the following opinion from Khayr al-Din suggests:

> QUESTION: There is a minor girl whose brother married her off, and she came of age and chose *faskh* [annulment] in her "coming-of-age" choice. Her husband claimed that her brother had acted as the *wakil* [agent] of her father and she does not have a choice. She then claimed that [her brother] married her off during [her father's] brief absence on a journey. If the husband provides evidence for his claim, is her choice canceled or not? If he does not have evidence, and wants her oath on that, must she swear an oath?
>
> ANSWER: Yes, if the husband proves his claim, then her choice is canceled. . . . Only the father's and grandfather's marriage arrangements cannot be canceled . . . [and] if the marriage was arranged by way of a *niyaba* [proxy] for her father, then she has no choice. If the marriage was arranged as a result of [the brother's] *wilaya* [guardianship], then she has a choice.[28]

Still, all muftis reiterated the same general principles: only arrangements made by the father or paternal grandfather were inviolate; arrangements made by other individuals were subject to review by the qadi; and a minor girl (or boy for that matter) could not exercise any choice of partner until she reached her majority, but she could then choose to reject arrangements made by any other *wali* even if that meant annulling a marriage that had already been consummated.

The family's right to manage the affairs of minors in its own household was thus tempered, in theory and practice, by the right of the individual to exercise free choice once she or he reached the age of reason. It was also modified by the position of the muftis that only the family's patriarch, in the person of the father or grandfather, could operate with a free hand. All other members of the community were constrained by standards imposed and enforced by the jurists to serve the interests of the individual minor, especially in the absence of a father. The jurists took their charge to protect the fatherless child seriously, and their defense of the rights of orphans figured among the most impassioned of their opinions. Khayr al-Din made no attempt to conceal his wrath when asked about a village head who had intervened in a marriage arrangement made for a girl from his village by her mother, who had legally assumed the position of *wali* (a possibility I shall address in chapter 4). The shaykh had wrested the girl away from her mother, forestalled the arranged marriage, and then arranged a marriage for the girl himself and pocketed the *mahr*. Khayr al-Din soundly reprimanded the shaykh, who had no business interfering with a valid arrangement made by the mother of a fatherless girl. Nor did the shaykh have any right to act as marriage *wali* himself, and the marriage he arranged was therefore not legal. And, thundered Khayr al-Din, "his eating of the *mahr* is like filling his belly with fire and blazing flame."[29]

Once a child reached his or her legal majority (at the time of puberty), that child's right to choose a marriage partner took clear precedence over the family's right to arrange a marriage. The muftis all agreed on the basic principle that men and women in their legal majority could choose their own mates. Such a woman could exercise this choice in two ways. First, she enjoyed a right of refusal: were she informed of a marriage arrangement made by her *wali* or anyone else for her, she could refuse the match, regardless of who arranged it. Second, she was entitled to take a more active role in her own fate, by appointing an agent to arrange a marriage for her, thus bypassing her *wali*.

A woman who wanted to refuse a marriage had to do so as soon as the news of the arrangement reached her. As long as she stated her opposition to the marriage when she learned of it, the marriage was canceled. And if some question arose concerning whether or not she had refused in a timely fashion, her own testimony under oath to her immediate refusal carried the day. This right of refusal clearly extended even to marriage arrangements made by her father, or by other relatives.[30] al-ʿImadi contrasted this position with non-Muslim (*dhimmi*) marriage practices when he was asked about the legality of a marriage arranged by a *dhimmi* woman for her daughter without her daughter's consent. We do not intervene, he stressed, in "the disreputable marriages of *dhimmi*s," for we have no jurisdiction over such *dhimmi* affairs; if, however, a *dhimmi* came to an Islamic court and wanted a judgment on this issue, we would rule according to Islamic law and invalidate this marriage, which was made without the woman's consent.[31] The jurists seemed intent on guarding against hidden coercion in marriage arrangements. A man pressed a claim against a woman on the basis that her father had married her to him when she was a minor, and now she refused to honor the arrangement. She replied that she had been in her majority at the time of the arrangement, and that she had not been informed of it. Her testimony, according to al-ʿImadi, should be accepted, and she, not her putative husband, can testify to the fact that she had already reached her majority (puberty) at the time of the marriage.[32]

Consent was signified by the absence of refusal. If a woman learned of a marriage arrangement made for her and kept silent, she thus signaled her consent. The muftis agreed that this consent, however silent, must be informed consent. al-ʿImadi weighed in on the issue of informed silence:

> QUESTION: A virgin in her majority was married by her *wali*
> legally, but without her permission, to a man who was suitable
> and paid a fair *mahr* [dower]. Then the *wali* informed her of
> the marriage and of the groom and of the *mahr*, and she was silent

concerning her choice and she did not reject the marriage. Is her silence acceptance of him?

ANSWER: Yes. But if the *wali* marries her off without consultation and then informs her after the marriage and she remains silent, and he does not mention the [name of the] groom and the [amount of the] *mahr*, then it is different and not [legally] sound. And likewise if he consults her before the marriage but fails to mention the [name of the] groom and the [amount of the] *mahr*, and she is silent, this too is not a legal marriage.[33]

A woman thus needed to enter a marriage willingly; coercion invalidated marriage arrangements. Such a position did not, however, preclude a firm family hand in marriage arrangements. Families were free to marry off their women as long as their consent, even if of a passive nature, had been obtained.[34] Women in their legal majority still had marriage *wali*s, those people who were legally entitled to arrange their marriages for them, but the *wali* had to communicate fully all details of a proposed arrangement and honor a woman's refusal of a marriage. The special interest of the family in the marriages of its members was thus affirmed and buttressed in legal opinion, while at the same time the practice of coercion was strictly prohibited.

A woman in her legal majority also had the right, so far as the Hanafi jurists were concerned, to arrange her own marriage. Again and again the muftis affirmed that a woman of sound mind in her legal majority could directly, or through an agent of her choosing, select her own husband and make her own marriage arrangements. Such a marriage might take the form of an oral agreement made directly between two people to marry with a stipulated *mahr:* as long as the *mahr* was fair and the agreement was properly witnessed, the marriage was legal. Sometimes such a woman would appoint her own agent (*wakil*) to arrange a marriage for her, a perfectly valid approach that might neatly bypass the plans of her male relatives. A woman in her legal majority need not rely on, or even consult with, her marriage *wali*; it was her prerogative to arrange her own marriage.[35] Her "patriarch," in the person of her father, paternal grandfather, or paternal uncle, had no power of intervention in such arrangements, and their objections would be overruled.[36] All the jurists were careful to point out, however, that the legal *wali* (the father or grandfather, or other paternal relative in the absence of both) could raise objections to a marriage if the groom were not suitable, or if the *mahr* were not fair. If the *wali* were to raise such valid objections, the qadi would have to annul the marriage.[37]

Legal discourse on marriage arrangement, then, displayed a certain duality. On the one hand, marriage was a family affair: every female had a legal marriage *wali* and, in the case of a girl in her minority, the *wali* enjoyed broad powers of discretion in making arrangements. Once a woman attained her majority, however, legal discourse emphasized her freedom to refuse a match and even to arrange her own marriage.[38] The muftis often elaborated these views in response to situations manifesting palpable tension between the family's interest in controlling marriage choice and the individual's right to choose a partner, within limits. Many of the opinions on marriage arrangements pitted the jurists against irregular social practices, especially those whereby a family attempted to arrange a marriage without taking proper account of legal procedure and a young woman's rights. There seems to have been no question in the minds of the muftis about their proper role: as the upholders of Islamic legal norms, they took a firm position on a woman's right to participate in choosing a mate. This right was a feature of life, at least theoretically, in the Muslim community, and could not be put aside for the convenience of the family.

The idea that social harmony would be served and gender difference softened by choice of marriage partner lurks between the lines of many of these opinions. In choice of partner, at least, the differences between the male and female were minimized, though still present. Minors, whether girls or boys, were under the same form of family control. Once in their legal majority, however, young women, unlike young men, still remained under the aegis of a marriage *wali* who could arrange a marriage for them. On the one hand, the muftis maintained the position that a woman could be married off with minimal (silent) consent; on the other hand, they also repeatedly elaborated the Hanafi position that women enjoyed the right to choose their mates just as men did. Gender difference was surely a significant factor in marriage arrangement, but the difference was tempered by clear acknowledgment of a woman's right to choose.

ENTERING A MARRIAGE

The muftis' view of marriage as a means for promoting harmony between the sexes provided the context for their elaboration of the ways men and women should enter marriage. They devoted considerable effort to detailed discussion of the rights and obligations of husband and wife, aiming all the while at gender harmony through close attention to the precise requirements of both parties. What was owed and what could be expected structured much of this discussion as the material aspects of the marriage arrangement were implemented.

An initial obligation on the part of the husband was the provision of a proper *mahr*. The *mahr* (dower) was a necessary component of any marriage contract, whether or not it had been specified in the contract itself. The *mahr,* usually stated in the contract in this period as a specified amount of money, or money in addition to certain goods, had to be delivered to the bride herself. None of her family members, or her husband, had any right to the *mahr.* In the marriage contracts recorded in Damascus, Jerusalem, and Nablus in the eighteenth century, the Hanafi practice was always to divide the *mahr* into two portions, a *muqaddam* (prompt dower, consisting usually of about one-half to two-thirds of the total) to be paid at the time of the signing of the contract and a *mu'akhkhar* (deferred dower, making up the balance) to be paid at the time of termination of the marriage, whether by death or divorce. The amount of *mahr,* although it varied enormously by social class, was usually a substantial sum.[39] The prompt receipt of the *muqaddam* was a right of the bride and, as we have seen, she could refuse to consummate the marriage until it was in her hands.

The muftis agreed that the *mahr* must be stated and must be paid. It might happen that a woman married and had the marriage consummated without a *mahr* having been paid. In such a case, the groom owed her a fair *mahr*, to be paid immediately. Once any marriage contract was concluded, the husband was obligated for the *mahr* as a debt to his wife. Should he have died before he had delivered the *muqaddam* of the *mahr*, his wife could take this amount from his estate or, in the case of an impecunious or minor husband, she could demand that amount of the *mahr* from her husband's father, if the father had served as *wali* or *wakil* for his son.[40] Upon the termination of the marriage through death or divorce, a woman could also lay claim to the *mu'akhkhar*. And in the case of a deceased husband, this claim would be made against his estate and had to be honored despite the disclaimers of his other relatives, unless they could produce legal proof that the debt had already been paid. Even if the woman were to have died shortly after her husband, her heirs could bring a claim against the husband's estate in the amount of the *mu'akhkhar*.[41]

The *mahr* had to be paid to the bride herself, not to any of her relatives. In the case of a girl in her minority, her *wali* was authorized to receive the *mahr* on her behalf, and she would be permitted to take possession of it when she came of age. Once a woman was in her majority, however, she was entitled to receive and control her own *mahr*: the muftis agreed that her father had no right to receive or keep the *mahr* over his daughter's objection.[42] Khayr al-Din, who handled many cases from the rural hinterland, where a free and easy attitude toward the *mahr* seemed to prevail, repeatedly took families to task for such lax *mahr* practices. To pay the *mahr* to a woman's mother or uncle, whether or not they subsequently spent it on the bride, was as good as not paying it at all: it was like paying the *mahr* to a "stranger." The husband in such a case still owed his wife a *mahr*, and he had to pay it, even if he were not successful in recovering the money he had given to his wife's mother or uncle.[43]

Nor could the prompt payment of the *mahr* be held hostage to bargains a family might strike over the marriage of their daughter. A man who married a woman and paid 85 (*ghurush?*) to her father, 5 to her paternal uncle, and 20 *ghurush* worth of clothing to the bride was informed that the entire amount had nonetheless to be paid to the bride as her legal *mahr*.[44] Khayr al-Din also actively discouraged the practice of exchanging brides for token *mahr*s:

QUESTION: A man said to his brother: "Arrange a marriage for my minor daughter and you can marry using her *mahr*," and [the uncle] married her off to a man with [the father's] permission and a *mahr* was named. And then [the uncle] married [the groom's] sister and a *mahr* was named for her. But the two marriages were consummated before the *mahr*s were received. Then the minor came of age and her father died. Can she authorize her brother or someone else to demand her *mahr* from her husband, and is the husband required to pay it? Likewise, can the husband's sister appoint an agent to collect her *mahr* from her husband, and is he obliged to pay it?
ANSWER: Each of them can appoint someone to receive the *mahr*, and it is not legal for the father to give the minor's *mahr* to her uncle or anyone else . . . for it is not his property, it is her property . . . and the groom must pay his debt, the *mahr*.[45]

Khayr al-Din also insisted that the *mahr* stated in a marriage agreement could not be reduced on a whim. A man who married his wife with legal witnesses and then decided to go to court with the bride's father to redo the marriage with a discounted *mahr*, "out of fear of the size of the first *mahr*," was informed that the first *mahr* could not be changed once it had been agreed upon.[46]

Through these opinions the jurists, especially Khayr al-Din, waged a campaign of sorts against the manifold ways in which family interests worked to erode a woman's right to her *mahr*. They were acutely aware that illegal practices existed, and they were consistent in upholding the principles that the *mahr* must be proper, must be paid, and must become the enduring property of the bride. Although none of the three muftis was willing to countenance social practices that interfered with the proper disposition of the *mahr*, they all demonstrated a greater willingness to accept local community practice when it came to other property transfers that took place at the time of marriage.

It seems to have been customary, although not required by law, for the groom to send the bride and her family a number of presents after signing the marriage contract and before the marriage was consummated. These presents, which could include clothing, jewelry, and money with which to purchase food for wedding-related entertaining, did not form part of the *mahr*, but rather were voluntary and customary gifts. The groom was under no legal compunction to send these gifts, though we can imagine that social pressure to do so must have been considerable. The muftis turned their attention to this custom of engagement presents when conflicts arose over the ownership of this property, usually in the context of the cancellation of the marriage before consummation. al-'Imadi noted that whereas a groom could expect the return of the *mahr* if the bride's family withdrew from a marriage arrangement, the presents he might have made to her of money, food, and clothing were not part of the *mahr* and therefore did not need to be returned to him.[47] Khayr al-Din took a similar position, at least on money that was spent on providing food for guests. As long as the groom had given this money in the knowledge that the family of the bride was going to use it to feed guests, then it was as if he had entertained the guests himself, and the money would not need to be returned.[48] Both jurists noted that such presents were made in accord with local custom and did not fall under the rules governing the *mahr*: in this instance, at least, the expectations arising out of standing customary practice loomed large in the reasoning of the jurists.

They took a like approach to questions concerning the bride's trousseau (*jihaz*). Brides were often fitted out with house furnishings and clothing by their families of birth when they first embarked on married life. But families were not legally required to provide a *jihaz*: if the mother of the bride or the groom himself complained that the bride's father had not given a sufficient *jihaz*, they were told that the father could not be compelled to do so.[49] Once such items were given, however, they normally became the property of the bride herself. A father or mother or both often furnished a daughter with a trousseau, which the daughter took with her to her marital domicile. If the giver of the trousseau subsequently died and his or her heirs tried to claim that trousseau items formed part of the estate of the deceased, they were told that the *jihaz* was the personal property of the bride and no longer that of her parents—it formed no part of the parents' estates.[50]

The muftis were sensitive, however, to local customs that might modify the bride's claim to this property. al-'Imadi worked from the notion that a bride could expect to receive a proper *jihaz*. If a mother fitted out her daughter with clothes and such clearly in excess of what could be expected, in one case double the value of her *mahr*, then the mother's claim that some of these things were given only on loan should be credited.[51] He was also willing to accept legal evidence that weakened the bride's claim to this property, such as a legal agreement between a father and his daughter stating that certain materials she took with her upon marriage were not *jihaz* but a loan. al-'Imadi in particular also bowed to the "custom in the community," where it was present, of making the *jihaz* a loan, a form of property shared by the bride with her family. When a family could demonstrate that such was local custom, the items of the *jihaz* were regarded as being on loan from the bride's family and would therefore revert to that family upon her death.[52]

The muftis, then, upheld the right of a woman to enter her marriage with certain endowments. Legal discourse held that the *mahr* was an absolute requirement of every marriage, and that a bride's family had no right, once a woman reached legal majority, to receive or control the *mahr*. Juristic discussion of the *jihaz*, however, was more nuanced. Discussion of the *jihaz* was permeated by the tension between, on the one hand, a woman's right and need to enter a marriage with independent means and, on the other hand, the family's desire to minimize the loss of family property occasioned by the marriage of their daughter. Although the muftis usually affirmed the bride's right to the *jihaz* as her private property, they also proved willing to bow to social practices that retained effective family control of this property.

The gendered transfers of property that accompanied a marriage were strictly regulated. The bride, but not the groom, was to be endowed by her husband's family through the *mahr,* and by her own family through the *jihaz.* In supporting her right to these endowments, and to full control of them, the muftis endorsed the idea that a woman should enter marriage as an empowered individual. At the same time, however, the jurists recognized and accepted the fact that local communities might adjust these transfers. The bride as propertied individual must be weighed against the need and desire of the bride's family to retain some control over their property: the custom of "lending" or "sharing" bridal trousseaus was accepted by the jurists as a legitimate community practice. Still, the bride was always to be launched into marriage with some clearly defined property of her own: the strongly gendered notion that the husband was to be the head of the marital household was thus tempered at a practical and significant level by some required provisioning of the new wife.

The importance of the dower, however, should be kept in perspective. The courts provide ample testimony to the fact that women acquired property in a variety of other ways, as well: they had legal rights to shares in family estates, for example, and were frequently named as beneficiaries of *waqf* (religious endowment) properties. For many women, then, the marital rights to property were supplemented by other forms of wealth. Indeed, estate records for women in eighteenth- and early nineteenth-century Nablus demonstrate that the amount of the dower named in a marriage contract represented roughly 15 to 25 percent of a woman's estate at the time of her death, and tended, not surprisingly, to be a more significant part of a poor woman's estate, since the middle and upper classes had far more access to other forms of family wealth.[53] Still, the *mahr* and *jihaz* could lend a new bride, especially one in a modest household, crucial control over money and goods central to the well-being of the new family.

LIVING A MARRIAGE

Once the marriage contract was agreed to and the marriage had been consummated, the bride and groom each acquired a set of rights and obligations, all of which were strongly gendered and therefore asymmetrical. The muftis took pains to delineate the legal expectations and requirements of husbandly and wifely behavior, which strongly differentiated male and female roles in the household. In such precise regulation of gender difference lay the key to gender harmony: men and women must understand their responsibilities to each other, responsibilities based on innate differences. Legal discourse did not view such difference, however, as justification for gender-based oppression since marital rights and obligations seemed to be aimed at achieving social harmony between two gendered individuals by assigning them distinct roles, while ensuring that the potential for abuse of these roles was limited.

The husband's role, first and foremost, was that of provider. Legal discourse held the husband responsible for the material support (*nafaqa*) of his wife. Once the marriage had been consummated, and for as long as he was married to her, a man was required to support his wife. Moreover, a wife was entitled to receive *nafaqa* before consummation of the marriage if she was refusing consummation because of nonpayment of *mahr*. Should the husband divorce her, he was also required to support her for the following three months of her waiting period (*'idda*), a period that was extended for a pregnant woman until after the birth of her child. If the husband should die, the responsibility for *nafaqa* was terminated, except for a pregnant wife who could claim *nafaqa*, through to delivery of her child, from her husband's estate. Such support must be provided only if requested during the period of the marriage or the *'idda*; no retroactive requests could be made.[54]

All the muftis agreed on the principle of *nafaqa* for a wife. The matter of how she was to claim this support was rather more complicated, however, and occasioned considerable discussion. We may assume that in the usual course of events the food, shelter, and clothing that comprised *nafaqa* were provided routinely, as a normal part of the life of a marital household in which husband and wife lived together, sharing food and shelter. A man might have taken it upon himself to name an amount of *nafaqa* to be paid to his wife as part of an agreement he had made with her at the time of the marriage or later. Although such an agreement was not legally required, once made it could be enforced by the court.[55] The muftis and courts would take up the issue of *nafaqa* only when something had gone wrong, as when a husband for one reason or another was not fulfilling his obligations, or when some unusual arrangement had been made and was not honored. The absence of a husband, or his failure to provide adequately for his wife, could throw the question of support into the laps of the jurists.

If a man were to leave the vicinity without leaving his wife the proper means of support or naming a substitute provider for her, she could choose to approach the court and ask for an assignment of *nafaqa*. The judge would then require that she swear that her husband had neither left her support nor named a provider, that she was not a "disobedient" wife (a category we will explore below), and that she had not been divorced. She might also be asked to produce, if the judge had no personal knowledge of her marriage, evidence that she was indeed married to the man from whom she claimed *nafaqa*. In response to her request for *nafaqa*, the judge was then authorized to fix an appropriate amount of support, expressed in money to be paid on a daily basis.[56] According to Khayr al-Din, certain procedures and standards of evidence had to be met before *nafaqa* could be assigned. He offered one terribly flawed case as an example of how it should not be done:

QUESTION: There is a man in Egypt who has a wife in Ramla, and she has a brother in Jerusalem who came to the qadi and asked that he assign *nafaqa* for his sister in Ramla from her husband in Egypt. The man did not present evidence of the marriage or of his agency [for his sister], nor did he have legal guardianship [of his sister]. She was not present, and she did not swear that he had not left her *nafaqa*. He [the judge] did not ask if they were poor or

rich or if one of them was rich and the other poor. . . . But he imposed on the absent man a sum of *dirham*s without first determining
the man's situation, and he wrote a document that contained an
assignment of a sum of *nafaqa* to so-and-so and her children
for the costs of meat, bread, oil, bath entrance, soap, laundry, and
all their needs, and the sum was, each day, 8 *qita' misriyya* [Egyptian
coins] imposed on the absent husband, and the judge gave her permission to provide for herself and her children, and the husband
will owe the money, and this permission was given to her brother,
her agent, "so-and-so." And it is the case that the children are in
no need of their mother and the daughter is weaned. . . . Is this
assignment legal?[57]

Khayr al-Din pointed out, in a lengthy response, that this case lacked
almost all the legal conditions for assignment of *nafaqa:* there was no evidence that the wife had made this request herself; she had not sworn that
her husband had not left her *nafaqa* and that she was not legally "disobedient"; and the judge had not investigated the material circumstances
of the couple and their children in order to assign a proper level of support. Elsewhere, Khayr al-Din reminded a judge that unless the husband
were away from his "hometown" (*balad*), he had to be present in court
when the judge assigned *nafaqa.*[58]

Once such conditions were met, however, and a judge had made an
award of *nafaqa*, a husband was legally required to make the payments,
and could be imprisoned until he did so.[59] If the husband could not be
found or reached, the woman who had been assigned *nafaqa* by the court
was authorized to borrow money in the amount of the assigned *nafaqa*,
and the debt devolved on her absent husband. The muftis were firm in
their position that any debts incurred by a woman for her awarded *nafaqa*
were the sole responsibility of her husband, once he became available.[60]
In this manner, the right of a wife to material support from her husband
could be activated and enforced by the legal system. The jurists underscored the central role of the qadi and court in the regulation of this support should problems arise: it was essential that a woman obtain a legal

assignment of *nafaqa* if she wanted to force her husband to meet his obligations, or if she needed to borrow money in his absence.

The muftis did not limit their discussion to legal procedure; they were also ready to give detailed instructions concerning what a wife could expect and require as appropriate *nafaqa* in terms of food, clothing, and shelter. A woman could not demand more than what was considered necessary to the customary standard of living of her social group, as we saw above in the question of food consumption. Thus the jurists were careful to guard a wife's right to *nafaqa*, but they were equally firm in limiting this support to a reasonable level. *Nafaqa* for clothing for the wife of a poor man of the Ramla vicinity, according to Khayr al-Din, should be sufficient for two gowns, a veil, and a cloak, the customary clothing of the poor. These clothes, along with a diet of barley bread, corn, and oil, were all that a poor woman might demand.[61]

al-'Imadi's opinions, by contrast, dealt with questions of a rather more exalted lifestyle, in keeping with the Damascus milieu. A woman from a comfortable background might refuse the hard work of making her own bread and processing other food at home; if such a woman did not have a household servant, her husband had to provide her with prepared food bought in the market as part of her *nafaqa*. A woman of respected status, such as a *sharifa*, whose husband was affluent, could demand a servant to help with household tasks. The *nafaqa* owed to a woman could also extend to her personal slave, if her husband was of sufficient wealth to maintain a household with slaves.[62] *Nafaqa* was not conceived of, then, as simply provision for subsistence: wives had to be supported in the manner to which their social group was accustomed, and the legal system was mandated to divine the standards of any social group in a given community.

In the matter of housing in the legal marital domicile, the muftis followed what they held to be very distinct guidelines. A wife had to be lodged in a house "separate" from the dwellings of other people, defined as one with a door that could be locked and that was fully equipped with its own conveniences, including a private toilet and kitchen. The house had to have its own water supply—a well or cistern—or the husband had to be prepared by other means to supply all the water his wife needed. The house had also to be located among "decent" neighbors where the wife's person and money would be secure.[63] The human need for same-sex companionship also figured into housing requirements: a woman had to have *mu'anasa*, companionship or conviviality, which could be provided, we may infer, only by female relatives, friends, or servants. A man might need to lodge a female companion with his wife if she lived without servants, but trustworthy neighbors would usually suffice.[64]

One form of companionship a woman might legally refuse was that of a co-wife. The muftis agreed that co-wives were entitled to separate dwellings, that is, dwellings that fit the definition of a legal marital residence, complete with locks and private bathroom and kitchen facilities. Such a dwelling could be located right next door to that of a co-wife—off the same courtyard, for example—so long as it fulfilled the requirements of separate locks and facilities.[65] A woman could not refuse, however, to live in the same house with other members of her husband's family, including his concubine, his mother, or his children by another mate as long as they were not yet old enough to "understand sexual intercourse."[66] She was not obliged, however, to suffer undue noise or annoyance as a result of living with her husband's family.[67] Although a wife could be expected to live with her husband's family members, the reverse was not at all the case. A man had no obligation to house his wife's children by a former marriage. Nor was he required to lodge his mother-in-law in the same house with her daughter; on the contrary, he could forbid her the house altogether with the exception of a weekly visit.[68]

The muftis, then, not only held the husband responsible for the *nafaqa* of his wife, but also elaborated in some detail on the form this support should take. The obligation of the husband to support his wife entailed a provision of food and clothing of a quality appropriate to her social background, an issue particularly prominent in the more urbanized and stratified locales. Much of the discussion of shelter, by contrast, focused on the strict legal requirements of the marital domicile. The gendering of space, and particularly of marital space, emphasized the married woman's need for privacy and relative autonomy, needs shared by all women regardless of social class. Spatial arrangements that allowed a woman to lock herself away from her husband's kin in order to perform her toilet and to prepare her food in private were an absolute minimum standard for a marital household, and were enforced by the jurists.

The muftis, in attending so earnestly to the details of *nafaqa* arrangements, signaled a serious commitment to the husband's obligation to support his wife and the wife's right to demand support commensurate with her status as a married woman of a given social class. A strongly gendered vision of male as provider and female as recipient of support, indeed one with well-defined rights to a certain level of comfort and privacy, underlay this discourse. There was a bill to be paid, not surprisingly, for this support: husband as provider for the marital family was also husband as ruler of the marital family. Upon marrying, a man acquired certain rights vis-à-vis his wife, rights that the jurists worked to clarify for their time and place.

The muftis agreed that a wife owed her husband obedience. The woman who did not obey her husband, the *nashiza* (disobedient) wife, forfeited her right to *nafaqa*. Such forfeiture was, indeed, the only penalty mentioned by the muftis, the sole disciplinary action they appeared to sanction. On a practical level, a husband could, of course, choose to divorce a disobedient wife, or to take a second wife as a form of discipline, but neither of these acts was suggested as sanction by the law. What exactly constituted disobedience (*nushuz*), and thus justified cancellation of *nafaqa*, involved the jurists' understanding of what a man could and could not demand of his wife.

The basic purposes of marriage—social harmony and sexual satisfaction—could not be fulfilled unless husband and wife lived together. The muftis agreed that a wife must inhabit the marital domicile. At the same time, however, there was room for some difference of opinion on the extent to which a woman must accommodate her husband if, for example, he decided to travel or move. As a general principle, a wife had to move with her husband, but the jurists found that the distance involved as well as the location of the woman's hometown and her place of marriage were factors to be considered. A wife could be required to move with her husband if the distance was not considerable. al-'Imadi, in giving the nod to husbands who wanted to move their wives from one-fourth to one-half a day's journey away, cited the positions of two different fatwas for guidance. The first stated that a man could move his wife as far as he liked so long as it did not constitute "exile." The second defined the maximum distance as that which one could travel in a day before nightfall.[69] Khayr al-Din also noted that the fatwa literature varied on this problem, especially when there was a considerable distance involved: past muftis had differed over whether a woman could be declared *nashiza* if she refused to move a "distance of travel" with her husband.[70] When a "distant place" was involved, however, the question was clear as far as al-Tamimi was concerned: the husband was absolutely forbidden from insisting that his wife move.[71]

Legal discourse recognized a certain level of ambiguity in the rule that a wife must live in her husband's house, an ambiguity that arose from the idea that a woman should not be asked to make a move that entailed undue hardship. The woman's hometown, defined as the place where she was married, was a factor to be considered in assessing the hardships of a move. Although a woman did not enjoy the unconditional right to remain in her hometown, she could refuse to move too far abroad.

A wife had far less latitude, however, in her ability to leave her husband's house against his wishes. All the muftis agreed that a woman who defied her husband by leaving his house was *nashiza* and had therefore forfeited her *nafaqa*.[72] A man might grant his wife permission to leave on an extended visit, but she should return in the time agreed. One woman left her husband in Lidd to attend her sister's wedding in Nablus with the understanding that she would return in a month. When, after a year had passed, she still remained in Nablus, Khayr al-Din found that she had clearly disobeyed her husband and had lost her rights to *nafaqa*.[73] Nor was illness a valid excuse for absence from the marital domicile. In the case of an ill woman who had moved to her parents' house and remained there despite her husband's demand that she return, al-'Imadi ruled that she should return to her husband "if it is possible for her to move to her husband's house on a litter or similar thing." If she refused, she would lose her *nafaqa*.[74] And in the most extreme yet permissible of behaviors, a husband was within his rights to forbid his wife to leave the house or to receive visitors, with the exception of her parents.[75]

There is little question that the marital domicile was the husband's house, that he was the proprietor, and that he set the rules and the tone. His comings and goings were not to be scrutinized so long as he fulfilled his obligation of providing for the household. It fell to the wife, on the other hand, to make such moves and other accommodations to life in her husband's house that might be necessary to realize the marital purposes of sexual companionship and social harmony. There was no hesitation on the part of the jurists in requiring wifely obedience as the key to this harmony, but a husband's demands were also subject to some constraints. His wife must live in his house, but the house must be equipped and located in such a way as to ensure her comfort, both material and emotional.

The muftis were mostly silent, however, on the question of the rules governing a husband's physical abuse of his wife. Only Khayr al-Din addressed this question directly:

> QUESTION: There is an evil man who harms his wife, hits her without right and rebukes her without cause. He swore many times to divorce her until she proved that a thrice divorce [a final and irrevocable divorce] had taken effect.
> ANSWER: He is forbidden to do that, and he is rebuked and enjoined from her. If she has proved that a thrice divorce has taken place, it is permissible for her to kill him, according to many of the *'ulama'* [jurists] if he is not prevented [from approaching her] except by killing.[76]

Elsewhere Khayr al-Din included decent treatment of a wife among a man's marital obligations: in addition to the expected requirements of a separate and secure domicile with conveniences, respectable neighbors, and so on, Khayr al-Din expressly forbade any "intentional ill treatment" of a wife.[77] He further noted that any battery of a wife that resulted in injury could be a matter for legal compensation: the man who knocked out three of his wife's teeth had to pay her the legal indemnity prescribed for such an injury.[78] Although there are no such explicit statements in al-'Imadi's or al-Tamimi's work, all the muftis did agree that such advantages as a husband may have secured from his wife by using force or threats of force were ill-gotten gains with no legal standing in court. A husband had no right, automatic or otherwise, to his wife's property. Men who coerced their wives to give them legal agency, to pledge their property as security for a husband's borrowing, to hand over their *mahr*s, or to forgo the balance of a *mahr*, were reminded that coercion invalidates such transactions.[79] The jurists were certainly conscious of the fact that the assignment of strongly gendered roles in marriage risked just this kind of abuse, but they relied on moral exhortation, as well as sanctions against gaining legal advantage through abuse, to lend protection of a sort.

The rights and obligations of a married couple heightened and ordered gender difference. A man was to provide; a woman was to consume. A man was to decide; a woman was to obey. The idea that such net differentiation ran the risk of fostering hostilities, of producing social rifts if not outright conflicts along gender lines, lurked between the lines of the legal discourse. The task of a legal thinker thus was not only to distinguish the male from the female, but also to elaborate on distinctly gendered rights, many of which privileged men but some of which worked to temper male dominance. The legal discourse on marriage was being constructed, of course, by men who themselves had a vested interest in male dominance. Marriage, however, was more than an individual male-female affair: it was a relationship with broad social resonance. As part of their responsibility for the welfare of the community, the muftis were pledged to harmonizing gender interests as much as possible and reducing what they termed abuses. It was in this spirit that they attacked the thorny problem of entrenched social practices that violated the letter and the spirit of the law, many of which tended to disregard female rights in marriage.

CAMPAIGNING AGAINST CUSTOM

On occasion, the jurists could find themselves locked in combat with social custom when custom threatened to undermine the harmony in gender relations they sought to achieve. The three muftis were unanimous, for instance, in their condemnation of the practice of testing a bride's virginity on her wedding night and then returning her to her family should she fail. The fact that all three jurists addressed this issue suggests that at least some communities in all three locales did integrate tests of a woman's virginity into the ceremonies surrounding the consummation of the marriage. But virginity or the lack thereof on the part of the bride was irrelevant, according to the muftis, to the constituting of a marriage. Men who found that their brides had been previously "deflowered" were informed that they could not cancel the marriage, send the bride back home, or demand the return of the *mahr*.[80] Khayr al-Din offered the most thorough critique of this practice when confronted with the situation addressed in the fatwa opening chapter 1 (a man who found his bride deflowered on their wedding night sent her back to her family, and then abducted her sister). In a sizzling response to this drama of honor, shame, and violence, Khayr al-Din made two distinct arguments against the practice of testing virginity. First, he averred that the condition of a woman's hymen had nothing to do with the legal contracting and consummating of a marriage. Indeed, once a marriage was legally contracted and consummated, the only way to dissolve it was by legal divorce with all the concomitant obligations of payments both for the balance of the *mahr* and for support during the wife's waiting period. A man cannot simply return a woman as damaged goods. Second, Khayr al-Din questioned exactly how a man would know that his bride was not a virgin. In a sophisticated and compelling discussion of female anatomy, he added that a hymen can be damaged or destroyed in a number of ways, including by accident or illness. A groom is not an expert on such matters, and is in no position to make such judgments. It is the woman's testimony that takes precedence.[81]

The virginity test, and the consequent rejection of the deflowered bride, thus had no place, according to the muftis, in Muslim marriage practices. It was a social practice that not only lay outside the pale of the laws governing marriage, but could also result in the active violation of Islamic law: a woman returned to her family after her wedding night was not, in these circumstances, properly divorced, and was, by the letter of the law, still married. If she were nonetheless treated as a divorced woman, that status would mean that her rights to *mahr* payment and support had in turn been summarily abrogated, an entirely unacceptable and illegal outcome.

The practice of marriage by capture incurred equal opprobrium. In the following instance, Khayr al-Din was consciously addressing the practice of abducting a bride as a not uncommon rural phenomenon:

QUESTION: A man approached a woman, a virgin in her legal majority who was married to someone else, abducted her in the month of Ramadan, and took her to a village near her own village. He brought her to the shaykh of the village, who welcomed him and gave him hospitality and protection. There the man consummated the "marriage," saying "between us there are relations." Such is the way of the peasants. . . . What is the punishment for him and the man who helped him? . . . Should Muslim rulers halt these practices of the peasants . . . even by combat and killing?

ANSWER: The punishment of the abductor and his accomplice for this grave crime is severe beating and long imprisonment, and even worse punishment until they show remorse. It is conceivable that the punishment could be execution because of the severity of this act of disobedience to God. This practice—and one fears for the people of the region if it spreads and they do not halt it—will be punished by God. The one who commits this act, and those who remain silent about it, are like one who punches a hole in a ship, [an act] that will drown all the passengers. . . . It is the obligation of Muslim rulers to commit themselves to putting an end to this revolting practice . . . even if it means punishment [of the offenders] by combat and killing.[82]

Here and elsewhere the jurists acknowledged the existence of a marriage practice that not only negated almost all the Islamic rules governing marriage arrangements, but also circumvented both family participation and female choice, a practice that nonetheless was accepted not only by the general population of a given area but even by those in authority, the village shaykhs.[83] In his use of the dire analogy of the sinking ship, Khayr al-Din assailed such a practice as hostile not just to the interests of a bride and her family, but also to the moral fiber of the community as a whole. The alarm in his response undoubtedly reflected a very real fear that parts of the Muslim community for which he felt responsible could slip out of his control, that is, out of the orbit of Islamic law and legally sanctioned Muslim practice. The importance of marriage as a central Islamic institution, lying at the heart of the social life of the community, was abundantly clear to Khayr al-Din.

Another local practice addressed with disapproval by the muftis was that of bartering brides between families, or of bartering a bride for other favors, from another family. Such arrangements usually involved the waiving of a *mahr:* the fathers or guardians of two girls would agree to exchange them as brides between the two families without incurring any expense. Alternatively, a girl might be given to another family as a "gift," for purposes of goodwill or material gain. According to the muftis, this bartering of brides could not be squared with Islamic law. Every marriage had to meet the basic requirements of the marriage contract, including a *mahr,* proper guardianship or consent, and witnesses. Every marriage arrangement had to be able to stand on its own: it could not be made contingent upon the arrangement of another marriage or the delivery of goods or favors, and it could not be such as to deprive a bride—or, worse, two brides—of proper *mahr.*

The muftis were consistent in their opposition to any such external, contingent conditions.[84]

Although legal discourse on marriage evolved in response to concrete social conditions, it did not accommodate all existing social practices. On the contrary, certain persistent customs, including the testing, abducting, and bartering of brides, were consistently and heatedly denounced by the jurists, but not thereby eradicated. In an institution constructed to recognize, and yet harmonize, gender difference, practices that reduced women to chattel, whose sole worth lay in their usefulness to immediate family honor or gain, could not but be viewed as destructive. Men and women came to marriage as distinct people with asymmetrical rights and obligations reflecting innate biological difference. On such difference lay the foundation for a stable and harmonious relationship, one that was central to the overall good of the Muslim community. The jurists, in their recognition and elaboration of gender difference, did not, however, countenance practices that translated this difference into unbridled male domination. The legal discourse existed, in large part, to regulate gender relations, to ensure that both males and females understood the proper parameters of their social roles, and to prevent abuses in gender relations, most of which occurred at the woman's expense. The presence of this discourse, and its accessibility in the form of a local mufti or other *'ulama'* who was learned in the fatwa literature of the past, provided a firm basis for claims to gender-based rights, as well as protests and appeals of gender-related abuses.

MARRIAGE IN THE COURTS

The fatwa literature was, at least in theory, a literature reflecting legal practice: the muftis were usually responding to concrete problems either raised by members of their own communities or referred to them from other Muslim communities by judges in the Islamic court system. All problems pondered were supposed to refer to actual situations: jurists were not to invent interesting questions in order to solve them. We cannot be sure, however, that such was the case. Probably many, or most, or even almost all of the questions the muftis answered did originate in real life, but we cannot rule out the possibility of embroidery or invention. The fatwa literature, then, cannot be read as a straightforward record of events in the life of a given community, so much as a reflection of the concerns of its learned hierarchy as they constructed a social discourse within and for that community.

The Islamic courts provided a forum for the multiplicity of voices in the community. Qadis listened to the plaintiffs who came to the court, weighed the evidence of witnesses and documents, and ruled on the issues. They did not indulge in juristic discussion and, indeed, rarely justified or explained their rulings. The minutes of the court proceedings are much more a record of the uses the population made of the Islamic court. The problem is often presented by a plaintiff in some detail, complete with explanations, evidence, and narrative, but the judge's reply is sparse and unadorned, usually a simple thumbs up or down, perhaps with brief instructions on the implementation of the decision. The fatwa literature captures the contours of an intellectualized legal discourse, and the court records demonstrate, in part, how that discourse was understood and mobilized by members of the community in the pursuit of their own ends.

In part, too, the courts acted as a marriage registry. In Jerusalem, and to a lesser extent in Nablus and Damascus, marriage contracts were entered into the court records. In each case, the titles and lineages of the bride and groom, their agents or guardians, the type and amount of *mahr*, and the witnesses to the agreement were included in the written form of the contract.[85] People of various social backgrounds registered their marriages in the courts, but in Damascus and Nablus only a minority of the population appears to have bothered to do so. The advantages of such registration included the establishment of a permanent written record of the marriage agreement. To register your marriage in court was to place marriage and its consequent rights and obligations squarely under the jurisdiction of the Islamic court, in anticipation of the court's playing a role in any later disputes concerning marriage arrangements or *mahr* payment. Such registration was not essential for subsequent claims or complaints concerning a marriage, but could no doubt lend strength and substance to testimony on amounts of *mahr* and other matters. A written record of the marriage agreement might also have served to obviate the need for court action: if the facts of the marriage were readily available to all, many potential disputes simply would not arise.

Indeed, people did not often bring questions about marriage arrangements to the court, although occasionally the issue of whether a marriage had actually occurred came up. A Muhammad b. Kamal explained to the court in Jerusalem that he had married off his minor son to his sister's minor daughter through a legal agreement with the girl's guardian that included a fair *mahr*. He went on to complain that the girl's guardian had subsequently refused to deliver the girl to her husband, claiming that there had been no such marriage. There was no written agreement in the court for anyone to consult, but there were witnesses to the marriage who could testify that it had indeed taken place as claimed, and the guardian was ordered to deliver the bride to her rightful husband.[86] Another Jerusalem bride claimed through her agent that she had never been married to a plaintiff, but both her maternal and paternal uncles testified against her, saying that she had been married off as a minor eight years previously, and she was "delivered" to her husband.[87]

In these cases, men who sought to claim their brides were relying on the court to enforce dictates concerning marriage arrangements. They were careful to bring evidence that demonstrated their adherence to the legal requirements of marriage arrangements, and in the case of the marriage of minors, they were conscious that the proper assignment of guardianship and fair *mahr* payment were mandatory.

Not all court decisions worked against the interests of females. Women relied on the privileging of *mahr* in the legal discourse to collect the balance of the *mahr* after marriage was ended by death or divorce. In theory, a woman was to receive any unpaid *mahr* from her husband's estate as a first claim against his property. In practice, a woman might have to resort to the court to collect unpaid *mahr* from recalcitrant heirs. In cases where a woman came in person (a not uncommon practice among the less affluent) or sent her agent to court to claim such a debt, the judge was quick to instruct her husband's other heirs that her claim took priority.[88]

A woman might also go to the court after her husband had divorced her in order to collect unpaid *mahr*. A Maryam bt. 'Abd Allah appeared before the judge in Damascus and complained that her husband had just divorced her but would not pay her either the 15 *ghurush* he still owed her from the *muqaddam* of her *mahr* or the 70 *ghurush* he now owed for the *mu'akhkhar*. The judge then stepped in to regulate the payment of this money as well as other divorce obligations.[89] Such claims, of course, did not always go the woman's way. If a man could produce evidence that he had paid the *mahr*, or if he took a formal oath that he had paid it and the woman could not produce oral or written evidence to the contrary, the court would deny the woman's claim.[90]

The fear that claims for unpaid *mahr* might be made at some point in the future seemed to underlie the practice of registering the payment of *mahr* in the court. Upon occasion, couples would come to court so that the husband could testify that he had divorced his wife and she could testify that she had received the balance of her *mahr* and had no further claim on her husband.[91] There was no ostensible legal reason for testifying, in court, to *talaq* (divorce) and the subsequent payment of *mahr*, save for the avoidance of dispute in the future. That some men chose to protect themselves in this fashion suggests the degree to which *mahr* obligations were taken seriously.

In the care with which the court registered *mahr* amounts, entertained *mahr* claims, and oversaw *mahr* payment, we discern the fine hand of the muftis, whose consistent position on the enforcement of *mahr* obligations resonated in court practice. There were a multitude of ways, no doubt, by which female rights to a fair amount and timely payment of *mahr* were abridged in social practice, but the courts were not ready to countenance deviation from the legal discourse on the sacrosanct nature of this female right and male obligation. Women did not bring this matter to the courts very often, but the fact that at least a few women continued to do so suggests that they were conscious of the legal position on this issue.

The greatest proportion of court cases that were related to marriage, outside of the contracts themselves, were those concerned with the *nafaqa* (support) that a husband owed his wife. Most *nafaqa* cases consisted of an award of *nafaqa* that was expressed as a certain sum of money each day to provide for the woman's needs. These needs varied but often included the costs of her clothing, rent, meat, oil, bread, drink, soap, henna, and bath admission, valued at anywhere from two to eight *qitaʿ misriyya* in the eighteenth century. The judge awarded a stated amount of *nafaqa*, authorized the woman to spend this amount of money on herself, and made the husband responsible for the payment of this sum and possibly any debts the woman might incur should she have to borrow money to cover awarded but unpaid *nafaqa*. A typical *nafaqa* award read as follows:

> The shariʿa judge award *nafaqa* for clothing, house rent, toiletries, soap, bread, oil, and other things, and the rest of her legally prescribed needs, to the *hurma* [lower-class woman] Amna bt. Darwish al-Ghazawi on the date below [in the amount] of two *qitaʿ misriyya*. He permitted her father Darwish to borrow the money, and the debt incurred will be owed by her husband, Ahmad b. Subah, who was away from the city and had left her with neither *nafaqa* nor anything else, nor had he delegated a legal provider for her in the prescribed legal fashion.
>
> Recorded at the beginning of Rabiʿ I 1138 H. (1725 A.D.).[92]

Women like Amna came to court seeking *nafaqa* awards when their husbands were absent and had failed to leave them with support. Often the woman appeared in person to swear that her husband was indeed gone and that he had not left her with adequate means, although on occasion she might send an agent to present her case. In some instances, provisions had seemingly been exhausted, such as in the case of one Saʿda, who told the judge that her husband had left her two jars of oil, some fabric, and some fabric, and some greengroceries. He had been gone, however, for a year and a half, and these supplies were manifestly inadequate. In this case, and in virtually all the others that reached the court, the judge accepted the woman's testimony and made an award of *nafaqa*.[93]

Just as many awards of *nafaqa* were made when the husband was not absent at all, but rather appeared in the court with his wife to be assigned his responsibilities. In these cases, the women did not testify to their husbands' absence or lack of support, but did receive an award and the same kind of permission to borrow up to the amount of the award, if necessary, against the husband's repayment. *Nafaqa* was awarded for the same items and in the same amounts as would have been the case with an absent husband.[94] Lacking explicit explanation, we can only speculate on why some couples sought an award of *nafaqa* from the court. In some instances, a woman would ask for a legal award on the eve of her husband's departure on a trip, as a means of protecting herself against his failure to return in the expected time period. Once she had the award of *nafaqa* in hand, she could then borrow the money she needed without incurring personal debts. Women also used the court forum for redress. If a husband was not supporting his wife adequately, she could come to court, have her *nafaqa* awarded, and thus obtain legal backing for a specific level of support. Once *nafaqa* had been awarded, the failure to pay it in the specified amount was punishable by imprisonment, a situation affording her a powerful means of enforcement.

That women came to court, with or without their husbands, to seek awards of *nafaqa*, strongly suggests that the legal discourse on marital *nafaqa* was taken seriously by the court. The Islamic court system acted to buttress a wife's right to material support: there is no record of refusal of such requests. Women came to court in expectation that the court would, in fact, back them up and act effectively in securing them proper support. By repeatedly raising this issue, women also contributed to its centrality in the discourse on marriage. Here as elsewhere it is impossible to draw a neat line between the discourse being fashioned by the muftis and the activities of the judges, plaintiffs, and defendants in court. We must assume a reciprocity between an intellectualized legal discourse and the more diverse discourses of the court system, as the muftis responded to social concerns and the courts and the people took heed of past juristic responses and anticipated those of the future.

The court system embraced the binary opposition of gender in marriage that was elaborated by the muftis. The judges and the court's clients accepted this gender difference as the foundation of the marital relationship. They also cooperated, however, in the larger project of ensuring that this difference promoted the harmony and stability of the community rather than breeding its disarray. By acting as a marriage registry where the details of marriage agreements could be recorded for future reference, by enforcing legal procedure and rights to *mahr*, by ensuring that *nafaqa* obligations were met, and, above all, by supplying a dependable space in which people could express their grievances and expectations, the courts helped elaborate the legal discourse on gender and served as the arena for the intersection and interaction of different levels of that discourse.

The marital relationship that the muftis and the courts described and defined served as a potent symbol of women's place in society. The distinctness of male and female roles in marriage, the clear denotation of the marital household as the locus of male authority, and the expectation of wifely obedience as fulfillment of a primary marital duty all point to a gendering of the marital relationship in which male was equated with power and command and female was equated with subservience and obedience. Embedded in the muftis' discussions of marriage and the courts' judgments, however, were nuances that suggest the ways in which social relationship softened and transmuted symbol. A woman was expected to come to a marriage endowed with property; she could choose her own spouse; she had well-defined and well-enforced expectations of support; and she enjoyed certain protections from coercion and abuse. She acquired through marriage a number of important rights—to property, to material and psychic comfort, to sexual satisfaction—that could not help but hedge the gender dichotomies of marriage under law. A woman's ability to call up these rights and privileges was circumscribed to a great extent, however, by the extent to which she could exercise control over the duration of her marriage, that is, by her power or lack of power in the face of the ever-present threat of divorce.

CHAPTER 3

Release Her with Kindness

Divorce

QUESTION: There is a poor man who married a virgin in her legal majority, but he did not pay her stipulated *mahr* [dower] expeditiously, nor did he provide *nafaqa* (support), nor did he clothe her. This caused her great harm. Must he follow one of God's two commands: "Either you maintain her well or you release her with kindness?" And if the judge annuls the marriage, is it on account of the severe harm being done to her?

ANSWER: Yes, the husband should do one of the two things, according to God's command: "maintain her well or release her with kindness." . . . You cannot sustain [indefinitely] such needs through borrowing, and it appears that she does not have anyone to lend her money, and the husband has no actual wealth. They [the shari'a and Hanafi legal thinkers] prefer that the qadi appoint a Shafi'i *na'ib* [assistant judge] to separate [*fasakha*] them. Many of our [Hanafi] legal thinkers [*fuqaha'*] chose this path in cases of extreme necessity, and it pleases the *faqih* [legal expert] because it spares him an awkward situation and saves the woman from harm. And God knows best.[1]

The decidedly promarital position taken by Ottoman-period muftis is not to be confused with the notion that marriage is a permanent arrangement. The muftis did try to ensure that marriage arrangements were made in such a way as to minimize gender conflicts and promote the stability of matches. All three muftis, however, as well as the judges and clientele of the courts, recognized that some marriages were not made to last. As is apparent in the opinion of Khayr al-Din presented above, they helped develop a legal discourse that addressed the question of defective or unwanted marriages and regulated the termination of marriages. This discourse was strongly gendered, in the sense that it defined male and female rights and obligations differently, proceeding from a clear appreciation of the net distinctions and asymmetrical relations between husbands and wives.

Legal discourse accepted a range of situations in which divorce could provide the remedy for a marriage that was either defective or unwanted. The multiplicity of types of divorce corresponds, in legal reasoning and social practice, to the different meanings of divorce: divorce was the corrective for a "bad" marriage; divorce solved problems of incompatibility; divorce functioned as a form of social control.

First, marriages that were not fulfilling the purposes of marriage should be annulled. As we shall see, a woman or a man confronted with basic defects in a marital relationship, defects that rendered the fulfillment of fundamental rights and duties impossible, could seek the remedy of divorce. This type of divorce or annulment (*faskh*) could only be granted by a qadi in a court setting: the aggrieved party must come to the court, present the grounds for annulment, and abide by the qadi's decision. Just what constituted sufficient grounds remained an area of considerable discussion among the muftis, as we shall see.

A marriage need not be defective, however, for one or both parties to seek a divorce. Indeed, a husband enjoyed the right to divorce (*tallaqa*) his wife for any or no reason. *Talaq* took effect with the pronunciation of a proper divorce formula, and, though there were a number of rules governing the husband's obligations to his wife in the wake of such a divorce, a man was free to divorce his wife without recourse to judge or court. For this reason, *talaq*, although undoubtedly the most prevalent form of divorce, was not entered into the court records as such. The obligations a man incurred with *talaq*, however, might well become a source of litigation, and it is in the disputes surrounding the aftermath of such a divorce that we encounter the reasoning of the muftis and hear the voices of divorced wives and husbands.

Unlike her husband, a woman could not divorce (*tallaqa*) her spouse where and when she pleased. Legal discourse provided a way, however, for her to leave an unwanted marriage. A woman could ask her husband to divorce (*khul'*) her in return for a compensation. Such a divorce, of course, required the cooperation of her husband and entailed some material sacrifice on her part, but it did constitute recognition of the fact that a woman might have reasons of her own to leave a marriage. *Khul'* was often recorded in court, although no reasons for the divorce needed to be offered.

We encounter also one other type of divorce, the meaning of which was not so transparent. In a significant number of cases, a divorce (*talaq*) results from an oath the husband has sworn. Typically, a man would swear that if he did or did not perform a certain act, or if his wife did or did not obey some command, or even if some unrelated person did not fulfill an obligation, then he would divorce his wife. Once the oath was sworn, it could not be retracted, and divorce became contingent on whether or not the condition of the oath was fulfilled in due course. Neither defects nor incompatibility were at issue here, since *faskh, khul'*, and simple *talaq* sufficed for those purposes. This type of divorce, or threat of divorce, appears to have been, in part, an accepted form of male social control, rather than a way to resolve intractable marital problems.

Just as men and women had many distinct, indeed opposite, rights and obligations in marriage, so too was their access to divorce largely gender based. The male power of *talaq*, the power to end a marriage at any time and without offering justification, stood at the center of a system of divorce that privileged men. The muftis, the Islamic courts, and the population who used them, however, were enunciating a legal position on divorce that hedged this male power with certain responsibilities even as it elaborated on the ways in which women could seek recourse in the case of an unwanted marriage. And in so doing, they modified and reinterpreted certain aspects of Hanafi doctrine. Legal discourse did not reverse the strongly gendered character and male bias of Islamic legal precedent on divorce, but it did work to soften this bias by defining female rights and strictly regulating divorce procedures.

ADDRESSING DEFECTS

Jurists of the Hanafi legal school, the school adhered to by all three muftis under consideration, authorized qadis to annul (*fasakha*) marriages if they exhibited certain defects that made realizing the purposes of marriage impossible. The mutual right to sexual fulfillment meant that certain absolute impediments to sexual intercourse could be grounds for the termination of a marriage. A husband's impotence, for example, as discussed in the preceding chapter, was grounds for an annulment if the condition lasted more than a year, as opined in long-standing Hanafi doctrine. Less predictably, however, the muftis agreed that should a husband contract leprosy, his wife could seek an annulment.[2] Serious communicable illness and insanity raised insurmountable barriers to the enjoyment of marital intimacy and therefore, at a spouse's request, constituted grounds for an annulment, despite the fact that authoritative Hanafi texts appeared to limit the grounds for annulment to impotence.[3]

Defiance of the requirements for the suitability of matches, for the appropriateness of the groom in terms of religion, caste, and class, could also lead to divorce. Under the law, a Muslim woman could not be married to a non-Muslim (*dhimmi*). When a woman converted to Islam, therefore, and her husband remained a *dhimmi*, the qadi was forced to annul the marriage. Moreover, the ex-husband was required to assume all the responsibilities of a Muslim divorce, that is, the paying of any deferred dower and the costs of support during the *'idda* (waiting period).[4] The absence of suitability by caste or class was also grounds for annulment if a woman's marriage had been arranged by anyone other than her father or grandfather. The woman herself, or her marriage *wali*, could ask the qadi for a *faskh* if the absence of suitability were to be proved. A woman could also obtain an annulment if she had been coerced into marriage, again by someone other than her father or grandfather.[5] *Faskh* was seen, at least in part, as a remedy for defective marriage arrangements that had united unsuitable couples.

A woman might also have chosen to exercise her right to refuse a marriage made while she was in her legal minority, by asking a qadi for an annulment when she reached her majority. In order to obtain a *faskh*, she had to fulfill several conditions. First, the marriage had to have been arranged by someone other than her father or grandfather. Second, she had to choose divorce as soon as she reached puberty; she could not delay. Third, she had to testify to her choice and apply to the qadi for the annulment. This final condition could be waived, according to Khayr al-Din, in the event that her marriage had been arranged by someone other than the most appropriate marriage *wali*.[6] Although the muftis were clear and unequivocal in their support of a woman's right to choose annulment upon coming of age, we cannot be sure to what extent this right was exercised. While, as we shall see, the Damascus, Jerusalem, and Nablus courts of the period granted annulments for other reasons, we did not uncover any instances of *faskh* as a coming-of-age choice in those courts. It may be that few minor marriages were arranged by people other than a girl's father or grandfather. Moreover, we may assume that there was considerable social pressure on a young woman not to reject a marriage arranged by her family, to say nothing of the fact that the marriage she sought to reject would have been one she had already been living in, and therefore accommodating, for some time.

All in all, the Hanafi jurists of the time entertained few valid reasons for *faskh*. A husband's impotence, insanity, or virulent disease, a *dhimmi* woman's conversion, grave defects in marriage arrangements made by someone other than the family's patriarch, and choice upon coming of age were the only grounds for requesting an annulment from the qadi. In point of fact, however, the vast majority of *faskh* decisions found in the courts of the period were not based on Hanafi jurisprudence at all, no matter that we are dealing here with Hanafi courts. In a striking instance of juristic accommodation, all three muftis accepted *faskh* as a remedy when a woman's husband was not supporting her, either because of poverty or because he had disappeared and left her without adequate support.

Our three Hanafi muftis did not claim that Hanafi law and Hanafi judges could grant an annulment if a husband was not providing for his wife. They did, however, point out that the Shafi'i and Hanbali schools of law used *faskh* as a remedy for this situation, and that Hanafi judges, though not authorized to apply Shafi'i or Hanbali rules themselves, should accept the rulings of Shafi'i and Hanbali jurists and treat them as legally binding. Khayr al-Din, in the chapter's opening fatwa and in the following, sums up this position:

QUESTION: There is a poor woman whose husband is absent in a remote region and he left her without *nafaqa* or a legal provider, and she has suffered proven harm from that. She has made a claim against him for that [support], but the absent one is very poor. The resources [intended] for her *nafaqa* were left in his house and in his shop, but they are not sufficient for her to withstand her poverty. She therefore asked the Shafi'i judge to annul [*fasakha*] the marriage, and he ordered her to bring proof. Two just men testified in conformity with what she had claimed, and so the judge annulled the marriage. . . . Then, following her waiting period, she married another man. Then the first husband returned and wanted to nullify the judgment. Can that be done for him, when it was all necessary and had ample justification?

ANSWER: When the harm is demonstrated and the evidence for that is witnessed, the *faskh* of the absent [one's marriage] is sound. . . . It is not for the Hanafi or others to nullify this, as our *'ulama'* have said in their *fatwa*s.[7]

Here, and elsewhere, Khayr al-Din outlined his position on annulment in cases where a husband had left his wife without arranging for the *nafaqa* she was due, or where extreme poverty prevented fulfillment of the marital obligation of support. The Shafi'i and Hanbali approaches to this problem, based as they were on the Qur'anic injunction to maintain a wife properly or let her go, were seen as an acceptable solution, so long as the rules of evidence for the discovery of the wife's need and the husband's absence and nonsupport were followed. Although Hanafi judges could not preside over such a proceeding, they were enjoined by Khayr al-Din to accept the resulting divorce as legally binding; not only should they refrain from nullifying such a divorce, but they should also be ready and willing to sanction the remarriage of a woman who had been so divorced. The other Hanafi muftis concurred. A Hanafi judge should respect the Shafi'i or Hanbali *faskh* and permit such a woman's marriage to a second husband.[8] There is even a palpable sense of relief, in Khayr al-Din's opinions, that the Shafi'i and Hanbali options existed, so that a remedy for a difficult and painful situation could be found.

The Hanafi qadis who staffed the Islamic courts in Damascus, Jerusalem, and Nablus, as well as the courts' clientele, were certainly cognizant of the muftis' position, and behaved accordingly. All three courts routinely granted women annulments, particularly in the case of desertion. A Hanafi qadi, however, could not easily annul a marriage when a husband went missing. For him, the marriage could be terminated only if the woman had received news that her husband had divorced her, had died, or had become apostate. The news had to be reported to her by trustworthy people, and she had to "believe it in her heart." Otherwise, she was still married, regardless of the length of her husband's absence or her material conditions, according to the Hanafi muftis.[9] The inability of the presiding Hanafi judge to grant an annulment on other grounds was easily circumvented, however, by allowing a Shafi'i or Hanbali *na'ib* to preside over such cases. Indeed, in all three towns it is clear that such a pinch hitter was invited by the Hanafi judge to oversee such cases, thus allowing *faskh* in cases of desertion or nonsupport to become a common ruling, despite the absence of support for such a ruling in classical Hanafi jurisprudence. In Damascus and Nablus, the Shafi'i or Hanbali assistants appeared usually without comment, whereas the Jerusalem court might specify that the regular Hanafi judge had given his permission to bring in the assistant. All three courts, however, accepted this practice.[10]

Such an annulment usually read more or less as follows:

> The *hajj* [one who has performed the pilgrimage] 'Ali b. Jadallah al-Maghrabi, the *hajj* Ahmad b. 'Amr al-Maghrabi, and the *hajj* Ahmad b. 'Ali testify to their knowledge of the *hajj* Ramadan b. 'Ali b. 'Abdallah al-Maghrabi and his absence, and to [their knowledge of] his wife, the *hurma* Fatima bt. ? b. Ahmad ? who is present in court. [She says] that he [the *hajj* Ramadan] married her and then traveled and left her without *nafaqa* and without a legal provider for a period of four years, and no news of his whereabouts has reached her. She swore to all that and asked the judge's permission for a *faskh*, and he gave permission and annulled the marriage.
>
> 12 Sha'ban 1154 H.(1741 A.D.)[11]

This document contains the essential minimum information for a *faskh*: the husband is absent and his absence is attested; the wife has been left without sufficient support for more than a year; the woman swears that her husband has left her no support (or insufficient support), and that she has not received news of him. Variations found in other *faskh* decrees include required testimony from witnesses that her statements about the duration of absence and the lack of support were true, and her own statement to the effect that she had suffered harm as a result of the lack of *nafaqa*. Upon occasion, the presiding judge might ask her to wait and be patient; she would refuse; and he would then give her three days to reconsider the matter before invariably issuing the *faskh*. There are no instances in which a judge refused a request for *faskh* in the case of desertion: the rules of procedure and evidence for such an annulment clearly were well understood by all parties.

More rarely, *faskh* might be used to end a marriage in which the husband was present but not fulfilling his material obligations. Such a possibility was clearly envisaged by Khayr al-Din in the fatwa opening this chapter, but it was by no means commonplace in the courts. That it was possible to procure an annulment if the groom did not pay up on the *mahr*, for example, was amply attested to by the activities of a woman known as the *hajja* Amna on behalf of her granddaughter, the minor Khadija. The *hajja* Amna first appeared in the Jerusalem court to ask for payment of the *muqaddam* of her granddaughter's *mahr*, owed by the minor husband's guardian, a man named Sha'ban, father of the groom Hamuda. Sha'ban, who appeared in court with Amna, agreed that he had not paid the required *muqaddam* on Hamuda's behalf, and further testified that he did not have the money to do so. Amna then stated her intention to ask a Shafi'i judge for an annulment of her granddaughter's marriage, and Sha'ban raised no objections. In the subsequent case, presided over now by a Shafi'i judge, this same Amna appeared armed with a fatwa she received from the mufti in Jerusalem, which stated that if a husband cannot support his wife or pay the stated *mahr*, then the wife can go to court and request that a Shafi'i judge annul the marriage. This fatwa was written into the court record, and Amna requested, and not surprisingly received, an annulment of Khadija's marriage.[12] In a case like this, where the husband was not missing, Amna felt the need for care and clarity. She first established beyond doubt that Khadija had not received her *mahr* and was not likely to receive it in the foreseeable future. She made sure, by appearing in court with Sha'ban, that the absence of objection on the groom's side had been clearly demonstrated. Finally, she took the added precaution of procuring, from an authoritative source, a fatwa that expressly supported her request for annulment. In the process, Amna demonstrated not only that she knew her granddaughter's rights under the law, but also that she knew best how to go about securing them.

The idea that a marriage in which an impoverished husband was not fulfilling his obligation to support his wife should be terminated was an idea that percolated through even to the minority communities. One Niqula, son of Niqula, a Christian living in Nablus, came to the Islamic court to testify that he had divorced his wife, the Christian woman Hilana, daughter of Saliba, because he was too poor to support her.[13] Niqula was probably taking advantage of Islamic law and the Islamic courts to secure a divorce that would have been prohibited in his own community, a not uncommon practice. The fact that he chose to justify his decision in the terms he did, by referring in the Hanafi court to the Shafi'i grounds for *faskh*, suggests how widespread was the knowledge of these grounds as well as their acceptance by the court and community.

Faskh existed, however, primarily as a remedy for women who wanted to terminate a defective marriage. A husband who failed to *be* a husband, in the sense of sexual companionship or material support, could be divorced. It was also possible to address the problems of the suitability of a match, the presence of coercion in the marital arrangements, and the absence of choice in minor marriage, so long as the woman's father or grandfather had not made the arrangement. That women knew and availed themselves of most of these options is made clear by the record of litigation. Although *faskh* was available to men as well, it was extremely rare for men to request annulment, for the simple reason that they could easily divorce their wives without arguing any defect or recourse to any judge. That the exclusively male *talaq* was a far more flexible instrument of divorce than the equal-opportunity *faskh* does not mean, however, that it was not governed by certain clear rules of procedure that, if violated, would be enforced by the courts and jurists.

DIVORCE AS A MALE PREROGATIVE

The muftis and courts were not, of course, called upon to adjudicate *talaq* in the sense of weighing a man's right to divorce his wife in given instances, or examining the quality of his evidence. Quite simply, a man could divorce (*tallaqa*) his wife at any time, in any place, and for any or no reason. He could threaten divorce once or twice with impunity, but once he pronounced the proper divorce formula, the divorce took effect immediately. He could retract his divorce declaration, but only if he had made it revocable, that is, had pronounced the divorce formula only once or twice, and only if he had uttered his retraction before the end of his wife's prescribed waiting period. With the third iteration of the phrase "I divorce you" (the three stated over any span of time) or the phrase "I divorce you thrice," the divorce became final and irrevocable. A man could not then remarry his divorced wife until she had married and been divorced from another man, after which events he would have to enter a new marriage contract and pay another *mahr*. It was understood, and accepted, that a man might deal with the problem of second thoughts by arranging a marriage with a *mahr* and an immediate divorce for his ex-wife, as discussed by al-ʿImadi:

> QUESTION: There is a woman whose husband divorced her thrice, and she completed her waiting period. Then he married her to his adolescent slave in a legal marriage, and the slave consummated the marriage by inserting the tip of his penis into the meeting point of the lips of her vagina. Then he withdrew from her. The marriage was annulled, and her waiting period ended. Is she permissible to the first [husband]?
> ANSWER: Yes, and the matter is fully explained [in the following sources].[14]

Such a procedure posed certain difficulties: the husband had to have a slave on hand to do his bidding, or be able to recruit a cooperative and trustworthy man, and the woman had to agree to this brief marriage and the minimal intimacy required by law. In short, it was not a loophole wide enough to undermine the meaning of irrevocable divorce.

When the muftis and courts got involved in *talaq* as referees, it was usually when some question arose about whether or not a divorce had actually occurred, and what type of divorce it was. In order to pronounce a *talaq*, a man must be mentally competent. Evidence of mental illness that affected rationality might therefore render a divorce invalid. Khayr al-Din outlined the mental states that a judge should look for to decide on mental incompetence and therefore nullify a divorce:

QUESTION: A man was behaving at times like an insane person, to the extent that he was brought before a judge and imprisoned in an asylum [*maristan*]. But his insanity was not confirmed. Does this mean he is imbecilic [*ma'tuh*]? If he pronounced an irrevocable divorce, is the divorce valid or not?

ANSWER: If, when this state seizes him, his speech and actions are not proper except in rare moments, and if he hits and curses, he is insane [*majnun*]. But if he is dim-witted and confused, and unable to manage but does not hit or curse, then he is imbecilic [*ma'tuh*]. At any rate, the divorce is invalid, because all divorces are invalid if pronounced by the insane, the imbecilic, the mentally confused, the unconscious [*sic*], or the epileptic during a seizure. If he had once been insane, and then he claimed under oath that he had been seized by the madness again [and had therefore pronounced an invalid divorce], then his oath is accepted. But if he had never been insane before, then his claim should not be accepted except with evidence, and God knows best.[15]

al-'Imadi agreed that a man whose speech showed signs of diminished rationality could not divorce his wife while he remained in this condition.[16] Any divorce pronounced by a man deemed not in his right mind was not recognized by the law, and his wife would continue to receive marital *nafaqa*, and could not ask for the balance of her *mahr* or remarry. A sane man who pronounced a divorce in a fit of anger, however, was bound by his words and could not retract: if he became enraged by his wife's calling him a "cuckold" or "riffraff" and pronounced a divorce in a moment of pique, he had to live with the resulting divorce.[17]

The provision nullifying divorce by the insane undoubtedly protected women from the whimsical behavior of unbalanced husbands, but one suspects that it could also be used by men to wriggle out of divorces pronounced in haste and repented at leisure. A man went to the Nablus court on behalf of his daughter, 'Aisha, to complain that her husband, Ramadan, had quarreled with her and divorced her irrevocably. She wanted the divorce to be recognized, but Ramadan was claiming that the divorce did not really take place because he was habitually seized twice a day by uncontrollable rages, during which time he lost his mind and did not remember what he said or did. Since he was able to produce two witnesses who testified to the pattern of insanity brought on by these fits, the judge ruled the divorce invalid, citing a fatwa that nullified any divorce pronounced by an insane man. 'Aisha, no doubt to her great disappointment, remained married.[18]

Nor could a man divorce his wife during an illness that led to his death. It was very much in a divorced woman's interest to prove that divorce had occurred as her ex-husband lay on his deathbed, particularly if there was much of an estate involved. If she could establish that her husband had died from the same illness that he had when he divorced her, she could then inherit her legal share (one-eighth) of his estate; otherwise, she would be effectively disinherited. The muftis accepted a woman's testimony to this effect unless the ex-husband's other heirs could produce witnesses to the contrary.[19] If, however, she could be shown to have *requested* the divorce, she forfeited her rights to inherit from her ex-husband.[20]

The muftis and courts dealt not only with the question of whether a divorce was binding, but also with the issue of whether a divorce had occurred at all. Sometimes the problem arose because of the absence of notification. Khayr al-Din discussed a situation in which a woman had been deserted by her husband and left without *nafaqa*. She had gone to court to have an amount of *nafaqa* assigned to her so that she could borrow what she needed to support herself, as a debt owed by her husband to the lender. Apparently her husband had divorced her while he was away, although she had not learned of it at the time; when the news finally reached her she still did not "believe it in her heart." Until such time as she received confirmation of this divorce, either by a written document or legal oral testimony, said Khayr al-Din, she was not, from her point of view, divorced at all, and could continue to collect *nafaqa*, which her husband would eventually have to repay.[21] The choice was hers to make, however, and women who received news of divorce pronouncements were free to believe the news and consider their marriages at an end.

Because *talaq* did not require a court or witnesses, disputes could also arise about whether a man had actually pronounced the divorce formula. When the parties in such cases disagreed about what had transpired, the muftis and courts were asked for a ruling. Not surprisingly, it was usually the woman who wanted to force her husband to honor a divorce he had pronounced and then rued. The position of the muftis was clear: once an irrevocable divorce was pronounced, it took effect immediately and irretrievably; a husband could not renege.[22] Should such a dispute come to court, the judge would ask the woman or her agent to produce witnesses to the divorce. One such case led a notable family of Jerusalem to air marital troubles in public. The lady (titled *al-sitt* and *khatun*), Saliha, sent her uncle to court as her agent to press a claim against her husband, the "shaykh of skaykhs" 'Isa. She testified, through her uncle, that some two years previously her husband had quarreled with her, insulted her, and pronounced a divorce. Although it was a revocable divorce, we must assume that he had not retracted it during her waiting period, and thus, according to Saliha, she was no longer married to him. 'Isa denied everything, but Saliha's uncle produced witnesses who testified to the divorce, and the judge ruled the divorce valid.[23] We can only guess at the circumstances surrounding this case. Why had it taken Saliha two years to seek judicial sanction for this divorce? Had she been separated from her husband since the time of their quarrel, and was she now resisting a renewed attempt to force her to return to him? Was the court process a final step in her attempts to collect the balance of her *mahr*? Although we will never know the background of this case, we can see that, with the support of her family, Saliha was able to enlist the court in her bid to hold her husband to a divorce he sought to deny all knowledge of.

Although women were not free to repudiate (*tallaqa*) their husbands, the legal position that divorce pronouncements, once uttered, had the full weight of law enabled them to force their husbands to honor such pronouncements, even those made lightly or in jest, if it seemed to a woman's advantage. This was not perhaps a very powerful weapon, but it did provide one way for a woman to choose divorce. From the point of view of the legal discourse on divorce, such a provision signaled the graveness of any talk of divorce. A man had the right to repudiate his wife, but he must beware: this was not a right to be exercised causally. If he misspoke, he could be held to his word by a wife who had been waiting for just such an opportunity to leave him. And as soon as the *talaq* was pronounced, the bills came due: a woman could demand payment of the balance of her *mahr* and continued support during her waiting period. Indeed, a great deal of the litigation surrounding *talaq* involved disputes about these accounts.

Once a "thrice" or irrevocable divorce was pronounced, a woman could demand immediate payment of the balance (*mu'akhkhar*) of her *mahr*.[24] If the divorce was revocable, she could make this demand at the end of her post-*talaq* waiting period (*'idda*), so long as her husband had not taken her back.[25] In the case of a divorce declared before a marriage was consummated, the man was to pay half of the total *mahr*, as stated in the marriage contract, but could retain the other half.[26] The muftis and courts agreed that any owed *mahr* constituted a debt that must be paid immediately and in full. Should a man fail to pay, his ex-wife could petition the court to imprison him until he settled the debt. A man might of course plead poverty, in which case he was not jailed, unless his ex-wife produced evidence of his ability to pay. Impoverishment did not cancel his debt, however, and the judge was instructed by the muftis to arrange a payment schedule by attaching any wages or other income the man earned, leaving him only enough for subsistence. And should his fortunes improve, he became immediately liable for full payment.[27]

The man who pronounced a divorce was also responsible for his wife's support during her waiting period, a period that endured for three of the woman's menstrual cycles (three months if she was no longer menstruating), or, if she were pregnant, until she had delivered (or miscarried). If the marriage had not been consummated, this waiting period and the costs of its support were waived. But as long as a woman remained in her *'idda*, she could not remarry. Her husband was responsible for her full support (*nafaqa*) during this period, and she, in turn, had to remain in the marital domicile. Should she leave this house to live elsewhere, without strong justification, such as the imminent collapse of the house, her husband could terminate support payments.[28]

Such, then, were the husband's clear obligations in the wake of *talaq*. Some couples (at the husband's behest, we can only assume) came to court after a divorce to record the fact that the divorce had taken place and that the husband had discharged his obligations.

> 'Abd al-Rahim b. *al-hajj* Ashur al-Zahki [?], the mature youth, came
> to court and acknowledged that he had divorced [*tallaqa*] his wife,
> Rabiyyah bt. *al-hajj* ? who is present in court. She acknowledged that
> she had received from him seven *ghurush*, the amount of the
> *mu'akhkhar* of her dower and the *nafaqa* of her waiting period. . . .
> And that neither one has any further claims on the other.
>
> 17 Jumada II, 1154 H.(1741 A.D.)[29]

The couple's appearance in court is not required, of course, for the legitimation of the divorce; the main purpose to be served, it would seem, was to establish a written record that could subsequently protect the husband from future claims. This case is typical: it simply reports that the divorce has taken place and registers the woman's receipt of what she was owed. That many Muslims and even some Jews would on occasion use the court to document payment of divorce obligations suggests that the possibility of future litigation loomed large.[30]

Indeed, women did take their husbands to court after *talaq* had occurred in order to press claims to the balance of the *mahr*, the costs of the *'idda*, and other debts owed by their husbands. A woman named Nafisa, for example, claimed that her ex-husband Muhammad had not paid her the 10 *ghurush* he owed her from her *mahr*, or the costs of her *'idda*, or an old debt of 35 *ghurush*. Muhammad allowed that he had divorced his wife, and that he did owe her the *mahr*, but he denied her claim for repayment of the old debt. Upon being asked by the judge to produce evidence for this claim, Nafisa brought two witnesses to the debt, and Muhammad was held liable for all three claims.[31] Women also went to court to ask the judge to assign a specified amount of *nafaqa* for their *'idda*. The judge would calculate the support money just as he might in the case of marital *nafaqa*, awarding the woman sufficient money to cover the costs of food, shelter, bath entrance, and other necessities as would be appropriate to her class.[32]

As often as not, however, women who pressed post-*talaq* claims in court lost their cases. The principles of male financial obligations so clearly enunciated by the muftis were not in any way abridged in these cases, but women often ran up against the difficulty of proving their claims. If a woman could not bring evidence to offset her husband's claim that he had paid the *mahr* and any other monies owed her, his disavowal was accepted. Often a husband could produce his own evidence, either witnesses or a written document recording the *talaq* of the kind we have seen above, to support his contention that he had previously settled all claims.[33]

Some of these cases seem to test our credulity, particularly when a woman was denied a claim she had pressed with compelling detail. One Maryam testified that her divorced husband owed her a great deal of valuable property, consisting of furnishings and personal items of clothing and jewelry. She presented a long and detailed list of the property, retained by her husband, that was rightfully hers, including such things as eight pillows, seven silk covers, a braided bed cover, a braided chair cover, 40 Chinese plates, 14 cups, 15 brass plates, a brass basin, four boxes covered in velvet, eight kaftans, a silver belt, a necklace of 190 old gold pieces, and so on, adding up to a total value of 1,206 *ghurush*. All these decorative household and clothing items were typically a woman's property, given to her at the time of marriage as presents from the groom or as part of her trousseau. In order to negate her claim, however, her husband was able to produce written evidence from a court appearance a few months earlier stating that his wife had received all her property at the time of *talaq*.[34] It is difficult to know if the cause of justice was served in this case, but the presence of the husband's evidence canceled the woman's claims without further discussion.

Talaq was a male instrument, a way for a man to extricate himself from a marriage without having to make his case to any authority. Neither the jurists nor the courts questioned this male prerogative, which endowed almost any man with the power to divorce his wife at any time. The muftis did, however, devote some of their time to the regulation of *talaq* by examining male capacity, enforcing rules of procedure, and policing the fulfillment of post-*talaq* obligations. Although any given *talaq* did not need the approval of the jurists and the courts to take effect, there were certain rules and responsibilities connected with the act that would, if necessary, be enforced by judicial authorities. The courts and the population who used them acted in ways that suggest that they knew these rules and felt compelled to observe them, at least at a formal level. *Talaq* was part of a gendered legal discourse that accorded men privilege, but the privilege was not to be construed as license.

KHUL‘: THE WOMAN'S DIVORCE

Women could not, of course, pronounce a *talaq*. Faced with an unwanted marriage that exhibited none of the defects that might qualify for *faskh*, a woman had one legal option: *khul‘*. In this form of divorce proceeding, a wife would request that her husband divorce her in exchange for a compensation she offered, which always included the waiving of any balance of her *mahr* owed by her husband and could entail additional payments as well, payments that might, for example, aim at reimbursing him for the customary marriage gifts. *Khul‘* thus provided a way for a woman to extricate herself from a marriage, albeit at significant cost. The muftis all accepted this type of divorce as legally binding, and issued fatwas that outlined the rules governing such a female-initiated divorce.

al-‘Imadi defined *khul‘* as essentially a *talaq* done with a wife's agreement and with compensation for the husband. As in *talaq*, the pronouncement of the divorce had to take a certain form: a man might say "You are divorced" or "I divorce you" and name a compensation, or the woman could say "Divorce me" for a stated compensation, followed by the husband's "I divorce you." In either case, *khul'* required a wife's agreement, both to the procedure and to the amount of compensation.[35] The naming of a compensation was not, however, absolutely necessary to the act of *khul'*, according to al-'Imadi:

> QUESTION: There is a man who divorced his wife with the pronouncement of a *khul'* but without [mentioning] money. He wants, after that, to take her back without her agreement, without a new marriage, and without a legal procedure. Can he not do this?
> ANSWER: *Khul'* is an irrevocable divorce and he cannot take her back except with her agreement, and the holding of a new marriage and its [taking] legal effect. With or without money, it is an irrevocable divorce [*talaq*].[36]

So long as the divorce was cast in the form of a *khul'*—that is, as a divorce with mutual agreement—it could not be retracted, regardless of whether compensation had been named and paid to the husband or not. Even if no compensation had been stipulated, then, the divorce was legally binding. A woman could be required, however, to pay a compensation after the fact: she would be required to waive payment of the deferred dower or, in lieu of any balance owed by her husband, she would have to repay him the prompt dower. The court could also insist that she make good on any promises she had made, whether of dower repayment or of additional sums of compensation money.[37]

The muftis were careful to note that a *talaq* divorce should not be taken for a *khul'* and used as a way to abridge a woman's rights. If a woman's father, for instance, asked her husband to divorce her for 60 *ghurush* and the husband then pronounced a "thrice" divorce, what had transpired was no *khul'* at all. Without the express consent of the wife and the proper *khul'* pronouncement, the divorce was a *talaq*, the 60 *ghurush* need not be paid, and the woman could demand the balance of her dower.[38] But if a *khul'* had indeed taken place, the *khul'* agreement canceled all the ties and obligations associated with marriage, including any outstanding *mahr;* the husband did owe his wife the costs of *nafaqa* during her waiting period, however, unless she had specifically waived her rights to this support as part of the *khul'* agreement.[39]

Most of the other rules of *talaq* applied equally to *khul'.* A woman who had been divorced by *khul',* for example, could not remarry until the end of her waiting period.[40] If, however, a woman was divorced (*khul'*) with her consent by an ill husband who then died from that illness, the divorce was valid, unlike the case in simple *talaq,* and she would not be one of her ex-husband's legal heirs.[41]

Khul' represented a means by which a woman could initiate divorce proceedings if she found herself in an unwanted, although not legally defective, marriage. To be successful, she needed the cooperation of her husband, who must either share her dissatisfaction with their marriage or be swayed by the waiving of debts and, sometimes, the further offer of a lump-sum payment. *Khul',* the woman's divorce, was not at all a unilateral and flexible instrument like *talaq,* the man's divorce. The male prerogative to enter and leave a marriage at will was not extended to women: male control of the marital relationship included male domination of divorce proceedings.

Still, *khul'* did offer women a way to try to leave a marriage, and many women of the period availed themselves of this opportunity. Although the muftis did not seem to require that *khul'* be certified in court to be binding, many couples did register their divorce agreements in court, most likely to establish a record that would militate against the wife's bringing future claims for divorce payments. Such agreements typically read as follows:

> The woman [*hurma*] 'Aysha bt. Muhammad ?, [whose identity is attested to by two male witnesses], asked her husband 'Amr al-Hamami b. ? b. 'Abd al-Qadus to divorce [*khul'*] her in exchange for his debts to her of the *mu'akhkhar* of her dower in the amount of 50 *ghurush* and the *nafaqa* of her *'idda* and the cost of her dwelling, and

all other wifely rights before and after separation. He divorced her and she is responsible for the *nafaqa* of her son by him for a period of three years from this date.

    19 Sha'ban 1152 H.(1739 A.D.)[42]

'Aysha had come to court with her husband 'Amr to register their divorce agreement, an agreement made at her request. She came veiled, and therefore two men who knew her had to testify to the judge that she was, in fact, who she was claiming to be.[43] She clearly specified what compensation she was making for this divorce: she waived the deferred dower and all the costs of her support during her waiting period. She also pledged to take on the cost of supporting their child for the next three years, a cost that would usually be borne by the father.

This kind of agreement seemed to be fairly standard, with certain variations. In some cases, like that of 'Aysha, a woman agreed not only to waive the deferred dower and the costs of her waiting period, but also to take on the support of her young children, undoubtedly those who were still too young to live with their father and thus had to remain in her care.[44] The most common *khul'* agreement, however, entailed only the woman's abdication of her rights to the deferred dower and the costs of the waiting period.[45] In a very few instances, a man could drive a harder bargain, such that the woman would have to surrender not only the deferred dower and the *'idda* costs, but also forgive back *nafaqa* or other debts, or surrender her share in some property, or pay a small monetary compensation.[46] Finally, in cases where the bride or her family requested a divorce before the marriage had been consummated, it was standard to waive or return the entire amount of the *mahr*.[47] There were relatively few agreements, however, that required more than the forgiveness of the deferred dower and *nafaqa*. In short, in almost all *khul'* agreements a woman could obtain her divorce in exchange for forgoing modest payments from her husband. The impediment, of course, was that her husband had to agree to her request for divorce, for otherwise she could not leave the marriage. The record shows, however, that women did know about *khul'* and did manage to use it.

If a man wanted a divorce, *khul'* offered him some distinct advantages: he could terminate the marriage and avoid the financial obligations of *talaq*. It is quite conceivable that he might try to persuade his wife to agree to *khul'*, or might claim that a *khul'* had taken place when his wife had not, in fact, agreed to the divorce. The position of the muftis on this matter, as we have seen, was crystal clear: a woman had to have given active consent before a *khul'* was valid. Some women did claim in court, however, that they were owed dowers and property in the wake of *talaq*s that their husbands asserted were *khul'*s. Fatima came to the court in Damascus with her ex-husband Yusif, claiming that he had divorced her three days previously and had not paid her the 24 *ghurush* he owed on her *mahr*. Yusif claimed that the divorce was a *khul'*, which thus canceled all his debts to her. Fatima, when confronted in court with the question whether or not she had discharged him of all his obligations at the time of divorce, was forced to admit that she had, thereby losing her claim.[48] If a woman persisted in her claim that the divorce was *talaq*, her ex-husband could bring witnesses to testify that they heard the divorce take place and that it was a *khul'*.[49]

The man did not always carry the day, however, in such disputes. Zaynab, daughter of the shaykh Muhammad b. Juma' al-Far, claimed that her ex-husband Muhammad had divorced (*tallaqa*) her five days previously, and that he had failed to pay what he owed her: substantial amounts of property, including a deferred dower of 50 *ghurush*, the costs of her waiting period, and personal goods, including gold earrings, a silver belt, a braided scarf, a black (cat?) pelt, a loom, a rug, and so on. Her husband Muhammad countered that the divorce was a *khul'* pronounced in exchange for the cancellation of all debts, and he produced two male witnesses to support his claim. Zaynab responded by bringing in three witnesses of her own, two women and a man, who testified that the divorce was a *talaq*, and thus won her claim: Muhammad was required to pay all his debts.[50] The fact that Zaynab was the daughter of a shaykh (an honorific title denoting any of several possible positions) and, to judge from the amount of her deferred *mahr* and her possession of luxury goods, a woman in comfortable circumstances may well have helped her realize the intent of the law that *khul* never be imposed on a woman.

Finally, the courts supported the muftis' position that *khul* was irrevocable, and that once pronounced, a man could not retract it. One 'Aysha bt. *al-hajj* Khalifa brought her ex-husband Muhammad b. *al-hajj* Mustafa to court in Damascus and stated that they had undergone a *khul* divorce for which she had not only absolved him of her deferred dower and support for her *'idda*, but had also given him a mattress, blanket, and pillow in compensation. Now Muhammad was harassing her to remarry him, and she wanted the judge to instruct him to stop bothering her. Indeed, the judge confirmed very clearly the position of the muftis: after a *khul* had taken place, a man could not remarry his wife without her agreement and a full new marriage contract. The *khul* could not be withdrawn.[51]

The part of the legal discourse on divorce formed by *khul* tempered, to a degree, the male prerogative. The idea that women could initiate divorce proceedings, albeit only with their husbands' consent, demonstrated that women could have reasons of their own to be dissatisfied with a marriage that was not, strictly speaking, legally defective. A husband's failure to live up to his legal obligations for support and sexual intimacy could serve as grounds for annulment. *Khul*, however, enabled a woman to leave a marriage despite the fact that these obligations were being met and the stated purposes of marriage were being served. Although the jurists never made their views on possible reasons for *khul* explicit, their endorsement and regulation of the procedure could not but reflect an acknowledgment that a marriage could go wrong, from a woman's point of view, for more than the minimalist reasons of sexual access and support.

DIVORCE AS SOCIAL CONTROL

One other form of divorce much discussed by the muftis was the divorce by oath, a variation that became a possibility when a man swore (*halafa*) to divorce (*tallaqa*) his wife if certain events did or did not take place. This form of divorce took effect the moment the conditions specified in the oath were (or were not) realized. All three muftis were called upon repeatedly to determine whether the activating conditions of an oath had been fulfilled, and thus whether such a divorce had in fact occurred.

The one standard form of this divorce masked several distinct sets of circumstances surrounding the taking of such an oath. In some instances, men appear to have taken such an oath in order to discipline their wives; the activation of the divorce in these cases was usually contingent on the wife's failure to obey her husband.

> QUESTION: There is a man who quarreled with his wife and they were both living in his house. He swore to divorce her thrice if she left the house without his permission (and he was referring to the above-mentioned house) except to go to the baths. Then he took her to his mother's house. While he was gone [from his mother's house] she left his mother's house to go to her father's house, without her husband's permission. Does the above-mentioned divorce not take effect because he swore his oath in [his own] house?
> ANSWER: Yes [it does not].[52]

The husband's intent here—to punish his wife in the wake of a quarrel by confining her to the house—seems obvious enough. At the same time, he was exercising his prerogative to control his wife's movements, even to the extent of forbidding her any exit from the marital household, except that absolutely necessary for basic hygiene. This threat of divorce could be used to regulate a wife's activities in a number of ways. The husband could prevent her from visiting her own family's house by taking an oath of divorce if she entered her father's house within, say, a one- or two-year period.[53] He could also use this type of divorce as extortion: one man swore to divorce his wife unless she immediately handed over a ring he claimed belonged to him.[54] Another man might require his wife to grind grain on a certain day or forbid her to cut out a garment on that day, demands buttressed by his oath to divorce her if she did not do as he demanded.[55] In all these cases, the husband was not only activating his right to divorce his wife, but tying the divorce to wifely obedience, an obedience he could claim, as we saw in the preceding chapter, as his marital due but had little means of enforcing.

Many of these oaths of divorce are linked to what appear to be relatively minor matters: surely the day on which a woman grinds her grain or cuts out a garment is not a matter weighty enough to justify a divorce. In most of these oaths, then, the issue at hand was not some particular activity so much as the power of a husband to exert control: the male prerogative of *talaq* was being turned to its logical advantage as a weapon of domination. The muftis accepted this practice without much substantive comment. In general, their discussion was limited to the technicalities of the procedure. Did the man pronounce the oath properly? Were the conditions of the oath stated clearly and unequivocally? Did the woman's actions or failure to act, which would precipitate the divorce, conform to these conditions as precisely stated? So long as the rules were followed, this kind of oath taking and the resulting divorce were viewed by the jurists as legal and binding.

Such a divorce could, upon occasion, reach the courts. A man in Damascus named 'Ali took an oath to divorce his wife 'Aysha if she left the house without his permission. She did indeed leave without his approval, and the divorce took effect. 'Ali brought the matter to court three days later, not to register the divorce but to press a claim against 'Aysha for money she took with her that he thought was rightfully his.[56] There was no question about the validity of this divorce or about what had actually transpired: 'Ali had laid down conditions for 'Aysha's behavior that could trigger divorce, and she had knowingly activated the divorce by her refusal to accept his dicta. We cannot know with any certainty what calculations lay behind this series of events. Perhaps 'Ali was finally throwing down the gauntlet after a history of difficulties in exerting his authority. Perhaps 'Aysha was as happy as not to seize upon this opportunity to be divorced. Whatever the dynamics in this case, there is little doubt that such an oath of divorce often entailed a man's attempt to control his wife's behavior and, above all, to underscore male authority in marriage.

Not all such divorces were made conditional upon the wife's behavior, however. In a second, and quite distinct, form of this divorce, a man would make divorce contingent upon his own actions, usually upon the nonfulfillment of promises he had made to his wife.

> QUESTION: A woman claimed against her husband (who had yet to consummate the marriage), after his return from an absence from her, that he had made it conditional upon himself that if he were absent for such a period and left her without *nafaqa* or a legal provider, then she would be divorced. And [his] absence took place without *nafaqa* or a legal provider, and she had found herself impoverished by his absence. He denied the condition [of divorce] and the lack of *nafaqa* and a legal provider. She then produced a document written in Damascus that recorded all this. Is the document alone proof of [his having made] the condition of divorce, or not? If she presented proof of the aforementioned condition and he claimed the conveyance of *nafaqa* and the assignment of a provider, whose testimony has precedence? If his absence took place before consummation, is the aforementioned condition legally sound or not?[57]

This was clearly a very different situation. In making a divorce conditional upon his providing *nafaqa*, the man was promising his wife either to fulfill his marital obligations or divorce her. In this case, the matter was complicated by the rules of evidence and the fact that the marriage had not been consummated. Khayr al-Din, in his response, cited a number of conflicting fatwas and refrained from taking a clear position himself. The taking of such an oath was not, in itself, a problem. The muftis were often

asked about this type of divorce, one in which a husband might swear
(*halafa*) or make conditional (*'allaqa*) a divorce as part of his promise to
deliver on certain marital obligations, most commonly the provision of
nafaqa. He might take such an oath before departing on a journey, or
swear to remedy a present deficiency, such as inadequate housing, within
a certain period of time.[58] This type of conditional divorce was thus another road to what was in effect a *faskh*, or annulment for reasons of nonfulfillment of marital obligations. Rather than resorting to a Shafi'i or
Hanbali judge, however, to annul a marriage in which the husband was
not providing, some women managed to have their husbands swear a
special oath to support them properly or divorce them. Should that support not be forthcoming, the divorce would be automatic, and require no
adjudication. Of course, a husband might deny that he had sworn to divorce, and then, as we have seen, the woman would have to shoulder the
burden of proof. Still, it was possible for conditional divorce to operate
very much to a woman's advantage.

This form of divorce could also be used to underwrite promises that
went beyond the delivery of required marital support. Men might employ conditional divorce as security for loans from their wives. In such
cases, a man would swear divorce if he did not repay a loan of money or
property within a certain period of time. If his wife could demonstrate
that he had made the oath and had then failed to repay her by the appointed date, the divorce would stand up in court.[59]

Other promises took the place of inscriptions of special conditions in
the couple's marriage contract. Couples did not, in this period, take advantage of the legal provision, recognized by the muftis, of including divorce conditions in their marriage contracts that could work to expand
and clarify a husband's obligations. Extant marriage contracts almost
never list any conditions, such as the wife's right to choose divorce
should her husband take a second wife. The divorce by oath, however,
offered another avenue for the extraction of such a promise. A man
could, at his wife's request, swear to divorce her should he take a concu-

bine or a co-wife, with results just as binding as if that condition had been written into the marriage contract.[60]

Just how prevalent this practice was—securing promises from a husband through an oath of divorce—is difficult to determine. It did not require the intervention of a judge at any stage unless there was some difference of opinion between husband and wife concerning what had transpired. It could reach the court when a woman wished to have a divorce recognized over her husband's objections, as was the case of one Hamida, who came to court to claim her divorce from her husband Mustafa. She related that her husband used to live with her in a house she owned in Bab Tuma (a quarter of Damascus). Two years previously he had sworn an oath of divorce that was to take effect if he did not move out of her house, an oath sworn, we must presume, because of the inappropriateness of his residing in her house—he, as the husband, was supposed to provide the marital domicile. He did indeed move out of the house (she did not say whether she moved with him) and took up lodgings elsewhere. Eight days prior to the court appearance, however, he moved back into her house, thus activating the divorce. She was able to produce two witnesses to the oath, the divorce was ruled final, and Mustafa was informed that he must pay her the balance of her *mahr*.[61]

The divorce by oath, then, took on an entirely different cast when its conditions regulated the husband's, not the wife's, behavior. A man made promises to his wife, promises to support her properly, to repay debts, or to refrain from taking a second wife, and he backed up these promises by swearing divorce should he fail to live up to his word. In this context, divorce was not viewed as a hardship on the wife, as a weapon that could be used to punish and control her. On the contrary, the penalty of divorce here is a penalty to be suffered by the husband.

Although all three muftis discussed cases involving these two rather different types of divorce by oath, most of their fatwas on divorce oaths actually dealt with a third variant, one in which a man would swear to divorce his wife if he or others failed to perform certain acts that were entirely unrelated to his relationship with his wife. It was not uncommon, for example, for a man to swear to repay a debt to another by a certain date, and to seal his promise with an oath of divorce.[62] In these circumstances, the man was invoking the gravity of divorce implied by the enormous potential cost to himself of risking the loss of his wife by making her the security for his loan. He ran the risk, that is, of having the oath activated, of actually finding himself divorced should he be prevented from repaying his loan on time. This practice, in the abstract, affirmed the value of marriage by positing divorce as a powerful and impressive oath; at the same time, however, it seemed to trivialize marriage by suggesting that men would jeopardize this relationship in the interests of a business deal.

It may well be that many such oaths were not very serious, in the sense that neither the oath taker nor the hearer expected the oath ever to take effect. Indeed, we have found no evidence of such oaths resulting in divorce in court. The muftis, however, considered it a serious matter, and when asked their opinion on the nature of such an oath, they invariably found it legally binding, so long as it had been pronounced clearly and properly and the conditions of nonpayment had been fulfilled. As often as not, the issue was brought to their attention in the context of a woman's claim that her husband had sworn such an oath and later refused to acknowledge that the divorce had taken effect.

A man could also employ the oath to divorce his wife as a sort of moral exhortation for others.

QUESTION: There was a group of people who made [cooked] soap. A man placed his oil with them and ordered them to make it into soap for him. They put him off with excuses, and so he swore by divorce that if they did not make it for him after the batch that was currently on the fire he would take his oil away and complain to the *Basha* [Ottoman official]. If they were to make it for him with even one jar of his oil after the batch that was currently on the fire, did the divorce take effect on the strength of his oath?

ANSWER: No, the divorce would not take effect if even the smallest part [was used], because even the smallest part was covered by the oath, and God knows best.[63]

A man has sworn here to divorce his wife, but the entire weight of fulfillment of the oath has been shifted from his shoulders to those of the soap makers. In his frustration over the slack response to his soap order, he threatens to withdraw his business and to report them to the authorities, threats backed up by an oath of divorce. What is different in this case is that the man cannot control the outcome of his oath, for the oath is taken contingent on the actions of others. A fatwa of this sort, dealing with a man who had knowingly abandoned control over the outcome of an oath, is not unusual: all three muftis delivered opinions on similar divorces. A man might swear an oath of divorce if someone simply stole his quince, or if a man declined to enter into a business partnership with him, or if a man failed to return a chair he had taken from him.[64] There is not only loss of control in such a case, there is a pervasive sense of the casualness of the whole affair.

What did it mean to reduce the oath of divorce to a form of pressure to be used with recalcitrants in business or social situations? Again, this kind of oath might have been understood as a purely formal statement of a high level of frustration or anger, designed to capture the attention of the hearer but not meant to result in actual divorce. Still, the muftis always took these oaths seriously, no doubt to make absolutely clear that the precepts of the shari'a were not to be trifled with. If a man swore a divorce in technical conformity with the law, his intentions at the time would not avail. The fact that he had used the oath merely to signal his earnestness about some matter at hand did not diminish the force of the oath, and if such an oath came to the attention of the muftis or the courts it would be ruled legally binding, so long as it adhered to proper form and procedure. There was no place, in the dominant legal discourse, for such unauthorized, personal appropriation of the law.

The practice of divorce by oath, taken as a whole, expands our understanding of the complexities of marriage. An oath of divorce could be sworn for a number of quite different reasons: to assert male authority in marriage and punish female disobedience, to clarify or augment a husband's marital obligations, to signal seriousness of intent in social or business dealings. By positing divorce as one of the most weighty and consequential of oaths, this practice underscored the centrality of marriage to the life of the community. But reducing divorce to a convenient tool for the exercise of discipline, for expanding the terms of a marriage contract, or simply for demonstrating serious intent in routine business matters surely devalued the marital relationship. The muftis, by taking the position that all such oaths were to be treated as deadly serious, communicated, albeit in indirect fashion, their opposition to any pronouncement of divorce so casual as to trivialize marriage.

Some women, of course, took a more subversive approach to the matter of divorce by oath. Many of the cases of this sort reached the muftis or the courts because a woman had seized upon the opportunity offered by her husband's oath. Some women, surely, were cowed by the threat of divorce and the loss of marital home and support it entailed. But for others, as we have seen, such an oath offered quick exit from an unwanted marriage: a woman could choose to hold her husband to such an oath, even if he had not intended to follow through on it. Because of their position on the binding nature of such pronouncements, the muftis and courts had little choice if a woman asked for such support, and the woman usually won her case unless there had been some technical flaw in the way the oath was pronounced. The oath of divorce thus proved a double-edged sword.

ESTABLISHING THE LIMITS

That the muftis recognized and facilitated various divorce proceedings did not mean, however, that they had abandoned their distinctly promarital position. Not all marriages were meant to last forever. If a marital relationship suffered from some defect, if a man or woman were unable to fulfill marital obligations, or if either party actively and earnestly desired to end the marriage, there were legal means of divorce that carried no recognizable stigma. Marriage was not, however, a relationship to be severed casually or extralegally. It constituted not only a legal contract, but also a basic source of social stability and harmony, and any termination of the marital bond must therefore conform to the letter of the law. The muftis bridled at any suggestion of high-handed interference in a marriage, or of divorce that did not conform to legal requirements:

> QUESTION: There is a man who attacked his sister while she was in her husband's house, unsheathing his knife and demanding to take her away by force and coercion, and he [the brother] coerced him [the husband]. He [the husband] said: "Take her, she is thrice divorced," and [the brother] thus triumphed over him [the husband]. He [the brother] took her by force, and it was not possible to free her from him. If [the husband] intended to stop [the brother] but could not, is she thrice divorced or not?
>
> ANSWER: If he meant to stop him but could not, and the wife testified to that, whether by oral testimony or by her actions, she is not divorced.[65]

Here, the usually binding and irrevocable pronouncement of divorce is rendered null and void by evidence that the husband was forced to pronounce the divorce by threat of physical violence. The mufti looked for evidence of such coercion, and for signs that the husband had not wanted his wife to leave but could not prevent it. Interestingly enough, the wife was the key witness: if she were to testify to these events, or to demonstrate by her actions, such as her unhappiness with her brother or her willingness to return to her husband, that he had divorced her under threat, then the divorce did not take effect. This fatwa took a clear position against family interference in a couple's marriage; divorce was a matter to be settled between husband and wife, and if family intervention and coercion could be proved, the divorce was not valid. Dependence on the wife's evidence did, however, open the possibility of a woman's colluding with her family members to secure a divorce she desired. Above all, the fatwa underscores juristic opposition to a tendency among some to take matters into their own hands and make a mockery of the law: surely a divorce at knife point violates the spirit as well as the letter of the law.

Even more disturbing were cases where a sly deceiver would circumvent the law altogether and lure a woman away from her husband without even a bow to legal procedure.

> QUESTION: There is a man who duped [*khada'a*] the wife of a man, claiming that he was her relative, and he separated her from her husband. Should she be compelled to return [to her husband] or not?
> ANSWER: She is compelled to return to her husband. Our *'ulama'* say that whoever dupes the wife of a man and causes her to be separated from her husband will be jailed until he returns her [to her husband] or dies in prison.[66]

Here the "separation" of the couple was accomplished without divorce proceedings of any kind; the marriage was terminated simply by the wife's leaving her husband. As long as there is no formal divorce, however, the situation cannot be found acceptable. The couple were still married under law and should be enjoying their marital rights and fulfilling their obligations by living together. Clearly, the only solution to this problem was for the wife to return to the marital domicile. The blame was laid at the door of a third party, a man who had somehow led the wife astray, had somehow estranged her from her husband. The responsibility for the unlawful separation caused by the wife's departure was thus not hers at all, but was assigned to the deceiver, who must deliver her to her husband or suffer the consequences.

The major issue confronted here, apart from the necessity of choosing between living a marriage and procuring a legal divorce, was that of outside interference in a marriage. Neither the husband nor the wife chose separation. True, the wife left her husband, but she was misled, turned against her husband by what means we are not told. Such female passivity was not the usual presumption, as we have seen in our discussion of *faskh* and *khul'*, but it was apparently conceivable that a woman could be manipulated in ways that a man could not. If a woman was tricked, or a man was coerced, as in the preceding fatwa, into wanting or pronouncing a divorce, they could not be said to have chosen to end their marriage, as one or both of them must do under the law. For the jurists, marriage was a relationship based on contractual agreement between two people, and its fate could not be determined by others.

Through their discussion and treatment of divorce, the muftis and courts of the period expanded and elaborated the legal discourse on marriage and gender. Divorce was as highly gendered as the marital regime of which it formed a part. Male dominance was enshrined in *talaq*, the blanket right a man enjoyed to divorce his wife whenever he wished. The threat of *talaq* could be employed to discipline a wife and bolster male control within the marriage. The absence of any parallel female right underscored the extent to which male needs and desires were privileged by the rules of divorce. *Talaq* was not, however, simple license. As we have seen, the muftis and courts took seriously the obligations a husband incurred with the pronouncement of a divorce, and insisted that he pay his wife any debts, remaining *mahr*, or support monies due her. Women, buttressed in most instances by the rulings of the jurists, were fairly effective collectors of their ex-husbands' debts, and the muftis and courts were vigilant in ensuring that the privilege of *talaq* not be abused. A divorce pronounced in anger or jest, or as an oath or threat not intended to take effect, was nonetheless binding, and men who used this privilege as leverage against their wives or others were warned that they risked seeing a divorce lightly threatened actually take effect, despite their intentions to the contrary.

Nor were women without recourse should they wish to initiate divorce proceedings themselves. If in a defective marriage, a woman could ask the court for an annulment (*faskh*): the muftis and courts not only accepted the usual Hanafi grounds for annulment, but were prepared to approve the more liberal Shafi'i and Hanbali rulings when a woman requested them. The woman could also choose, with her husband's cooperation, to seek a *khul'* divorce and pay a compensation in return for the termination of the marriage. Neither *faskh* nor *khul'* was as flexible an instrument as the husband's *talaq*, but they did open avenues for female-initiated divorce, which was often pursued in this period.

The words and deeds of the muftis and courts thus tempered the gender oppositions of divorce law and supplied certain grounds for further female subversion of male-dominated divorce. Women, as we have seen, were quick to seize upon the opportunities presented by the legal discourse on divorce. A woman could transform the oath of divorce from a method of male control to a mechanism for expanding male obligation, by using it as a means of documenting marital promises. A *talaq* pronouncement, intended to enhance male power but not result in an actual divorce, could be turned to a woman's advantage if she wanted to leave her marriage. The unequal and gendered nature of divorce was not thereby changed in any fundamental way, but the muftis, the courts, and the members of the general population interacted to soften gender privilege and provide women with more latitude in matters of divorce than one familiar with the bare outlines of the law might have initially expected.

CHAPTER 4

The Fullness of Affection
Mothering and Fathering

QUESTION: There is a woman, the custodian of her minor son, who married a stranger [a nonrelative]. The minor boy did not have anybody [any relative] besides her except a paternal aunt who was also married to a "stranger." What does one do with the boy?
ANSWER: [One source says] . . . if the [custodial] rights of all the women are nullified, then the judge places the minor with whom he wants from among those women. The Khayr al-Ramli . . . in a case of this kind opined that the child is left with his mother because of the fullness of her affection.[1]

The muftis in Ottoman Syria and Palestine habitually discussed the rules governing not only the relationship between husband and wife but also those defining and regulating relations between parents and children. The rights and responsibilities of mothers and fathers were based in part on the jurists' understanding of the inherently different qualifications the male and the female brought to parenthood, of the ways in which they defined "man" and "woman." A woman, both emotionally and physically, was thought to be equipped for reproduction and the care of small children; and the muftis recognized a mother's special bond with her children, a "fullness of affection." A man, by contrast, was held to be more qualified to represent the interests of the child in the world outside the family, and to provide material support. Motherhood and fatherhood were thus defined along clear and strongly gendered lines: the rights and responsibilities of the mother and father displayed the same kind of complementarity of conception that we have seen in the marital relationship. In building on scant biological fact to erect the edifice of maternal nurturance and love, the muftis' discussions of motherhood constructed the woman as mother as well as wife. Similarly, the role of father as provider, protector, and guide amplified the concept of man already encountered in the marital relationship.[2]

The understanding of parenthood was not governed solely by perceptions of male-female difference in adults, however. The jurists' views of the capacities and needs of the child also entered into their deliberations. In the interstices of their discussions of parental roles, we find a nuanced, if somewhat fluid, ordering of the ages of the child, from the fetus to the fully mature and independent adult. As a child grew, he or she was seen as passing through a number of stages of development, each of which was marked by an advance in capabilities and a shift in the level and type of parental support required. The rights and responsibilities of the mother and father derived, at least in part, from an assessment of what the child needed from a parent at a particular stage, and which parent was best equipped, on gender-specific traits, to provide it. The child's needs were also held to be influenced by the child's gender. The muftis and courts viewed girls and boys through the gendered lens of their culture: after the brief androgynous period of early childhood, they were men and women in the making whose needs and welfare were to be served somewhat differently.

Although gender identity, both that of the parent and that of the child, permeated all legal discussion of and legal action on parenthood, the jurists and courts of the period did display a certain flexibility in approach and a willingness to temper many of the strictly delineated gender roles as the needs and situation of the child demanded. Again, we can divine here a strategy in which fundamental gender difference is being continually negotiated in order to head off serious social problems and conflicts. Without surrendering in any way the net distinctions between mothers and fathers, the muftis and courts allowed for a certain shading of the boundaries of parental roles when it appeared to be in the best interests of the child to do so. The power of the mother, carefully restricted by law and custom, could in various circumstances be permitted to expand beyond the period of early childhood to permeate and shape the entire experience of growing to adulthood. Moreover, such personal power was interwoven with the politics and economics of the day; the modern division of life by the capitalist system into private and public spheres was not known.[3]

The patriarchal nature of the law when dealing with the fundamental question of a child's identity was unmistakable. There was never any question in the minds of the jurists or the population about the ultimate allegiance of the child: any legitimate child was a member of his or her father's family, not the family of the mother. But despite such clear adherence to the rules of patrilineal descent, it is striking to what extent the jurists balanced the basic and irrefutable claims of the father's family against the specifics of a given child's situation. The rules of patriliny were never disregarded altogether, but the jurists and courts elaborated these rules in the context of their own understanding of the responsibility of the community as a whole for the well-being of the child. Mothering and fathering were constructed in legal discourse primarily in reference to child welfare—against the backdrop, of course, of strongly gendered social roles. In the normal course of events, when parents and children lived together in one household, the boundaries of motherhood and fatherhood did not require discussion. Death or divorce, however, scarcely isolated events in this society, prompted the muftis to address a range of issues surrounding parents and children.

AGES OF THE CHILD

The muftis' approach to the question of children vis-à-vis their parents was undergirded by their understanding of the different stages of childhood, the progression from fetus to fully mature and independent adult. But they did not usually define these stages by a child's age in years. Indeed, numerical age was rarely mentioned at all in legal discussion or court sessions, with the exception of occasional reference to the Hanafi rule that boys who reach age seven and girls who reach age nine should leave the custody of their mother, if she was divorced or widowed, and be given to their father or his family. Rather, the ages of the child were based on an appreciation of developments in a child's physical and mental states and capacities as he or she grew. Generally speaking, it was the jurists' sense of the age of a child in these terms, rather than knowledge of age in years, that dictated which parental rights and responsibilities were activated in a particular instance.

In the first stage, that of the fetus, the child was not yet a person, and the parents' rights and responsibilities were accordingly rather limited. For example, a fetus did not have a legal guardian as did a minor child: a father could not legally act as the guardian of a fetus, nor could he appoint someone else as its guardian.[4] If a fetus were born dead as a result of an injury done to its mother, the perpetrator was required to pay a special indemnity, the *gharra*, calculated at one-twentieth of the indemnity (*diya*) owed in the case of a murder. Should the fetus have lived outside the womb, however briefly, before dying, it was felt to have become a person, and the one who caused the miscarriage owed a full *diya*.[5] It seemed, then, that the moment of birth inaugurated a new stage of being, the fetus having become a child only when it lived outside the womb.

Khayr al-Din pointed out, however, that opinion differed on legal precedent when it dealt with the sensitive question of the religious identity of the fetus:

QUESTION: There is a Christian woman, married to a Muslim, who died while pregnant. Is she to be buried in a Muslim cemetery or in a polytheist cemetery?
ANSWER: ... The matter was one of controversy among the followers. Some say that she is to be buried in a Muslim cemetery and

[some] say a polytheist cemetery. . . . [Some say] in a cemetery by herself. . . . In some Maliki books, her back is to be placed toward the *qibla* [toward Mecca] because the face of the fetus is at her back. . . . [It is said] that if an unbeliever dies and a Muslim child died in her abdomen, by consensus you do not pray over her, but they disagreed about the burial. . . . Some say she is to be buried in a Muslim cemetery, and some say she is to be buried in an unbelievers' cemetery, and it is said that she is buried by herself, and God knows best.[6]

The difficulty of resolving this issue—and Khayr al-Din himself waffles here, in uncharacteristic fashion—arises from a number of questions about the nature of a fetus to which no clear answers are offered. A child fathered by a Muslim is born a Muslim, but is that child a Muslim in the womb? Can a fetus have a religious identity? If we accept the idea that the unborn is a Muslim, is the mother simply a vessel whose own religious identity is effectively canceled by or subsumed under that of the fetus? When the matter of religion arose, the line between the fetus and the child began to blur.

Once a baby was born, it shed the somewhat ambiguous status of the fetus and became a child. The second stage of existence was that of the small child, from birth to age seven for boys and from birth to age nine for girls. The personhood of this child was unmistakable: he or she could inherit and own property (under guardianship), and a full *diya* would be required if the child were to suffer wrongful death. This was the age, however, of total physical dependence: a small child needed a mother's care, initially as a wet nurse and subsequently as a caretaker who would feed, dress, and love the child.

The differences between boys and girls were highlighted by the distinctions made in determining when and for what reason a child was deemed ready to leave this stage of caretaking (*hidana*). For fundamentally distinct reasons, this stage was terminated at one age for boys and another for girls. It is at age seven that a child is ready to "eat and drink and dress and go to the toilet [by] himself."[7] A boy of age seven who has shown this level of independence is ready to leave the caretaking stage: if he is being cared for by a divorced or widowed mother, the father or his family may remove him from her care, so long as his survival skills measure up to those expected of a seven-year-old child.[8] For a girl, however, the caretaking stage was extended to age nine, well beyond the expected achievement of rudimentary independence. Although the reasons for this difference are not made fully explicit, the muftis did comment that a girl's caretaking stage ended at the age at which one could expect the beginnings of physical maturity, as demonstrated by her becoming *mushtahah*, or desirable in a sexual sense.[9] A boy left the stage of *hidana* when he could care for himself; a girl ordinarily left that stage when she began to show some signs of sexual development, and thus be ready for marriage. This did not necessarily mean, of course, that she would be married off upon the termination of the *hidana* stage, but her exit from early childhood was defined by her readiness for the role of wife, not by her ability to manage on her own without her mother. For both boys and girls, however, the assessment of their needs shifted with the end of early childhood from a nurturing love to a socialization appropriate to their gender.

After leaving the stage of *hidana*, both boys and girls entered a stage in which they were no longer looked upon as small children but were not yet in their legal majority. In this third stage, between, on the one hand, the complete dependence of early childhood and, on the other hand, the arrival of puberty and the sexual maturity (*bulugh*) that signaled legal majority, both boys and girls remained under the legal guardianship of one of their parents, usually their father or another adult relative on the paternal side. The boy at this stage, often referred to as a "youth" (*ghulam*), and the girl (*bint*) could not yet see to their own affairs: their guardians managed their property and provided for them.[10] Their guardians could also, as we have seen, marry the children off as minors, and these marriages could be consummated if the boy were capable of an erection and the girl were deemed physically ready for intercourse.[11] In this particular stage, boys and girls shared a similar legal status, although the muftis might assess their needs rather differently. In discussing the needs of a prepubescent boy, Khayr al-Din stressed the advantages of a male guardian who could shape him by inculcating the manners and character of men.[12] There was, however, silence on the special needs of the girl in this stage, though we have seen that she was left in female care for an extended period of *hidana*, perhaps so that she could reap the benefits of female socialization and learn the duties of a wife. The fact that a girl left the stage of *hidana* when she was approaching, at least in theory, a marriageable age suggests that her primary need in the post-*hidana* period was thought to be the arrangement of a good marriage.

Puberty marked the most dramatic shift in the status of the child. A physically mature (*baligh*) adolescent (*murahiq*) was considered in many respects a legally competent adult. He or she was no longer under guardianship and could exercise choice in marriage arrangements, if such an arrangement had not already been made.[13] A postpubescent youth could even act as the guardian for a minor.[14] An adolescent girl who had passed puberty could choose with whom she wanted to live, so long as she picked a trustworthy relative who could provide a safe home.[15] The majority or minority of a child was far and away the single most important factor influencing his or her legal standing: although numerical age was almost never given in court cases concerning matters of marriage, divorce, inheritance, property transfers, and such, the majority or minority of any young person involved in a case was always stated. In general, the attainment of legal majority was defined by puberty, and legal majority brought with it the legal competence required to arrange one's own marriage, manage one's own affairs, and even act as the guardian for others.

The Hanafi muftis agreed, however, that at least in Hanafi jurisprudence the onset of puberty did not necessarily usher in an age of full independence. A boy or girl might, for example, reach puberty but still be subject to the tutelage (*damm*) of a parent or other relation. This concept of formal tutelage recognized the fact that a child might reach physical maturity without necessarily having acquired the maturity of mind essential to full participation in the community as an adult. In order to ascertain whether a youth had reached mental adulthood, the muftis usually asked if he or she were rational (*'aqila*), of sound judgment (*ra'y*) or independent opinion (*mustaqilla bira'yiha*), able to manage without a parent (*yustaghni*), and responsible for himself or herself (*ma'muna 'ala nafsiha*). It seems that a child had to demonstrate all of these qualities in order to be judged adult: the youth who was rational but not yet responsible for himself had to remain under his father's tutelage, and his father could, if he wished, deny him permission to travel, punish him for misbehavior, and otherwise intervene in his affairs.[16]

A boy who had reached physical maturity but was still endowed with boyish prettiness presented special problems:

> QUESTION: There is a mature pretty [*sabih*] youth. Does his father have tutelage [*damm*] over him, and can he prevent him from travel-ing, and if he does something [bad], can he punish him?
> ANSWER: Yes. He has his tutelage and can prevent him from travel-ing and can punish him if he does something. [A source says] that a youth, if he is rational, of sound judgment, and able to manage with-out his father, [then] his father does not have tutelage, unless [the youth] is not responsible for himself; [then] his father has tutelage. He [the father] is not responsible for [the son's] support [*nafaqa*] un-less he takes it on voluntarily . . . and if one fears for him, the father has precedence over the mother [to keep him]. . . . It is up to the fa-ther to punish his mature son if he does something. . . . If he is *sabih* [pretty] and wants to leave to seek knowledge, his father can prevent him. . . . If the son is beardless and *sabih*, then the father can prevent him from leaving home until he has a beard. In any case, obedience to parents is required, and this is a clear ruling in the shari'a, and the verses and *hadith* about that are too numerous to mention.[17]

With a *sabih* (pretty) boy, the question was not so much one of mental maturity as of physical characteristics: an attractive, beardless youth could not be treated as a man even if he had reached puberty, and there-fore was still under his father's tutelage. Such restrictions, as we shall see in the next chapter, had more to do with the disruptive effects a desirable youth might have on male society than with the youth's own ability to function in the adult world. If a youth was too young and pretty looking, he had to remain under the firm hand of his father until his outward appearance matched his biological maturity. Khayr al-Din adds here that children should always obey their parents and respect their authority, whether under legal tutelage or not.

But despite such pious hopes, once a youth had passed the tests of mental maturity and physical appearance, he or she was an independent adult, one not subject, at least under law, to parental authority. A girl of divorced parents who was judged both physically and mentally mature could refuse her father's demand that she leave her mother and live with her father and stepmother.[18]

The rights and duties of parenthood, then, were shaped by a fairly complex vision of the capabilities and needs of the child as he or she moved from the womb through the dependency of early childhood and pre-adolescence to the qualified independence of physical maturity and then adulthood, as an individual with fully developed mental capacities. Each of these stages was gendered: the male fetus was more highly valued, for the purposes of an indemnity, than the female; the male child left his early childhood and the care of his mother at a younger age and for different reasons than the female did; and the evaluation of physical maturity was based, necessarily, on different criteria. Interestingly enough, the assessment of mental maturity appeared relatively gender free: the criteria of rationality and responsibility were determinant for males and females alike. But the separate rationales for the tutelage of girls and boys were stated quite distinctly: girls needed to be protected from harm (usually interpreted as sexual approaches), whereas boys required guidance in the acquisition of male culture.

MOTHERING

The roles of mothering and fathering, in the eyes of the muftis, were defined in terms of the needs of the child as he or she grew, the different strengths and capacities of women and men, and the notion that mothers and fathers, even in the same household, had certain distinct and gendered rights to the child.

In the fatwas and court cases that dealt with miscarriage, it was the parents' and other relatives' rights in the child that occupied pride of place. The wrongful death of a fetus was held to harm the parents and other relatives of the fetus, and they could claim the compensatory *gharra* from an assailant if they could prove that his assault on the pregnant woman had caused the miscarriage. The muftis agreed that some kind of physical assault had to have taken place shortly before the miscarriage in order for a claim to be accepted: the woman who miscarried after someone surprised her or yelled at her could not receive compensation.[19] When such claims were brought to court, the judges would look for evidence of physical assault. In the absence of such evidence, the assailant's testimony that he had not touched the woman was sufficient for the judge to conclude that the miscarriage had natural causes and the claim should be denied. The sex of the fetus was another important piece of information in these cases, because the *gharra* for males differed from that for females: one-twentieth of a male *diya* for the male fetus, and one-half of *that* for the female fetus, following the rule for all *diya*s.

In one such case, a couple, Mustafa and Jamila, came to the Damascus court from their village to make a claim against one *al-hajj* Salih. They recounted that Salih had come to their village looking for Mustafa, and, in the process of a fruitless search for him, had hit one of their young children with the back of his sword. Jamila had then intervened to protect her child, Salih struck her, and she miscarried a three-month-old fetus, "a male with recognizable features." Salih, however, denied all the accusations under oath, and Jamila could not produce evidence to support her version of the events. Mustafa and Jamila lost their claim.[20] Such claims could be pressed by both parents jointly, by a mother or father alone, or even by, in at least one case, a grandfather (in this case, the assault had resulted not only in miscarriage but also in the subsequent death of his daughter). Parents could ask to be compensated for the loss of the fetus, and this compensation was their property and that of other relatives who would in the course of time have stood as heirs to the child's estate.

The fetus, although attached to the mother's body, belonged in a significant sense to the father as well. The man who fathered the baby had certain rights to the fetus even while it was still in the womb.

> QUESTION: There is a free woman, pregnant by her husband, who intentionally struck her own stomach and aborted a dead male fetus [*janin*] of seven months, without the permission of her husband. Is the clan [*'aqila*] of the woman liable for the *gharra*, and does the woman not share in it? What is the amount of the *gharra*?
> ANSWER: Yes, her clan is responsible for the *gharra*, because she committed an offense and her clan must bear [the expense] of it. She does not share in it because she is a murderer without right, and the murderer does not have a share. The amount of the *gharra* is half of a tenth of the *diya* of 500 *dirhams*, and this sum is required within a year. . . . [In one source] the *gharra* is required from the clan of a woman who aborted [her fetus] purposely through [the use of] drugs or [her] actions without the permission of her husband. [Ibn 'Abidin adds that] . . . if [the husband] gives permission, there is no discussion.[21]

This unique fatwa made clear that the fetus is the possession of both parents. Ordinarily, the indemnity for the death of a fetus would be paid to the heirs, including, of course, the mother and father. In this case, however, the woman's unilateral decision to abort was illicit: she was thus to be treated like any other "murderer" of a fetus, and her relatives were required to pay a *gharra* to the heirs. The two salient facts here are, first, that it had to be shown that she had purposefully done something to herself in an attempt to abort the fetus, and, second, that she had done so without her husband's permission. al-'Imadi allows that if her husband had indeed given permission, the matter would be different, but exactly how different we are not told. Surely he could not then claim his part of a *gharra*, but would his permission have given his wife the "right" to abort? Would she no longer have been a "murderer" in the eyes of the law? These issues are not made explicit. What is clear, however, is the notion that the fetus belonged to both mother and father, and that the father could exercise some control over the child even while it was still in the womb. From the moment of conception, the mother was responsible for the child's well-being, a responsibility she bore to the father as well as the child.

Once the child was born, the mother had certain other rights and responsibilities, as the caretaker of young children. These were usually made explicit only when a mother was widowed or divorced, and the issue of child custody arose. In general, the muftis agreed that a mother was the best caretaker of her own young children. In the first place, she was her child's optimal wet nurse: a baby should remain in her care whenever possible for nursing, and the mother should receive a special allowance from the child's father until the child was weaned. A mother's testimony that she was nursing her child with her own breast milk, and therefore should receive her nursing allowance, should be given precedence over a father's testimony that she was using another's milk and therefore did not deserve the allowance.[22] But the mother's right to nurse her baby was also a responsibility: if the baby's father were too poor to pay the nursing allowance, the mother could be obliged by the court to nurse her child without compensation.[23]

The mother's right to nurse her baby for the sake of its health could become a point of litigation. A woman came to the Damascus court to complain that her ex-husband had taken their six-month-old daughter, still a nursling, out of her custody. The baby, deprived of breast milk, had sickened and died, and she held her ex-husband responsible. He countered that she had given him the child freely, and that he had hired a wet nurse to care for her; the baby's death, he claimed, was not the result of his actions and intentions. In this particular case, the mother could offer no evidence to override her ex-husband's sworn oath that he had not caused the death of the child, and her claim was dismissed. The form of her claim, however, underscored the custodian's legal responsibility to provide a baby with the breast milk it needed for survival. If the father had indeed taken the baby from her mother and had then failed to provide proper nutrition, the mother would have had a claim to compensation for wrongful death.[24]

Again, the mother was seen to be the person best equipped to raise young children, meaning, in Hanafi jurisprudence, boys up to the age of seven and girls up to the age of nine. Her right to the caretaking (*hidana*) of her small children, continually affirmed by the muftis, was justified by the "fullness of her affection" and by her natural nurturing abilities. The very young child, who needed to be fed, dressed, and toileted, was best cared for by his or her own mother.[25] Should the mother's right to *hidana* be canceled by, for example, her remarriage to a man who was not closely related to the child, the right then devolved upon another female relative of the child, with priority accorded to women from the mother's side of the family. As long as the child was in need of physical nurture, he or she should be, by preference, in a woman's care, because women, according to Khayr al-Din, "are more capable of *hidana* than men."[26]

The preference for women from the maternal side of the family, sometimes referred to as the "family of the *hidana*,"[27] extended the mother's right of *hidana* to the maternal family as a whole.

> QUESTION: There is an orphan girl, seven years old and about to turn eight, who is in the custody of her grandmother on her mother's side, thus of the family of *hidana*. She has paternal uncles who want to take her from her grandmother into their tutelage without a legal proceeding. What is the judgment?
> ANSWER: When the grandmother is from the family of *hidana*, the minor girl remains in her custody until she turns nine years old, and the uncles cannot take her before that time without a legal proceeding.[28]

The women of the maternal family, through their association with the mother, took on the role of nurturing this young child; the force of the family right to *hidana* was sufficient to turn away all claims to the child that the family on the paternal side might press. Although none of the muftis ever suggested that the ultimate allegiance of the child belonged anywhere but with the paternal family, the claims of patrilineality were suspended temporarily in order that the interests of the young child might be served best, by providing it the most competent and caring custodians. If, however, there were no female relatives on either side of the family, and the child had therefore to be entrusted to a man, custody devolved upon the closest male relative on the paternal side, the paternal uncle or older brother of the child.[29] And when the issue of female nurture had become no longer relevant, the claims of the patrilineal family won the day.

A mother or other temporary caretaker was not required to absorb the expenses she might incur in caring for her child. Rather, it was the child's father's duty to pay child support (*ujra*) for the duration of the caretaking period. The father or, if he were deceased, his family was required to make these payments to the child's mother as long as she was judged qualified and fit to care for the child; they could not evade this responsibility by supposing they could take the child out of the mother's custody. Only in the event that the father or his family were impoverished could they offer to take the child into their care in lieu of support payments.[30] Otherwise, the mother had to be paid at a level commensurate with her standard of living, enough to cover the costs of clothing, food, shelter, and even a servant if that were in keeping with her lifestyle.[31] A woman's testimony concerning the wealth of her ex-husband and his ability to provide support for the period of *hidana* was sufficient to override a man's claim that he was too poor to provide that support.[32]

The muftis discussed only one set of circumstances under which a father who was able to provide support might refuse to do so. If a woman had waived her right to child support as part of a divorce agreement (*khul'*), the responsibility for that support was hers.

QUESTION: There is a man whose wife asked him to divorce her in exchange for the [uncompensated] nursing of her son, with whom she was pregnant, and for his [uncompensated] keeping for a designated number of years. So he divorced her in exchange for that. Is she obliged to do that, and is the *khulʿ* judgment sound?

ANSWER: Yes. She is legally obligated. It has been explained that *khulʿ* is valid in exchange for the keeping of a child for a designated period of years and for his nursing if he is being nursed. If the period of time is not made clear, she nurses him for two years. The divorce that is based on compensation is the equivalent of *khulʿ*. . . . This [case] is within the category of *khulʿ*: it is a contract between the spouses in which money is given by the woman and he divorces her, [and] one of the five ways in which *khulʿ* is pronounced is "Divorce yourself for a thousand." Keeping the boy and his nursing for a period of time is a known benefit, and can be specified.[33]

If a mother had made a conscious and specific agreement to waive her rights to child support as the price of a divorce, the father was discharged from his obligations, but only for the specified period. al-ʿImadi added in one fatwa that should the mother fall on hard times and ask her ex-husband to help out with child support, despite the fact that she had assumed total responsibility as a *khulʿ* condition, he should come to her aid, presumably for the sake of the children. He could, if he wished, consider any such support payments a loan to his ex-wife, one that she would have to repay when she got back on her feet.[34]

A mother's right of *hidana* did entail certain responsibilities, the most important of which was the safeguarding of the lives of her children. Khayr al-Din discussed her liability should a child die in her keeping:

QUESTION: There is a minor girl, three years old, in the *hidana* of her mother. She [the mother] went out to enjoy herself and left [the girl] without a caretaker. She [the girl] fell into a hot cooking pot and died. Is the mother liable?

ANSWER: Yes. The mother is responsible for leaving her with a caretaker. It is explained [in two sources] . . . about a boy, three years old, whose mother went out and left him and he fell into the fire, and the mother was [made] responsible. . . . A [nother] mother left her son with a woman and said, "Take care of him until I return," and she went out and left him and the little one fell into the fire, and the *diya* is the responsibility of them both.[35]

In the event of the loss of a child through carelessness, the mother was liable for an indemnity to be paid to the child's heirs, underscoring her role as a custodian who was to safeguard the child, if only temporarily.

Certain limits were placed, as well, on a mother's ability to make decisions affecting the child. She could not, of course, manage her child's property, arrange his or her marriage, or whatever, because she was not the child's legal guardian (*wali*). Nor could she move wherever she wanted with the child. A divorced woman who intended to move from Damascus to Aleppo with her young son was informed by the mufti that because Aleppo was neither her homeland (*watan*) nor the site of her marriage, she could not move there with her child unless she had her ex-husband's permission.[36]

The mother's right to the care of her children could be canceled for several reasons. First, should she marry a "stranger," the child could no longer live in her house. A "stranger" was defined as any man who was not a *mahram* relation of the child's, that is, who was sufficiently unrelated as not to fall into a category of prohibition as a marriage partner. A new husband who was not the child's paternal uncle, for example, would cancel the mother's right of *hidana*, and the child would be turned over to the next closest female relative, with preference to female relatives on the maternal side.[37] In the event that a child had no surviving *mahram* relations, on either the mother's or the father's side, who were not married to strangers, then, according to Khayr al-Din, it was best to keep the child with his or her mother because of her loving care, even if this meant cohabitation with the mother's husband.[38] Ordinarily, a child was not permitted to live with adults who were not close relatives, but exceptions to this rule were permitted when they could be shown to be in the best interests of the child.

Second, should a mother prove unfit to care for her children, they could be removed: a divorcée who frequently left her children alone in the house in "a miserable state" was not a just caretaker, and could lose her children to her husband.[39] The right of *hidana* accorded to other female relatives was also conditional upon their fitness for the role of caring for young children; a caretaker had to be a woman in her legal majority who was rational, trustworthy, capable, and of free status. A woman who failed to meet these criteria could lose the children. A maternal grandmother who was "advanced in years, disabled, and blind" would lose the *hidana* of her grandchild in favor of a competent paternal grandmother.[40] A slave woman who had borne a child to her master, and was thus the mother of a free child, did not have a right of *hidana*; her child could be removed at any age by the paternal relatives.[41] A non-Muslim mother enjoyed somewhat circumscribed rights of *hidana* of her Muslim children:

QUESTION: A Jew converted to Islam and then died, leaving his Jewish wife and two girls by her, the older of whom is six, and his affluent Jewish father, but he left no estate himself. The wife is poor of the family of *hidana*. Does she get the *hidana* of her two girls when they are not yet conscious of religion and one is not afraid that they will become habituated to unbelief [*kufr*]. Is their support the responsibility of their grandfather?
ANSWER: Yes. When the situation is as mentioned: the non-Muslim [*dhimmi*] caretaker, even if she is a Magian [adherent of Mazdaism], is like a Muslim unless the child can comprehend religion, and the age [of comprehension] can be fixed at seven, because you can profess Islam at that age. [Another source says] . . . when one fears habituation to unbelief even if [the child] does not comprehend religion, then you can remove the child from her. . . . No support is required except from the mother . . . because the inheritance is discontinued [by conversion].[42]

Here a clear distinction is being drawn between the young child's need for physical care and affection, best met by the mother even if she is a non-Muslim, and the older child's need for moral guidance and religious instruction, which must, in the case of Muslim children, be supplied by a Muslim caretaker. The non-Muslim mother's right to *hidana* terminates when her children, whether male or female, reach age seven, the age presumably at which the child, regardless of gender, is ready for moral and religious education. The distinctions made between the needs of young boys and those of young girls thus tended to collapse in the face of such considerations. Acculturation as a male or female took a back seat to religious training: Muslim girls as well as boys had to be removed from the care of a non-Muslim mother as soon as they reached the age of minimum survival skills and the capacity for religiosity.

Finally, when a boy turned seven and a girl turned nine, they left the stage of *hidana* and thus the care of their mother, regardless of her fitness for the role. Although the law always assigned ultimate possession of the child to the father and his family, we do encounter many instances in which children, especially girls, remained with their mothers far beyond the legal period of *hidana*. As we shall see, if neither the father nor his family was interested in taking charge of the child, custody and indeed guardianship could devolve to the mother.

In law and general practice, however, mothering was bounded in time by the age of the child: very young children needed their mothers for survival and for affection, and women were the nurturers best equipped to provide for them. Indeed, the muftis even spoke of the child's "right" to care from a woman, a right that the woman herself could not invalidate, even though she might not be able to provide the care.[43] The mother's right of *hidana* was a conditional right, however, and could be abrogated should she not measure up as a nurturer. The children's father was expected to pay the bills, to subsidize *hidana;* the mother was a temporary caretaker and did not ordinarily acquire formal guardianship of her children. Her children, even during the period of their residence with her, "belonged" in a legal sense to their father and/or his family, a proprietorship that began as early as the womb.

Such was the vision of mothering elaborated by the muftis and enforced, in general, by the court system. The rules of *hidana* were activated when plaintiffs came to the courts. If a woman had remarried, her ex-husband might go to court to terminate her *hidana* on the grounds that the child should not live with an unrelated man, or he might ask to remove the child from maternal relatives at the end of the period of *hidana*.[44] Conversely, a maternal grandmother might successfully resist attempts by a father or his family to remove small children from her care.[45]

The most common situation concerning *hidana* in the courts, however, was that of a mother coming to collect child-support money from her ex-husband. Upon the mother's request, the judge would assign the amount of appropriate support:

> Support is assigned to Makiyya bt. Muhammad . . . , the minor, who is in the *hidana* of her mother, the woman Marwa. Support includes the costs of meat, bread, soap, bath entrance, and laundry, in the amount of two and one-half *qita' misriyya* each day. The mother has permission to spend this money, and the father of Makiyya, Muhammad b. Sa'ad, is responsible for its repayment. This assignment is made after a request for support was received.
>
> 18 Rabi' II 1152 H.(1739 A.D.)[46]

That the courts were sympathetic to such requests, and able subsequently to extract the support monies, was amply attested by the fact that women resorted frequently to the courts for support assignments.[47] Sometimes a woman would seek assignment of child support from an ex-husband who was absent from the city; specifically, she would seek permission from the judge to borrow money for child support, which her husband would then be required to repay. In most instances, however, the ex-husband himself would be present in the court and would receive his assignment in person, a proceeding that must have functioned as a form of registration of child support, which would result in a record that could then be referred to should disputes arise later. And indeed, a woman might return to the court if her husband lagged in his payments: one woman claimed that her husband had paid her only one and one-half *ghurush* each month for the last three years and eight months, instead of the two *ghurush* he had been assigned for child support. He was found liable for the difference.[48]

Consistent with the position of the muftis, the courts held that documented poverty of a child's father could be accepted as a reason for failure to pay child support. When 'Aysha bt. Isma'il brought her former husband Hasan to court and claimed that he was not paying child support for his young son Sulayman, Hasan pleaded poverty and produced four witnesses to testify to his situation. If 'Aysha had wished to retain custody without receiving child-support payments, she was, of course, free to do so. In this case, however, Hasan's mother agreed to take over the care of Sulayman without recompense, and the child was given into his grandmother's custody.[49]

Another way in which an ex-husband could evade child support was to make the mother's support of the child a condition of a *khul'* divorce, a practice known well to the population who frequented the courts, but one that could become a source of litigation. A woman named Zaynab came to the Damascus court and explained that her husband Husayn had granted her a *khul'* divorce in exchange for her waiving the balance of her *mahr* and forgiving him a debt of 40 *ghurush*. The question of support for their two boys, however, had not been part of the *khul'* agreement, according to Zaynab, yet Husayn was now refusing to pay child support by arguing that she had agreed to support the children for a period of five years in return for the divorce. The situation was further complicated both by the fact that she had now remarried and thus could not keep custody of the children, and by her poverty, which prevented her from providing sufficient support in any case. The judge, faced with no firm evidence that the *khul'* agreement had indeed included child-support arrangements, and the mother's inability, in any event, to provide support, assigned the boys' support to Husayn. He also insisted, however, honoring the rules of *hidana,* that the children remain in the care of their maternal aunt until they reached the proper age for transfer to their father's keeping.[50] A *khulʿ* agreement by which a mother assumed child support was entertained as a perfectly legal arrangement, but in this case questions about whether such an agreement had been made, coupled with the mother's poverty, threw the responsibility for child support back into the father's lap.

Women whose husbands had died would also apply to the court for the assignment of child support. Here they were not attempting to collect from a recalcitrant husband, however, but asking for a formal assignment of child support for as long as their children remained in their care. Once awarded a specific amount for support, they were authorized to collect that money from whomever was held financially responsible. The child's closest male relatives on the paternal side, paternal uncles, for example, were one possible source.[51] But in the absence of a sufficiently well-heeled paternal relative, a mother could receive compensation for this support directly from the child's inheritance money (usually from the child's share of his or her father's estate), or she might spend the money from her own resources against repayment by the child when he or she came of age and began to earn an income. These awards were most often made to the mother herself, but upon occasion the support money might be funneled through the hands of a child's legal guardian, who would be authorized to spend it on the child while he or she was in a mother's custody.[52] If the father's family lacked the means to provide support and there was no inheritance to draw on, the court might oversee the transfer of the children from the widowed mother to the care of female relatives on the paternal side who would agree to raise the children without benefit of financial support.[53] The mother herself, in keeping with her role as temporary caretaker, was never held responsible for child-support payments unless she had voluntarily offered to support the child in the face of poverty on the paternal side, or in exchange for a divorce.

Court practice also agreed with the muftis' position that child support should be provided at a level in keeping with the standard of living of the child's social group. Support awards in eighteenth-century Damascus, Jerusalem, and Nablus ran all the way from one *qita' misriyya* per child per day up to a high of fifteen: the costs of obtaining the necessities of food, shelter, clothing, and hygiene varied enormously among classes, and the courts assigned amounts of support commensurate with class position. A mother might come to court to request an adjustment of her child-support award if she felt that it did not accord with her class status. One titled lady (*al-sitt, khatun*) named 'Aysha, who was the wife of the (deceased) shaykh Muhammad, who had borne the official title of *afandi*, told the judge that the court's previous assignment of support monies for her son, in the amount of five *qita' misriyya* each day, was insufficient; she requested, and received, a revised award of fifteen *qita' misriyya* daily, which she could spend out of her son's inheritance from his father.[54] In this case, an upper-class woman had taken it upon herself to seek correction of what had been, according to her own assessment of her child's standard of living, a gross underestimation of the actual cost of supporting a child in her social circles.

The muftis and the court system thus constructed mothering as the nurture of young children, as the essential tasks of nursing, feeding, clothing, and otherwise caring for the physical needs of a child. The clear preference for the biological mother as caregiver during the child's early years was based not only on her ability to meet these needs, but also on her love for the child. If the mother were not available or were disqualified as caretaker, another woman, usually from the mother's family, was the second choice; women were indisputably best equipped for the role of nurturer, best able to provide, both physically and emotionally, for a child.

It was also abundantly clear, however, that a child ultimately belonged to the father and the paternal family: mothering was a temporary activity performed for both the good of the child and the ultimate benefit of the patrilineal family. Once a boy could fend for himself, and a girl had become marriageable, they were no longer in need of mothering and could be placed with their father (if the parents had been divorced) or with the patrilineal family to whom they belonged (if the father were deceased). Child support was thus the responsibility of the paternal family; by taking care of the child, the mother was performing a service for the child's father, and therefore was subsidized by him. Her own rights to her child were temporary, conditional, and partial, for it was the father who took over as parent when the child's needs reached beyond the mother's province of love and nurture.

FATHERING

From the moment of a child's birth in these communities, the father was responsible for supplying the goods or money required for all the basic necessities of life. That the father should provision all material support for the child followed the logic of the male responsibility for the costs of the marital domicile, as the family provider, and was buttressed by the fact that the child was identified as a member of the father's, not the mother's, family. *As long as the parents remained together,* the issue of child support did not usually arise: children shared the food and shelter of their parents. In the event of a divorce, however, a father's responsibility for child support could become an issue: he was legally required to provide full support even during the period of *hidana,* when the young child was in the mother's or another's custody. We have seen how actively mothers would pursue this support and how receptive the courts were to a mother's request for the assignment of a certain level of support.

In one of his fatwas, al-'Imadi outlined the full extent of the father's support requirements:

> QUESTION: There is a minor boy nursling whose mother has died, and he does not have money, and his father is impoverished. He has a grandmother, his mother's mother, from the family of *hidana.* Is his father required [to pay] the wage [*ujra*] of nursing, and the wage of caretaking [*hidana*] and the support [*nafaqa*] of the child?

ANSWER: The caretaking [*hidana*] goes to the mother's mother, and the father is required [to pay] the wages of nursing and the wages of caretaking, and the support of the child, of all types. [The sources say] that the wage of nursing is different from the support [*nafaqa*] of the child . . . and it is in compensation for that. If the mother hires [someone] to nurse, the child's *nafaqa* is not sufficient for that, because the child does not need milk alone, but also other things, as can be seen, especially clothing. The qadi decides on a *nafaqa* different from [in addition to] the wages of nursing and the wages of caretaking. And so there are three payments required of the father, the payment for nursing, the payment for caretaking, and the support payment [*nafaqa*] for the child. . . . [Ibn 'Abidin adds that] housing is to be included in the support payment.[55]

Here we see the clear enumeration and description of a father's financial obligations. He had, of course, to make support payments (*nafaqa*) to cover the living expenses of his child. But he was also liable for a payment to the caretaker of his child, if she were not the child's mother, of a "wage" (*ujra*) for services rendered. And should the child not yet be weaned, the third payment, that for the nursing wage, was added. The nursing wage was to be paid to the caretaker, who could either nurse the child herself or hire a wet nurse for the purpose; a mother was not compelled to nurse her child, but a father was required to pay the wage for a substitute.[56]

As we have seen, a father could be assigned a specific amount of support in a court registration proceeding. The money was to be sufficient to cover all the costs of raising the child in a manner in keeping with the father's social class: proper housing, clothing, food, and a servant, if appropriate, were to be covered.[57] Once a level of support was designated, either by being assigned by the judge in court or by the formal promise of the father, he was liable for the precise amount of this support. Should he not pay support promptly, or should he leave town, the child's caretaker was automatically authorized to borrow money in the amount of the awarded support; whatever was borrowed became a debt owed by the father to the lender. If the child's caretaker borrowed from other family members, whether on the mother's side or the father's side, the father was responsible for repaying those who had lent money for the support of his child. A man who refused to pay child support, or to reimburse others who had made his payments, was to be jailed until he met his responsibilities; only documented poverty could save him from prison. And should a father die owing child support, his estate was required to pay off the debt.[58]

In the event of the father's disability or death, responsibility for the material support of his child was usually assumed by the patrilineal family. The support of the children of a chronically ill man was assigned to their paternal grandfather, who was liable, in this instance, for the support of his disabled son as well as that of his grandchildren.[59] Male relatives on the paternal side, typically grandfathers or uncles, were always held responsible for the support of fatherless children or the offspring of the insane or otherwise disabled, if neither the children nor their mother had sufficient resources of their own.[60] The muftis also acknowledged, however, that circumstances might shift responsibility for support of the children from the paternal to the maternal family, and from males to females. If paternal relatives were poor and maternal relatives were rich, the mother or other maternal relatives were to assume the costs of support. An impoverished woman with a young son whose husband had been imprisoned for debt could ask her own father or brother to provide support payments, on the condition that her husband would be responsible for those payments when he recovered from his financial woes.[61] A poor, sick father might request, and receive, support payments for his children from his wealthy sister.[62] And if the father were deceased, the child who received support from his maternal relations would repay them him- or herself, for whatever they had spent on support, either out of inheritance monies or earned income after he reached maturity. Paternal relatives other than the father could also ask for repayment. The child may have "belonged" to the paternal family, but the family's responsibilities to the child were defined as contingent and relative, unlike those of the child's father.[63]

Although a father did not acquire custodial rights over the child he was supporting until he or she left the stage of caretaking (when a boy had reached age seven and a girl had reached age nine), he was considered the child's legal guardian. The child's relationship to the world of social and business affairs was mediated through the father from birth. As a guardian for the purposes of marriage arrangement (*wali*), or as a guardian with more general authority to act on behalf of the child (*wasi*), a father exercised considerable control over his child's person and property.[64] As we saw in chapter 2, a father as *wali* could arrange marriages for his minor children without their participation or consent. As *wasi*, he managed such property as his child may have acquired through inheritance: he could sell the property to himself or others, and he could buy other property with the child's money. He could also use the child's money to make improvements on the property, as he saw fit. So long as he bought, sold, and improved the property at a "fair price," and the proceeds of these transactions went to the child's account, he had a fairly free hand.[65]

Although a father acquired the guardianship of his children at their birth, without formal legal proceeding, his exercise of this office could become subject to the scrutiny of the court. al-'Imadi addressed the problem of a father, the guardian of two minor children, who managed the money they had inherited from their mother very poorly, "squandering it ruinously." In such a case, the qadi would intervene and appoint another guardian who could better care for the children's money.[66] A father's guardianship was thus a position of trust and responsibility, not an absolute right. If the interests of minor children were not being well served by their father, it was up to the court to protect those interests; the welfare of minor children could take precedence over the authority of the father.

A father normally exercised the power of guardianship until a child attained his or her legal majority, a sea change marked by the physical maturity of puberty. In some instances, a youth might be deemed incompetent despite his or her maturation. If a child reached the stage of legal majority but was insane or imbecilic, the father's guardianship over "his money and his person" was continued. Should a child attain legal majority and then later lose his or her good sense or sanity, the father's guardianship could be reimposed, although some authoritative sources held that guardianship should then pass to the state.[67] Formal guardianship was normally terminated, however, when a child reached legal majority and could exercise choice in marriage arrangements and make decisions concerning property.

Custody, as we have seen, was distinct from guardianship. A father acquired custody of a son when he was deemed old enough to feed, dress, and toilet himself, that is, to be able to do without a woman's care. It was felt that, at this age, a boy should live with his father (or another male relative) so that he could be raised to know the "manners" and "morals" of men.[68] A daughter, for her part, was to remain with her mother until she showed the first signs of physical maturity, thus until she had become an "object of desire" and "fit for men." The muftis were not explicit about why a girl needed to be in the custody of her father or another male relative at this point, but a concern about protection of her person from sexual advances occasionally surfaces. A female needs to live with people who are "trustworthy," in a place where one need not "fear for her."[69] It was her safety, in the sense of safety from corruption, rather than her need of training or education, that informed the discussion. Once she had become an object of desire, her father was deemed her best protector and, moreover, it was he as *wali* who would make the marriage arrangements that might soon follow. Should her father not be available, the range of appropriate custodial relatives was more limited than it was for a boy: she should not be placed with any but *mahram* relations, a ruling that excluded many male relations. She could not, for example, live with her paternal or maternal male cousins, who were, after all, potential marriage partners.[70]

A father's custody and guardianship as such were both terminated when a child reached his or her legal majority at puberty. As we have seen, however, if the child were not deemed rational and responsible for him- or herself, the period of custody and partial guardianship could be extended under the rubric of *damm*, or tutelage. For a boy, the issue was usually his mental maturity, but occasionally his physical maturity, as determined by the possession of manly physical traits. Until he was mentally and physically mature, then, his father could continue to exercise control over his living arrangements and his movements. Once he had reached the age of judgment, responsibility, and physical maturity, however, he was a fully independent adult, no longer to be committed to his father's keeping.

A similar set of considerations governed the relationship of a father to his mature daughter. The muftis assumed that an unmarried woman, regardless of the fact that she was physically and mentally mature, must live with "honorable" people in a place where one would not fear for her well-being. Her freedom to choose her place of residence, then, was circumscribed by these considerations in a way a youth's was not. Her father or other paternal relatives could not, however, *impose* a particular arrangement: once she was mentally mature, she was no longer under her father's tutelage and she could choose with whom to live, so long as her choice met the criteria of trust and safety. She could, for example, refuse to leave her mother's house to live with her father, her paternal uncle, or her mature brother, and she had freedom of choice of residence among, say, her own competing brothers, each wanting her to live with him.[71] She might even, according to Khayr al-Din, decide to live with her maternal uncle, despite her paternal aunts' protest that he lacked righteousness and they feared for her with him.[72] So long as a mature woman had chosen what was felt to be a safe residence, her father or other paternal relatives could not continue to exercise control over her life.

Fathering, like mothering, was located in time and constructed, at least in part, in response to the perceived needs of the child, as well as the jurists' understanding of male roles and capacities. It was the father who would best support a dependent child, in terms both of basic material needs and of business and social relations with the world outside the family. In the years of transition from childhood to full adulthood, a father supplied guidance and training to his sons, and protection to his daughters. It was as guardian, seeing to the physical and social development of the child, that the father found his central role, as envisioned by the muftis, a role to be assumed by other members of his family should he be unable to fulfill it.

Fathers were the natural guardians of their children and did not need to be appointed to that role by the court. Court records do refer often to the father as guardian in the many cases of marriage arrangements, property sales, and *waqf* business in which minors were principals. It was also not uncommon, in court practice, for paternal relatives to take on the guardianship of fatherless children (always referred to as "orphans," whether their mother was alive or not). Paternal uncles, grandfathers, or brothers were recognized as guardians, and often sought support awards for their charges.[73] Once a level of support was fixed by the qadi, these paternal relations could borrow or spend up to that amount against eventual repayment by the child. By thus recognizing the guardian, and setting a level of support for his charge, the court reinforced the juristic preference for vesting guardianship in male relations on the paternal side. The father (or, in his absence, a male relative on the paternal side) was felt to be the best choice for managing a child's affairs because of his central role within the patrilineal model of allegiance and descent.

MUTATIONS: THE MOTHER-GUARDIAN

The muftis and the courts were part of an environment in which any distinction between, on the one hand, a woman's world of childbirth, child rearing, and immediate family affairs and, on the other hand, a man's world of business and the social complexities of extradomestic life was not only tenuous, but often ill-adapted to the goals of social welfare and harmony that they set for their communities. Their vision of the nurturing mother and the guiding and supporting father, who divided up the tasks of child rearing according to their natural proclivities and the child's needs, was a vision of complementarity and order easily sundered by unanticipated events, including the premature demise of either parent. If the mother died, the substitute caretaker in the period of *hidana* was usually a woman from the maternal side of the family. If the father of a minor child died, the closest male paternal relative, a paternal uncle, grandfather, or mature brother, would step in as guardian. In some situations, however, women were able, after the death of their husbands, to expand their role of caretaker to that of full legal guardian.

The muftis recognized women as appropriate guardians in certain cases, particularly for children by a deceased husband: sometimes these widows were permitted not only to keep their children with them beyond the age of *hidana*, but also to manage their children's affairs until they attained their legal majority. The muftis dealt with the mother-guardian as a normal phenomenon, and held her to the same standards as they would any male guardian. Like her male counterpart, she had a free hand in the management of her children's property: she could use her children's money to make repairs on their property, or she could sell property so long as it sold at a "fair price" and the proceeds went to the account of the child.[74] She could arrange a marriage for her minor daughter so long as the *mahr* was "fair" and the groom was suitable.[75] Her power to act on behalf of her child was indistinguishable from that of a father-guardian, except that she could marry her daughter only to a suitable groom with a reasonable *mahr*.

Although the mother-guardian took on the powers of a father-guardian, she did not take on all the responsibilities. Unlike a father, she was not obliged to pay the costs of support for her charge out of her own pocket. Any money of her own that a mother-guardian spent on the child could be deducted from the child's present or future income. She might receive an assignment of *nafaqa* from the court specifying the amount she was authorized to spend, but the mother who overspent that amount in order to meet the needs of her children was nonetheless to be fully reimbursed. Normally, the mother's oath, testifying to the amount she had spent, would be sufficient evidence, but if it was "obvious" that she was lying about the amount, the judge could ask for corroborating testimony.[76]

How did mothers acquire this power of guardianship? A mother became a possible candidate for the office with the death or disappearance of her husband. She was not, however, automatically appointed as her children's guardian. On the contrary, the patrilineal rights of male relatives on the paternal side took precedence: a paternal grandfather would be named guardian of the children in preference to their mother so long as their father had not appointed anyone else before he died.[77] The mother-guardian was thus enough of a departure from the patrilineal norm to require special certification: a village qadi's appointment of a mother as guardian of her children was held to be invalid until it had been approved by the *qadi al-qudah*, the chief qadi of the district.[78]

The surest route to female guardianship, and the one that would best stand up to any challenge, was selection by the child's father. A *wasi mukhtar* was a guardian who had been chosen by the natural guardian, usually the father, to replace him if and when he died.

> QUESTION: There is a man who, in his death illness, said to his righteous wife, the mother of his children, "I entrust my children to you; arrange for their needs after my death," and then he died, leaving her and the aforesaid children. The deceased has a paternal nephew who opposes the mother's taking control of her children's property. If what was mentioned [above] is proved, is the mother the guardian for the aforesaid children, and [is it the case that] the nephew cannot oppose her in that?
>
> ANSWER: It is said [in the sources that] . . . if he said, "You are the guardian," and does not retract, or he said, "You are the guardian of my money," or he said, "I entrust my children to you after my death," or "Take care of my children after my death," or "Arrange for their needs after my death," any part of this wording, [this makes] a guardian.[79]

Once a father had appointed his wife guardian before his death, it was all but impossible for other relatives to contest her guardianship. Not even a paternal grandfather could displace a mother who had her deceased husband's blessing as a guardian.[80] As one of her prerogatives as guardian, a mother-guardian could, in turn, name a guardian to take *her* place should she also die, and she was free to choose whomever she liked. According to al-'Imadi, she could even decide to designate the son of her uncle (the children's cousin on the maternal side) over the protests of a paternal uncle who claimed the right of guardianship.[81] The father's stated wish to make his wife their children's guardian was sufficient, then, to cancel the privileges of the patrilineal family. Once a mother gained guardianship, she could effectively thwart any attempts by the father's family to regain control of her children.

A mother-guardian could register her guardianship in court, so as to obtain official authorization for the spending of her children's money on their own support during the period of her guardianship. Such registrations did not specify how a mother had obtained guardianship, but did serve as formal acknowledgment of her status as guardian and her power to manage her children's property and use that property to provide for them.

> The court recognizes the woman, Amna, daughter of *al-sayyid*
> Husayn, and her legal guardianship of her minor daughter, Khadra,
> daughter of the deceased *al-sayyid* Ibrahim. . . . Amna has permission
> to spend from her [Khadra's] inheritance from her father for her
> needs. The judge fixes support [*nafaqa*] for meat, bread, fat, soap,
> bath fees, laundry, and other necessities at two *qita' misriyya*. The
> mother is authorized to spend this on her [Khadra] and to be reim-
> bursed from the money the daughter inherited from her father.
>   17 Rabi' I 1146 H.(1733 A.D.)[82]

Here, and elsewhere, a mother sought the court's recognition of her guardianship in the context of the assignment of a specific amount of child support and the permission to spend this amount from the child's resources.[83] We can only assume that a mother would bring this matter to court to forestall possible future challenges to her guardianship, or to the way in which she tapped her charges' property to pay for their keep. By registering such guardianship, the courts would reinforce the muftis' position that female guardianship could be both appropriate and beneficial for the children in certain circumstances.

The mother as guardian was a role quite distinct from the mother as temporary caretaker: rather than simply nurturing the child until he or she was old enough to join the paternal household, the guardian exercised full control over all the child's affairs, a power to be relinquished only when the child her/himself was old enough to take control. Such a role defied the rules of the patrilineal society of which it was a part, and stood the strongly gendered vision of mothering on its head. The jurists' and courts' acceptance of the mother-guardian, and their willingness, in such cases, to conceive of mothering as an all-pervading power over the person and property of the child, suggest that they did not view inherent male and female capacities so differently. Yes, women made better caretakers for young children, but they were also well able to assume, if necessary, the responsibilities entailed in the management of businesses and other property. The duration, terrain, and power of mothering was bounded not so much by the capacities of woman as mother as by the jurists' perception of the needs of the child and who could best meet them.

Mothering and fathering in Ottoman Syria and Palestine were constructed with careful reference to the welfare of the child. The jurists' sense of community responsibility for ensuring that children were fairly treated and would grow to an effective adulthood informed their discussion of parenthood. All parents were subject to the oversight of the court, as principal guardian of the interests of the community. All parents had to fulfill their obligations of support and protection, or risk losing their rights of parenthood. By declaring a mother unfit for custody, or by removing a father as guardian, the jurists chose to champion the welfare of the child at the risk of weakening the claims of kin. Children were not just family property; they had rights, rights to decent care and to the protection of their interests. If their relatives failed to honor these rights, the muftis authorized the courts to step in and make other arrangements.

The muftis and the courts constructed mothering and fathering along clearly gendered lines by defining the mother as nurturer, best equipped for the tending of babies and young children, and the father as provider, best equipped to support all children and protect the older ones. The parents' complementary responsibilities were synchronized with the ages of the child. When the mother cared for young children who would eventually join the patrilineal household, she could and frequently did claim compensation from that household for her services. If the wishes of a father and the needs of a child so dictated, however, a mother might combine with the role of nurturer the duties of protector and educator of her child, a possibility often entertained by the muftis and abetted by the courts. It is here that we encounter the complexity of legal thought and courtroom activity that softened the harsh rules of patriliny in the interests of what was best for the child, and constructed motherhood and fatherhood with a fluidity sufficient to meet changing circumstances.

The roles and powers of mother and father also derived their flexibility from the location of mothering and fathering along the same spectrum. The world of reproduction, of the bearing and nurturing of children, was not a world isolated from the rest of social life. On the contrary, the child—as actual or potential possessor of family property, as present claimant on resources, as future principal in a marriage alliance—was a family member who was intricately involved in the family affairs that served as the basis for the economic and political life of the time. Mothering and fathering shared in the common project of raising the child from conception to maturity. Though there were divisions in time, the years of early childhood being given to mothering and the prepubescent years to fathering, there were no strict divisions of sphere. Children were mothered and fathered in the family, and the family served as the basis for all other social life. Reproduction and nurture belonged to women and men alike, though their roles were conceived as serial rather than interchangeable. Both were involved in child rearing, and that duality made permutations, particularly in the extent and power of mothering, possible.

Mothering and fathering in these times were gendered roles. The muftis drew on the accumulated wisdom of past jurists to further elaborate in their own fatwas the gendered version of motherhood and fatherhood that permeated activities in the Islamic court system, as well. The strictures of a patrilineal family system that rendered motherhood a relatively powerless and temporary position were reinforced by many of the muftis' opinions, and by the courts that were guided by those opinions. At the same time, the muftis and courts also proved able to envision, because of the unity of purpose of mothering and fathering, a female parent whose authority could cross the gendered lines they had drawn.

CHAPTER 5

If She Were Ready for Men

Sexuality and Reproduction

QUESTION: If a husband wants to consummate a marriage with his minor wife, saying that she can endure intercourse, and her father says she is not yet ready, what is the legal ruling?

ANSWER: If she is plump and buxom and ready for men, and the stipulated *mahr* has been received promptly, the father is compelled to give her to her husband, according to the soundest teaching. The qadi examines whether she is [ready] by [asking] whomever raised her and by her appearance; and if she is suitable for men, he orders her father to give her to her husband or not. And if there are none who raised her, then he requests a consultation from women. And if they say that she is ready for men and can endure intercourse, he [the qadi] instructs the father to give her to her husband. If they say she is not ready, then he does not so instruct the father. And God knows best.[1]

Legal discourse on sexuality and reproduction was predicated on the notion that human sexual desire, both male and female, was powerful and ubiquitous. Marriage was unquestionably viewed by the muftis as one way to contain sexual desire so that it could not threaten the stability of the community by leading to inappropriate pairings and the conception of children of uncertain parentage, children who would be se-

148

vere social and economic liabilities in a kin-based society. The muftis' pronounced promarital position thus stemmed, at least in part, from their view that the institution of marriage channeled powerful sexual drives that might otherwise lead to illicit unions, unclaimed children, and, at worst, a social anarchy bred by unregulated sexual contacts. Legal discourse on desire focused, then, not only on the power of desire, but also on the ways in which sexuality could be regulated, reproduction could be controlled, and transgressions of the rules for sexuality and reproduction should be punished.

The sexuality the muftis sought to tame was a sexuality that they had had a hand in creating, for "sexuality is constituted in society and history, not biologically ordained."[2] Indeed, despite the enduring sameness of the biological base of human sexuality, culture and history can produce understandings of sex, and practices born of those understandings, that defy generalization about the nature of desire. Michel Foucault, by calling our attention to the major discontinuities between kinship-based systems of sexuality and the modern systems of sexual categorization and stratification, alerts us to the chasm that may separate our views of sexuality from those of the legal discourse of—in this case— Ottoman Syria and Palestine.[3] Jeffrey Weeks has pointed out, for example, that in "the historical variability and mutability of sexual identity in general . . . a 'homosexual' (or indeed a 'heterosexual') is a relatively recent phenomenon, a product of a history of 'definition and self-definition' that needs to be described and understood before its effects can be unraveled."[4] Our ways of describing and understanding human sexuality, then, may not serve us well as a framework for exploring the muftis' approaches to sexuality, however much they necessarily inform the questions we ask and the ways in which we interpret the answers.

Indeed, the muftis reflected and elaborated notions of sexual desire that strike us as "different": they did not strictly differentiate between heterosexual and homosexual desire, they acknowledged the sexuality of young children, and they assigned the sexual urge an almost obsessive and uncontrollable power. Though the familiar and deeply rooted

Western view of sex as a negative, destructive force was not entirely lacking, we must not assume that the equation of sex with sin and the apposition of the spiritual and the sexual were therefore present. On the contrary, the muftis accorded desire a central and well-integrated place in their understanding of human character, however wary they were of its potential for creating social disturbance.

The muftis' approach to the control of desire was linked, of course, to their understanding of the nature of that desire. The sexual urge was held to be powerful and universal, certainly not a candidate for reform or elimination. The control of sexuality, then, could not be based on attempts to reshape the sexual urge per se; rather, social constraints had to be such as to ensure that desire did not wreak disorder, but instead would be channeled in socially useful directions. The promarital position of the muftis was one mechanism for turning desire to the purpose of social stability, but they also adopted and elaborated a number of other legal doctrines that gendered space in such a way as to erect barriers to extramarital contact between men and women. And, if prevention failed, the muftis were prepared to discuss in some detail the proofs and punishments pertaining to sexual transgressions.

Control of sexuality was exercised not only to minimize social conflict, but also, and above all, to oversee reproduction. The identity and paternity of children were key components of a strongly patrilineal family and a social system in which the patrilineal family undergirded most political and economic arrangements. In the context of such a kin-based system, the discourse of the muftis discussed sexuality as the determinant force in reproduction, largely because of the importance of establishing the legitimacy, and therefore the social identity, of any child produced by a sexual union. The legal discourse therefore examined reproductive processes with an eye to establishing the paternity of a child, and the muftis were called upon to consider aspects of human sexuality and reproduction that may strike us as not so dissimilar from modern understandings as we might have expected. At the same time, however, they grounded their arguments on issues of descent, on legitimating (or delegitimating) the offspring of a sexual relationship. They were, then, in the final analysis, the bestowers of birthright in a society where paternity established the familial identity, and therefore the class, status, and social networks, of any new member of society.[5]

DELINEATING DESIRE

The muftis viewed sexual desire from a distinctly male vantage point. Though they did not deny female sexuality, their fatwas focused on the power of male desire and the temptations that beset men at many a turn. The basic legal doctrines they had inherited differentiated male and female sexuality in seemingly unalterable ways. The male need for sexual activity and variety was recognized, in the law, in the permission granted to men to be married to as many as four women at one time—but women were not permitted a parallel privilege. The muftis did not comment much on polygyny: though it was clearly permitted, it was circumscribed, as we have seen, by the requirements of providing a suitable *mahr* in every marriage arrangement and of lodging and supporting all wives in the prescribed manner. The paucity of discussion suggests that the practice was neither widespread nor much contested. The muftis did, however, enforce the limits set by the law: should a man with four wives take yet another bride, the new marriage was to be considered *batil*, null and void.[6] Although the legal insistence on payment of *mahr* and full support to all wives put polygyny out of the reach of many, the legal accommodation of sexual variety for men openly reflected a discourse on the power of the male sexual drive.[7] Women, through divorce and remarriage, might have more than one licit sexual partner in a lifetime, but only men could enjoy several partners at once.

Another form of sexual license that underscored belief in the vitality of the male sexual drive was the legal acceptance of slave concubinage. A man could have sexual relations with an unlimited number of slave women, so long as they were his personal property, and any issue of such relationships were his legitimate children, as legitimate as any children born to a free wife. Again, the muftis had little to say about this privilege, except to point out that certain rules applied: a man could not, for example, keep two sisters as concubines at the same time, because sexual intercourse with sisters was forbidden, whether they were wives *or* concubines.[8] The muftis also recognized, and approved, the provisions men might make for the care of their concubines. A man could undertake formally to pay support (*nafaqa*) to his slave concubine, just as he might to a wife. He might also make legal bequests to his concubine to ensure that she shared in his estate, despite the fact that she would not otherwise be of his legally prescribed heirs.[9] Support of this sort was not required, however, and in legal doctrine a slave concubine was a sexual partner with few rights. As we shall see, it was only in her role as the bearer of legitimate children that she acquired even the minimal right of eventual manumission. Like polygyny, slave concubinage was expensive, and a realistic option for only a few. By making sex with multiple partners licit for men but not for women, however, the muftis elaborated a legal doctrine that constructed male sexuality as a more active and demanding force than that of females.

Likewise, any social interaction between a man and a desirable woman was fraught with sexual peril: a man was expected to attempt to have illicit sexual relations with any attractive woman with whom he might find himself alone. The muftis' view of privacy between a man and a woman (*khalwa*) was supposedly derived from two sayings attributed to the Prophet Muhammad: "A person should not be alone with a woman unless he is her *mahram* relative"; and "A man is not alone with a woman but that the devil makes a third."[10] Indeed, the muftis worked from the legal presumption that a man and a woman left alone together would have sexual intercourse. The simple fact that a husband and wife had enjoyed privacy (*khalwa*) was enough for a marriage to have been considered consummated: privacy was equated with sexual intimacy.[11] The contrary proved true as well: if a married couple had not been able to have *khalwa* because their house had an open door and anyone could walk in on them at any time, the marriage was not considered consummated.[12] The approach to *khalwa* rested, of course, on an understanding that women as well as men had strong sexual urges: it was not the possibility of male sexual violence that rendered *khalwa* a danger, but, rather, mutual attraction.

It was male desire, however, that occupied most of the muftis' thoughts about sexuality. Sexual arousal outside of licit marriage was a constant risk of social life. In his discussion of the problem posed by the *sabih*, the mature youth whose prettiness called for the extension of his father's tutelage, Khayr al-Din depicted male desire not only as powerful, but just as easily homoerotic as heteroerotic. In explaining why a father could continue to exercise control of a mature son, even to the extent of preventing him from leaving home to seek knowledge, Khayr al-Din spoke to the havoc an appealing youth could wreak in even the most pious of circles:

> Abu Hanifa, may God bless him, used to put one Muhammad ibn al-Hassan, who was pretty [*sabih*], behind a pillar for fear of the eye's betrayal. For if a boy reaches physical maturity and is not *sabih*, then he is judged a man, but if he is *sabih*, then he is judged like a woman and he is *'aura* [literally, genitals, i.e., that which evokes desire] down to his feet. . . . This means that men must not look at him with desire, but looking at him *without* desire is not bad. Therefore, the boy is not obliged to wear a veil, and in prayers he is like men. . . . According to legend, someone was seen in sleep [in a dream] and he was asked, "What did God do with you?" And he said, "He forgave me every sin I asked him to forgive except for the one sin I was ashamed to ask for his forgiveness for, and I was tortured for that sin." He was then asked, "What was that sin?" He said, "I looked at a youth [*ghulam*] with desire." . . . A woman has two devils and a *ghulam* has eighteen.[13]

In his discussion of the *sabih*, Khayr al-Din presents us with a topography of male desire. First, the resonant name of Abu Hanifa is invoked: Abu Hanifa, the renowned Muslim scholar and teacher, the founder of Khayr al-Din's own legal school, used to fear that he could not control his desires, that the sight of a radiant youth would stir him. All human beings, we surmise, even the most learned and pious, are subject to spasms of desire, and it is the wise among us who take the necessary precautions. Second, an attractive male youth may arouse a man's desire as easily as a woman might; his attractiveness, in fact, derives from his feminine appearance. Beardless and delicate, he is an honorary woman whose entire body, like a woman's, is a source of sexual excitement for a man. Unlike the attractions of a woman, however, those of the *sabih* are in the eye of the beholder. Men can look at him with or without feeling desire, because his seductive qualities are not inherent—he is not required to wear a veil or absent himself from men's prayers as women must. A woman's sexual attractions, to the contrary, are an essential part of her being, always present and powerful, always to be guarded against. Perhaps because the *sabih*'s appeal derives from his resemblance to a woman rather than from his own inherent sexuality, he is viewed as a more troubling temptation, and because men may or may not be attracted to him, the notion of voluntarism is introduced into the analysis. Moreover, a youth's powers of sexual attraction can be nine times that of a woman; for some, then, the seductiveness of the young man is no pale imitation of a woman's charms but rather stirs a passion far beyond anything a woman might kindle. There is no sense here, however, that heterosexual and homosexual desire are distinct impulses. Any man may desire a boy just as he desires a woman; the radiant youth, like the woman, must be safeguarded because of his appeal to most men. The notion that "'lust in the heart,' to which all men are susceptible, is as likely to be stimulated by boys as by women" was a standard assumption in the Arabic literary tradition, and one no doubt familiar to the Ottoman-period jurists.[14] Khayr al-Din was dealing here, then, with a form of desire considered neither marginal nor unnatural.

Sexual desire was seen as part of the male condition, among even the great and the pious. It was ubiquitous and troublesome, and a man must devise ways to avoid situations where his passion might be roused, as it well might be by the sight of an attractive woman or comely youth. But why must a man guard against desire? Khayr al-Din invokes the question of sin and divine sanction in a peculiar way. The story of God's punishment of desire is told as a "legend" or unauthenticated account of a dream: it thus stands at a double remove from the verifiable. By recounting the story, Khayr al-Din raises the issue of desire as sin, but leaves his reader in doubt about whether desire in and of itself is sinful. The rest of the fatwa, in its emphasis on the social disturbances produced by desire, for example, the possibility of distraction from the work of teaching and learning, suggests on the contrary that it is the results of desire that constitute the greater problem, not any inherent moral failing in experiencing desire itself.

Sexual desire, as a normal part of the male constitution, was thought to make its appearance early. The muftis assumed that boys began to experience desire in their youth, usually before they reached puberty. A prepubescent boy could consummate a marriage, so long as he was a *murahiq*, "one capable of having sexual intercourse with someone like him, whose instrument moves, and who desires sexual intercourse." A boy ordinarily developed these abilities and desires, the muftis said, at age ten.[15] Here the birth of sexual desire is linked not to full-blown puberty, but to the ability to have an erection and therefore to consummate a marriage. A ten-year-old boy was expected not only to be physically able to have sexual intercourse, but also to feel the sexual desire that would make him want to do so. This did not mean, of course, that prepubescent boys were married off as a rule; on the contrary, the marriage contracts registered in the Islamic courts rarely record a minor groom.[16] Still, sexual desire in boys as young as ten was considered the norm, even if child marriage did not appear to be an accepted channeling of that desire.

The question of sexual desire was posed quite differently for girls. The muftis did not assess female readiness for sexual intercourse in light of a girl's desire or active capabilities, but rather asked whether or not she could "support intercourse." If a prepubescent girl ran away from her husband out of fear and sought refuge in her father's house, she must be returned to her husband if she is "ready for intercourse."[17] Her own desires, and in this case her signaling of an active distaste for sex, did not enter into the deliberations. Indeed, a girl's readiness was decided entirely on the basis of her impact on male desire, not her own experience of desire. Sometimes the issue was clear, as in the case of a six-year-old girl who was deemed too young to be an "object of desire."[18] At other times the muftis were called upon to establish guidelines for determining when a girl seemed ready, as we saw in the chapter's opening fatwa, in which Khayr al-Din assigns to the qadi the task of assessing a girl's ability to "support intercourse" by studying her physical appearance or, if that is inconclusive, by relying on the opinion of delegated women.[19] It is the girl's shapeliness that signals her availability as a sexual partner, not her desires. The judge can ascertain her readiness simply by looking at her, because it is his desire, not hers, that determines her readiness for sexual activity. He might turn the decision over to women who could inspect the girl more closely, but the criteria they would use would be male criteria. They would look for the physical attributes that stimulate male desire, that make her literally an "object of desire." The girl's wishes are not relevant, and the subject of female desire is not broached.

Although the muftis did not deny the existence of female desire, they clearly did not find it a central concern. They discussed desire entirely in male terms. The awakening of desire in boys found its parallel in girls in the process of becoming desirable. The maps of desire are male maps, outlining the powers of male desire, the early interest in sex, the fluidity of the sexual object. They are also maps drawn not for the purpose of categorizing or stigmatizing sexual identities or behaviors but rather for devising controls. Unregulated desire was seen as posing real threats to the stability and harmony of a society where so much of social, economic, and political life was based on kin ties. The power of desire could not be changed or subverted, but it could be controlled.

CONTROLLING DESIRE

One way to control sexual desire was to eliminate situations in which illicit relations might develop. An unsupervised visit between a man and a woman who were neither husband and wife nor *mahram* relations was not a good idea. al-ʿImadi took a narrow view of the circumstances under which such contact might be permitted:

> QUESTION: A man entered the house of an unrelated woman and was alone with her, on the pretext that he was her legal agent [*wakil*] representing her interests. Her father forbade him [entrance]. Can the father forbid this, and are the man's pretenses of no consequence?
>
> ANSWER: Yes . . . being alone with an unrelated woman is forbidden, unless she is in debt and has fled the law [become an outlaw], or if she is old and deformed, or if there is a screen between them.[20]

It was only the woman whom age or illness had rendered totally unappealing or who was hidden from view that a man could be trusted with. Moreover, the woman who had defied the authority of the law was treated as a special case; as an outlaw, she was no longer a member of the community, and thus the rules of behavior concerned with the regulation of relations among members of the community no longer applied. Apart from these almost trivial exceptions, a man and a woman should not be alone together, even for legitimate business purposes.

Khayr al-Din dealt with a similar question regarding a man's intrusion upon an unrelated woman. When a man entered his sister's husband's house without the permission of his brother-in-law, he intruded upon his sister's co-wife, a woman unrelated to him. Such entry without permission and intrusion were illegal, and punishable by *taʿzir*, the qadi's discretionary punishment.[21] A man could not enter another's house in his absence and without his permission, and the crime of trespass was strongly linked to the problem of contact with the unrelated women who might live in the house. Furthermore, it was the husband, as in Khayr al-Din's fatwa, or the father, as in al-ʿImadi's fatwa, who could, and should, act to ensure that the women under his protection would not be at risk of contact with unrelated men.

There were some clear limits, however, to male authority. A mature, unmarried young woman whose parents and grandparents were deceased could choose to live where she wanted. If her paternal uncle wanted to assert his authority and take her under his tutelage, he had to argue that she ran a real risk of being "corrupted" in her present situation. Otherwise, he had no right to tell her where or how to live.[22] Men were styled the protectors of women—but only of those women for whom they had clear legal responsibilities, such as their wives and daughters.

Nor was proper female behavior viewed by the muftis as synonymous with seclusion. A young woman who was to be "taken in hand" by her mother might still run errands to neighborhood shops.[23] In fact, none of the muftis evince any marked preference for total female seclusion from public space. The avoidance of one-on-one contact was to be achieved by having both men and women honor the rule that they avoid being alone together. If women wished to seclude themselves they should be accommodated, but seclusion was not prescribed. A secluded woman (*mukhaddara*) was excused, for example, from coming to court in person. She might give indirect testimony in court by giving her testimony to two trustworthy men, who would then deliver it before the judge, and she could use an agent to bring a claim to court or to defend her.[24] The courts were thus expected to adjust their procedures to the special needs of a secluded woman, but they were not, by the same token, in any way told to discourage the nonsecluded woman from coming to court.

Indeed, women often came in person to the Damascus, Jerusalem, and Nablus courts to press claims, to transact business, or to testify. Some women, especially in the more conservative Jerusalem venue, would come to court veiled, and male witnesses would be required to confirm their identity in front of the judge. Most often, however, they appeared dressed in ways that made their identity clear to the judge. The secluded lifestyle was known and accommodated, but it was by no means universal or even, apparently, very widespread: women were much more likely than not to appear in court when a case concerned them.

The muftis also allowed the qadis a certain flexibility in interpreting the prohibition of contact between unrelated men and women. Khayr al-

Din dealt with the problem of such contacts in the context of his community's taboo against women's presence in a cemetery.

> QUESTION: There is a woman who died and she had no *mahram* relatives. Who should bury her?
> ANSWER: Her [male] neighbors, righteous ones, should bury her. And women should not enter the tomb to bury her, because the touch of an unrelated man can fall on a woman's robe when it is absolutely necessary, after death just as during her lifetime.[25]

Here, the custom of prohibiting women from entering a cemetery came into conflict with the problem posed by unrelated men touching a woman's body. Faced with this choice, Khayr al-Din opted to allow men to handle the woman's body as a practical necessity. Khayr al-Din also suggests, though he does not elaborate, that there are other times when such contact is acceptable, presumably in instances where the basic needs of the community and its citizens so dictate. In this show of flexibility on issues of sexual segregation and seclusion, the muftis did not hang the control of desire's harmful consequences entirely on the removal of women from male space. One rule, however, *was* made clear: a man and a woman should not be alone together; it was up to both men and women, and to no small extent to a woman's father or husband, to make certain that opportunities for the play of desire did not arise.

Another approach to the control of desire was the imposition of heavy sanctions for transgressions of the rules for sexual relations. It was unlawful sexual intercourse, and not sexual preferences and practices, that occupied the attention of the law and the muftis. In other words, it was acts of rape and consensual sexual intercourse between a man and a woman who were not husband and wife, acts that could result in illegitimate births, that were soundly condemned and criminalized, not the acts of sexual "deviance" so stigmatized in the modern era. It was not that homosexual acts were explicitly condoned; they were simply not discussed much at all. By contrast, the muftis were forceful and even strident in their condemnation of heterosexual transgressions, though they also trod lightly where the issue of evidence and punishment was concerned.

Strictly speaking, the rape of a woman other than one's own wife was a form of *zina'*, unlawful intercourse, and it was punishable, if proved, by the severe *hadd* penalty of death by stoning. Like all forms of unlawful intercourse, it was considered a crime against religion, and punishment was a right of God. No negotiated settlement was possible.[26] The rules of evidence and punishment allowed the muftis a certain flexibility, however, in dealing with specific cases:

> QUESTION: There is a *muhsan* criminal who kidnapped a virgin and took her virginity. She fled from him to her family and now her seducer wants to take her away by force. Should he be prevented, and what is required of him?
> ANSWER: Yes, he should be prevented [from taking] her. If he claimed *shubha* [judicial doubt], there is no *hadd* punishment but he must [pay] a fair *mahr*. If he did not claim *shubha*, and admission and testimony prove [his actions], the specified *hadd* punishment is required: if he is *muhsan*, then he is stoned; if not, he is flogged. In the event the *hadd* penalty is canceled, a *mahr* is required.[27]

Khayr al-Din here outlined his approach to the question of rape. First, the rape did not establish any recognized relations between the man and the woman: the rapist had no right to demand the return of his victim. Second, the crime of rape was a form of unlawful intercourse for which there were prescribed *hadd* punishments. A *muhsan*, or person who had already consummated a marriage and then had unlawful intercourse with someone else (whether consensual or not), receives the most severe punishment, death by stoning; but if the perpetrator had never been married, the law required the lesser but still severe and potentially lethal punishment of flogging. Third, the court had to have received either the confession of the accused or the legal testimony of others, who, in the case of unlawful intercourse, had to number no fewer than four male eyewitnesses. So far here, Khayr al-Din has not strayed from the straight and narrow of the legal tradition. Fourth, however, a wild card appears: the perpetrator will be given an opportunity to claim *shubha*, that is, to argue that the act he committed resembled a lawful one so closely that he had, in fact, acted in good faith. The claim of *shubha* in this instance could be based only on the notion that the accused thought he had contracted a legal marriage with his victim and had acted on that assumption. The doctrine of *shubha* had no doubt been designed to deal with the problems posed by defective marriages: if a man thought that he had contracted a valid marriage, it would be unjust to punish him severely for unlawful intercourse. Instead, if the putative marriage were discovered to be invalid, he would be allowed to compensate his sexual partner by paying her the equivalent of a *mahr*. Khayr al-Din was ready to accept the claim of *shubha* at face value, thereby canceling the *hadd* punishment in favor of compensation to the victim in the form of the equivalent of a "fair *mahr*."[28]

Such use of the concept of *shubha* was not altogether an innovation. Hanafi jurisprudence had long held that certain kinds of unlawful sexual intercourse "resembled" licit relations closely enough that *hadd* punishment was not appropriate. If a man had sexual relations with a slave owned by his wife, mother, or father, for example, or with a woman he thought he had married legally even though the marriage was not valid, some Hanafi jurists had ruled that he could escape *hadd* punishment.[29] What does seem something of a departure here is Khayr al-Din's very liberal use of *shubha*, his willingness to extend a very broad benefit of the doubt in some rather suspicious circumstances.

This concept of *shubha* allowed the muftis to convert the usually draconian punishment for rape into the relatively mild requirement of an indemnity. In the various cases they considered—most involving the willful abduction and rape of minor or virgin girls—the muftis strain our credulity by repeatedly accepting the claim of *shubha*, despite the fact that the actions of the accused are clearly described as "abduction" and intercourse with the use of "force."[30] Rape was clearly a criminal act, but punishment was routinely muted by the legal fiction of *shubha*. We cannot know with certainty why the muftis allowed virtually every rape case they considered to be treated as a matter of indemnifying the victim. They may have been advising a court system in which the judges had no sure means of implementing *hadd* punishments, and thus preferred to deal in indemnities whenever remotely possible. They may have felt that, in the case of rape, the victim was better served by receiving substantial material compensation than by knowing that the rapist would be physically punished, especially in light of the fact that the law was vague concerning whether the victim of a rape might also be found guilty of *zina'*. Perhaps they calculated that, given the difficulties involved in proving unlawful intercourse, the path of *shubha* offered a kind of plea bargain that benefited the victim as well. And it may be, of course, that they thought the crime of rape not sufficiently serious for its perpetrator to merit death. In any event, the common use of *shubha* shifted the meaning of the punishment away from an expiation owed to God, and toward compensation owed a victim.

We must also ask if the muftis, in commuting *hadd* punishment to indemnity, were following the lead of Ottoman criminal law. As Uriel Heyd has shown, as late as the early seventeenth century the judges in the shari'a courts were exhorted by the Empire to administer justice and punish criminals "in accordance with the noble shari'a and the exalted *kanun*."[31] The various and evolving Ottoman criminal codes (*kanun*) authorized the Islamic judge to fine a perpetrator of simple *zina'* in lieu of applying the *hadd* penalty of the shari'a, but in the case of forced abduction and rape, whether of a woman, a girl, or a boy, the criminal code prescribed castration of the guilty. We cannot be sure of the extent to which the muftis and qadis of seventeenth- and eighteenth-century Ottoman Syria were fully cognizant of the various provisions of the code, for they did not call upon the criminal code to justify legal decisions, nor did they mention the code's penalty of castration as a possibility. And, indeed, their invocation of *shubha* and the imposition of a payment equivalent to a *mahr* to be made to the victim make no appearance in the Ottoman criminal codes. The deliberations of the muftis in cases of rape thus tend to support Heyd's view that "in the course of the seventeenth and eighteenth centuries the Ottoman Criminal Code was gradually discarded as a source of penal law, and finally completely forgotten,"[32] if indeed the code ever guided the pens of the Syrian and Palestinian muftis.

Only once did Khayr al-Din call for harsh punishment, by beating or execution, of a rapist, curiously enough one who had kidnapped his victim and then "married" her in an extralegal village ceremony before he had intercourse with her.[33] In this case, his ire seems to have been driven chiefly by the way in which some peasants were taking the law into their own hands by circumventing the legal requirements for marriage and sexual intercourse, a crime against God and the community that deserved the full weight of *hadd* punishment.

Accusations of rape, however, were not often brought to court. In one of the few cases found in the court records, a woman named Khadija bt. *al-sayyid* ʿAbd al-Hadi, from a village near Damascus, related a tale of rape. She told the court that some six months previously she had gone to a house to bake her bread, and the owner of the house, Muhammad b. *al-sayyid* Yasin, had raped her, taking her virginity. After the rape, he married her with an appropriate *mahr*. Then, two weeks before Khadija came to court, he had divorced her. Muhammad, for his part, denied the rape by swearing that he had married her before intercourse took place, and his sworn denial took precedence over her testimony, in keeping with the rules of procedure.[34] The judge therefore ruled that the only outcome of this case was the confirmation of the termination of their marriage by divorce, and the husband's obligation to pay her the balance of her *mahr*: he paid half of the balance, ten *ghurush*, on the spot, and acknowledged his debt to her of the remaining ten *ghurush*.[35]

Why did Khadija bring an accusation of rape to court six months after its occurrence? Perhaps, in the wake of her divorce, anger had spurred her to attempt to procure for her ex-husband the punishment he deserved for his crime. Perhaps she hoped to be awarded some additional compensation. In either case, she was to be disappointed. Without witnesses to the rape, her accusation was effectively deflected by her ex-husband's sworn denial. Even if Muhammad had not denied the rape, he had already, by pledging a fair *mahr,* given her the compensation that the judge, following the lead of the muftis, was likely to have required.

The dearth of similar cases in the court records suggests that kidnappings and rapes, if they occurred, were rarely brought to the attention of the Islamic court. Indeed, many of the fatwas dealing with such crimes made it clear that in the eyes of the muftis it was in the village and among the peasantry that rape and forced marriage were seen as social problems. We cannot, of course, rule out an urban bias here that might have led the *'ulama'* to exaggerate the moral laxity of the rural setting. Still, such events probably did occur more frequently as one moved farther away from the urban centers, where the Islamic courts and jurists more assiduously upheld the law. And it was, moreover, the inhabitants of the rural areas who would be least likely to resort to an appeal to a distant urban court.

Consensual sexual intercourse between a man and a woman who were not married to each other was the other form that *zina'* might take. In the case of two consenting adults, the *hadd* penalty would be imposed not only on the man, as it would in the case of rape, but on the woman as well. Under the Ottoman Criminal Code, the *hadd* penalty of flogging and stoning could be replaced by fines, calibrated by both the wealth and marital status of the perpetrators, to be paid by both partners to the state.[36] But the muftis once again took a different course here, avoiding both the *hadd* penalties and the payments into official coffers in favor of compensation in the form of a *mahr* to be paid by the male partner to the female. They reasoned that the doctrine of *shubha* applied equally well to consensual sexual relations, and the remedy of a compensation could be applied if a claim of *shubha* were made.

In point of fact, however, prosecution of this form of *zina'* does not appear to have been a major concern of the muftis. Surely the rules of evidence, requiring four male eyewitnesses to prove *zina',* or four separate confessions on the part of the guilty parties, acted to discourage accusations. Testimony by witnesses that a man had confessed his *zina'* to them was not sufficient: either they had to have witnessed the act or the man had to have confessed it directly to the court.[37] Furthermore, any formal accusation that was not followed by a finding of *zina'* made the accuser liable to a charge of *qadhf*, the false accusation of *zina'*, a *hadd* crime punishable by flogging. If a *muhsan*, in the sense of a free person who had never been found guilty of unlawful intercourse, were so accused, and no guilt was found, the man who accused the *muhsan* of *zina'* would find *himself* receiving the punishment for false accusation.[38] Even insults that only implied *zina'*, such as calling another a "son of a fornicator," a " son of fornication," or other such insults that slurred his origins, could result in punishment for false accusation if the parents of the one so insulted (who were of course at the heart of the insult) wished to demand a trial.[39] Most of the fatwas dealing with *zina'* focused, indeed, on the pitfalls associated with bringing accusations.

Nor did the spouse or other family members enjoy any special responsibility under law to report, judge, or punish *zina'*. A husband could not conclude, for example, that his wife had committed *zina'* if he found her "deflowered" on their wedding night.

> QUESTION: A man consummated his marriage with his virgin legally major wife, and then claimed that he found her deflowered. He was asked, "How was that?" And he said, "I had intercourse with her several times and I found her deflowered." What is the legal judgment on that?
>
> ANSWER: The judgment is that all of the *mahr* is required, and it is fully and entirely incumbent on him. Her testimony on her own virginity [is sufficient] to remove the shame. And if he accuses her without [evidence], he is punished and his testimony is not accepted, as is her right. If he defamed her with a charge of *zina'*, he must now make a sworn allegation of *zina'* if she so requests, [and take the consequences]. Such is the case, and God knows best.[40]

In this fatwa and others like it, the right of the husband to judge whether or not his supposedly virgin wife had previously committed *zina'* is strenuously denied. It was her testimony, not his, that established her virginity. By offering such testimony, he had slandered the woman and for that offense alone was at risk of discretionary punishment (*ta'zir*). Furthermore, and at much graver risk to himself, he would have to be prepared to make a formal accusation of *zina'*, after which the prescribed punishment for false accusation would no doubt be his lot. The other muftis agreed: a man could not slander his wife on the basis of his experience on his wedding night. He had no right to voice or act on any conclusions he may have reached about her sexual history, unless he could meet the required standards of evidence for proof of *zina'*.[41] Nor did a brother have any special responsibility in the discovery or chastisement of a sister suspected of *zina'*; it was not up to the brother, as brother, to seek justice for his sister's sexual transgressions.[42]

In denying family members, specifically a husband or brother, any defined role in the punishment of women for sexual crimes, the muftis were adhering to the doctrine that unlawful intercourse was, as we have seen, a crime against religion, not an offense against one's relatives. The accuser in a case of *zina'* was any Muslim who had witnessed the crime, or who had evidence backed by four witnesses that such a crime had been committed. The muftis took a clear position here against social customs that assigned fathers, brothers, and husbands the role of enforcer of female sexual behavior. Men could guard their female relatives, especially minors, against involvement in situations that might lead to improper sexual contact, but an actual instance of sexual intercourse outside of marriage was a crime against religion: rigid rules of procedure and evidence did not allow for any special family role and, furthermore, implicitly condemned any unilateral family move to punish those presumed guilty. This does not mean, of course, that matters of sexual behavior were always, or even often, handled by the courts and according to the law. The wording of the fatwas suggests, on the contrary, that the muftis were engaged in a rearguard action so far as the issue of family policing and punishing of sexual activity was concerned. The fact that very few cases concerning *zina'* ever came to the court also supports the idea that the problem of illicit sexual activity was usually handled by families or communities and remained, at least in practice, largely unknown to, and outside the jurisdiction of, the Islamic courts.

In short, the law and the muftis criminalized desire only when it led to the act of sexual intercourse outside of marriage. Even then, the law concerning *zina'* made actual prosecution of offenders very difficult, and encouraged the muftis to develop the doctrine of *shubha* in ways that effectively subverted the imposition of corporal *hadd* punishments and replaced them with indemnification. The focus on illicit heterosexual intercourse persisted, however, reflecting an overriding concern about the problems of offspring of uncertain lineage. Sexuality was both criminalized and problematized primarily because of its procreative potential. An important part of the discourse on sexuality thus focused on issues of reproduction.

REGULATING REPRODUCTION

Much of the muftis' discussion of sexual matters dealt directly with issues pertaining to the legitimacy (or illegitimacy) of children born of a sexual union. As they discussed sexuality and sexual intercourse—whether in the context of a licit marriage, a master-slave relationship, or an illicit liaison—their overriding concern was to clarify rules for establishing the paternity, and thus the identity, lineage, and rights of any child born of that relationship. Procreation was not the only raison d'être of sexual intercourse, but it was always a potential outcome, one with profound consequences in a kin-based system. Children were born with certain entitlements and a future access (or lack of access) to wealth and power, all based largely on their family ties, and in pondering issues of sexuality, it was intercourse in its role as the ultimate creator of such ties that consumed most of the muftis' attention.[43]

Within a legal marriage, a man was presumed the father of any child born to his wife, so long as the birth took place at least six months after the time of the marriage. Indeed, even if he were to deny that the child was his, the child was his legitimate heir, and he was required to assume his fatherly duties of support.[44] Only in the event that his wife had committed *zina'*, and the crime had been legally proved, could he deny a child born six months or more after he had consummated the marriage. Paternity, at least within the context of legal marriage, was not a question of volition: the children of a marriage belonged to the father, whether he claimed them or not.

The question of children born after the termination of a marriage, the termination brought about either by the husband's death or by divorce, was slightly more complicated. Over time, the muftis elaborated a set of legal rules that helped establish the paternity of a child born after a marriage was ended. The linchpin of this system was the *'idda*, the statutory waiting period following a divorce or a husband's death during which a woman was not allowed to remarry. In the wake of a divorce, the *'idda*, as we have seen, was to last until three menstruations or, in the absence of menstruation, three months had passed; a widow was supposed to wait for four months and ten days. Should the woman prove to be pregnant during the *'idda*, then the waiting period was extended to cover the duration of the pregnancy, and the baby was presumed to have been fathered by her former husband. A husband's denial of a child was not accepted so long as the mother testified that she was indeed pregnant by her ex-husband.[45] These rules, when followed, eliminated all dispute about paternity.

One of al-'Imadi's fatwas demonstrated what could happen when people did not adhere strictly to the specified procedures:

QUESTION: A man died, leaving his wife, and she passed a waiting period after his death of more than two months [but not three] and did not appear to be pregnant. Then she married a man and lived with him for a month and a half, and it became evident that she was pregnant by her first husband. Is the [new] marriage null and void [*batil*] or not? And if it is null and void, and there was intercourse, should the dower which [the new husband] paid her and what he spent in *nafaqa* and other things be returned [to him]? Is there a penalty for the wife, or not, if she did not know she was pregnant? ANSWER: The marriage is null and void and they are separated. He does not get what he paid to her nor is what he spent on her returned. [But] there is no penalty for the groom or the bride if she swore that she did not know she was pregnant.[46]

The widow's failure to pass the *'idda* as prescribed after the death of her husband had resulted in the precise situation the *'idda* was designed to prevent: a potential confusion about paternity. In this instance, the question of paternity was settled summarily: the pregnancy became evident some three and a half months after the first husband's death and thus fell within the period of a widow's *'idda*. The pregnancy also required that the *'idda* be extended, and thus rendered the second marriage void, because it had been initiated during a waiting period. Although the woman had surely been aware that she was remarrying too soon after the death of her husband, and thereby violating her *'idda*, the mufti did not find this a punishable offense, so long as she could swear to her ignorance about her pregnancy. It was the pregnancy, not the violation of *'idda* as such, that had precipitated legal action and resulted in the cancellation of the marriage. The second husband, having enjoyed conjugal rights, however illicit they turned out to be, did owe his putative wife the dowry and support connected with a consummated marriage. As far as the mufti was concerned, the honoring of a wife's marital rights and a clear attribution of paternity were the desirable outcomes of this case.

Indeed, most of the fatwas that dealt with the violation of *'idda* focused on a paternity issue rather than on the violation itself. Elsewhere, al-'Imadi spelled out the rules for determining paternity in these cases. If a woman remarried during her waiting period and then bore a child less than two years from the time of divorce or her husband's death *and* less than six months from the time of the second marriage, the child was the offspring of the first husband. If, conversely, she gave birth *more* than two years after the termination of her first marriage *and* more than six months after her second marriage, the child belonged to the second husband.[47] Again, the concern was all for the lineage of the child, not the violation of the waiting period. A woman who failed to observe the proper waiting period was put on notice that she ran the risk of producing a child who might "belong" to her former husband.

The *'idda* thus served as a means for ensuring that the paternity of a child born in a licit marriage could not be disputed. In tying the *'idda* of a divorcée to a woman's biological rhythms, the law also placed a certain power in the hands of the woman herself, who alone could testify to her menstrual cycle.

> QUESTION: There was a woman whose husband divorced her thrice after consummating the marriage, and after a period of three months in which she menstruated three times, she married another [man] in a legal marriage after she had sworn [that she had completed] her waiting period. Her divorced husband contested that and accused her of lying about the end of her waiting period. Is her oath accepted? and the former husband's protest denied? and her marriage legal?
>
> ANSWER: Yes.[48]

A woman was empowered, within the limits of the feasible, to define her own waiting period, and it was her word, not that of her husband or others, that determined when the waiting period ended. A woman who was known to have irregular menstrual periods, for example, could also testify to the completion of three menstrual cycles, and her testimony would be accepted, so long as a reasonable period of time had passed.[49] The rules for establishing paternity in the wake of a divorce, then, removed most volitional elements: a man could not choose whether or not to acknowledge a child born to his wife or ex-wife; and a woman was granted some limited freedom of maneuver, in the sense that she might shorten or extend a waiting period in order to establish paternity unequivocally.

In a master-slave relationship, the issue of paternity was treated very differently. A master had sexual access to any slave woman he personally owned, and concubinage was a practice accepted and regulated by law. A slave woman who had sexual intercourse with her master was no different, juridically speaking, from any other slave: if she were not already pregnant, she could be sold or married off by her master and, unless she had been manumitted, her subsequent children were born slaves. If, however, a slave woman became pregnant by her master, and her master acknowledged that the pregnancy was indeed by him, the woman assumed permanently the status of an *umm walad* (mother of a child). Should the pregnancy have ended in the delivery of a child, that child would be born free and legitimate, equal in all ways and all rights to any child fathered by the man via a free wife. Even if the pregnancy ended in miscarriage or stillbirth, the woman retained the title of *umm walad*, with its associated privileges.[50]

An *umm walad* could not be sold, and upon the death of her master she would be manumitted automatically. If her master freed her, she would be required to pass a waiting period of three menstrual cycles or three months, a period analogous to that of a free wife, before marrying. In other respects, however, the *umm walad* was clearly a slave: she was her master's property and had no right to contract a marriage, for example, without her master's permission.[51] The possibility of bearing free and legitimate children, who would take their place in their father's household and secure for their mother a future of probable freedom and material ease, must have made many slave concubines covet the status of *umm walad*. A woman could not assume, however, that her master would claim her child, and the law and the muftis left the matter entirely up to the master's discretion.

QUESTION: There is a man who married an *umm walad* of "Zayd's" after he [Zayd] had freed her. The husband had intercourse with her and then, some months after the intercourse, it appeared that she was pregnant. Both the master and the husband denied that the pregnancy was initiated by them. What is the legal judgment if she gave birth less than six months after intercourse with her husband or more than that [more than six months]? And, assuming that she was pregnant at the time of the marriage and the master did not know, did he commit an offense or not?

ANSWER: The denial of the master is legal under any circumstances, for it is explained in the books of our *'ulama'* that without exception it is legal for a master to deny the child of an *umm walad*, whether she delivered in less or more than six months from the time of the marriage. As for the denial of the husband, it is not valid if she produced [the child] six months or more after [the marriage]. If it was less [time], then his denial is valid. His denial does not prove descent from the master, and there is no offense committed by the master in this case, and God knows best.[52]

The establishment of paternity, then, worked quite differently in the master-slave relationship, for the master was free to deny any child born to his concubine regardless of presumptive circumstances. If a master refused to acknowledge a child he fathered, not only would his concubine fail to achieve *umm walad* status, but the child would be born a slave like his or her mother. Furthermore, if a man impregnated a slave whom he did not own personally, then the woman could not acquire *umm walad* status even if the man subsequently bought her and acknowledged the child.[53]

A man was not supposed to have sexual intercourse and sire children with a slave woman whom he did not own. Such an act was, theoretically, *zina'* and therefore subject to *hadd* punishment. The muftis, however, were willing to give the usual benefit of the doubt in these cases, and ruled out *hadd* punishment so long as the "fornicator" later bought the slave woman.[54] Nor was it considered *zina'* to have sexual intercourse with a slave woman owned by one's grandparent, parent, or wife. Although this was not licit sexual activity, it was met with a certain forbearance, and the children born of such a relationship could be recognized as free and legitimate should the father wish to do so.[55]

The bestowal of the mantle of legitimacy on the children of a slave woman was very much in the hands of the man who owned, or had seduced or raped, her. A master could choose whether to incorporate the children of his concubine into his household or relegate them to slave status. A man could even acknowledge children born to a slave owned by one of his relatives. The fact that the legitimacy of the offspring of slave women rested entirely on the volition of their masters underscores the extent to which the law ceded control over the reproductive activities of concubines to their masters. As the literal possessors of these women, slave-owning men could assert a level of patriarchal control over female sexuality that was unthinkable, at least in legal doctrine, in the context of a man's marriage to a free woman.

A certain volitional element also crept into the discussion of the legitimacy of a child conceived through *zina'*. We might expect that such a child would be clearly illegitimate, because he or she would have been conceived by an illicit liaison, by sexual intercourse with a woman who was neither a wife nor a concubine. The question was not, however, always so clear-cut:

> QUESTION: There is a male fornicator who wants to marry his female fornicator, who is pregnant by him. Is this lawful?
> ANSWER: Yes. And he is permitted to have intercourse with her and the child is his, and he must provide *nafaqa*.[56]

The notion that a man and a woman who had committed *zina'* could subsequently marry and render the child of *zina'* legitimate was also supported by al-Tamimi, who approved of post-*zina'* marriage and was ready to accept the child as the legitimate offspring of his or her father just so long as the marriage had taken place at least one month before the birth.[57] The muftis further opined that these shotgun marriages should take place only between the parties who had the illicit liaison: a woman pregnant by *zina'* should not marry anyone other than her impregnator, an identity that could be established, we may presume, only by the man's assertion or agreement that he had, indeed, had sexual intercourse with the woman in the pertinent time frame. At the same time, however, the child could not be legitimated if a formal accusation of *zina'* had been made *and* proved, a development that likely would result, in any case, in a series of events that would have obviated the need to decide on legitimacy.[58]

This tolerance of premarital sex, to the extent of recognizing a baby as legitimate even though it had undoubtedly been conceived well before a marriage took place, was not always endorsed by later commentators. Indeed, Ibn ʿAbidin, in his nineteenth-century comment on al-ʿImadi's acceptance of the validity of marriage and the legitimacy of the offspring of two "fornicators," felt constrained to add that the child was not legitimate under all circumstances. In fact, according to Ibn ʿAbidin, it was only in the event that the child was born at least six months after the marriage that it could be considered legitimate.[59] By applying the standard legal rule for the legitimacy of any child, Ibn ʿAbidin departed from the position of his eighteenth-century predecessors, which had allowed for a certain acceptance of premarital sexuality and its consequences, so long as it was followed by the marriage of the partners.

In their concern for the regulation of reproduction, the muftis appeared to lean toward a flexible interpretation of the rules governing legitimacy. The issue of a legal marriage was almost always presumed legitimate, even if a husband denied that a child was his. In the case of illicit sexual intercourse, the offending couple was given ample opportunity to confer legitimacy on any offspring simply by marrying up to a month before the birth of a child. Finally, the children of a slave concubine easily acquired full legitimacy if their father acknowledged them. There is, then, a marked preference here for establishing the legitimacy, and thus the family ties and social locations, of all children born in the community. Extramarital sexual relations were a crime against God, but the muftis' interest in social harmony and stability once more led them to focus on the ways in which such relations could be transfigured, and thus result in children whose lineage and social position were not open to question. Male power over female sexuality and reproduction was elaborated by these legal doctrines: it was a man's acknowledgment of sexual intercourse with his slave or a man's admission of illicit intercourse and subsequent willingness to marry his lover that conferred legitimacy on the child conceived outside of legal marriage. But *within* the context of marriage, male power was tempered by clear-cut rules of legitimacy that eluded, at least in the view of the jurists, all forms of extralegal patriarchal control.

SEXUALITY IN THE COURTS

The dramas of sexuality and reproduction in Syria and Palestine were rarely played out in court. With the exception of a very occasional complaint about sexual misconduct, usually made in the context of a claim to compensation, such as in the Damascus case mentioned above, the court was not the venue for the trial of *zina'* or other sexual offenses, in any of their forms. Despite the fact that the muftis repeatedly lamented and condemned the prosecution and punishment of sexual offenses by family members, they do not appear to have been able to secure the jurisdiction of the Islamic court over matters involving sexuality, especially the control of female sexuality.

Abdul-Karim Rafeq found a signal exception to this pattern in the many court judgments in eighteenth-century Damascus against women of "bad actions and words." At the request of plaintiffs from her neighborhood, a woman could be accused of "facilitating association with strangers," a euphemism for prostitution, and be expelled from her quarter. Rafeq noted that, in the context of possible punishments for prostitution, such an approach seems rather "kindly," and, indeed, it was the only action the Islamic courts took in the face of what seemed to him a burgeoning problem of prostitution in the city.[60] By treating prostitutes as "mischievous persons" whose presence compromised the reputation of a neighborhood, the court neatly sidestepped all issues connected with the *zina'* in which these women must have been engaged.

We cannot be sure why the courts so infrequently handled cases that addressed *zina'* directly, but several explanations appear plausible. First, issues of sexuality and reproduction lay at the heart of a family-based system of social organization. A family's ability to control female sexuality was directly related to the acquisition of power and the preservation of family property by way of strategic marriage arrangements and the regulation of reproduction. The family's drive to harness its members' sexuality to the cartload of family interests could, and did, conflict with the jurists' approach to sexuality as a natural and normal part of human existence, but one that needed special forms of control in the interests of community stability. The jurists elaborated rules—for social contact, for marriage, for sexual relations—that expressed their views on the matter, and they also vested the responsibility for enforcing these rules in the Islamic courts. Families, however, proved unwilling to cede social power over sexuality. The muftis delivered fatwas that bemoaned high-handed and extralegal family maneuvers: families, they felt, should not judge or punish sexual transgressions. It is clear, however, from the very absence of litigation over sexual matters in the courts that families refused to allow a control so central to their political and economic well-being to slip through their fingers.

The muftis and qadis were, of course, fathers and brothers themselves, often members of educated families that formed part of the local political elite. To a certain extent we can, therefore, expect a level of complicity with families who needed to assert control over sexuality, particularly female sexuality. Such complicity might well have taken the form of a tacit policy of nonintervention, at least at the level of legal practice, into this realm of family life, despite the clarity of legal doctrines to the contrary. That so few court cases ever raised questions of sexuality suggests that the qadis did not encourage the airing of such issues in court. Even the muftis, in the various fatwas dealing with unacceptable family interventions, rarely tackled these issues close to home. They tended to present problems of illegal family regulation and punishment of sexual activity as matters distant from their own urban, educated world: it was the practices of the uneducated and largely rural population that drew their criticism. If the more affluent urban families were violating the law in the ways in which they controlled sexuality, we do not learn about it from their native sons.

Finally, the courts may have chosen to avoid these issues because of the thorny nature of prosecuting and punishing these crimes against God. We have seen how the muftis tended to recommend removing these crimes from the category of *hadd* punishment whenever possible, and we can expect that the qadis were equally leery of taking on cases that would invariably present problems of proof and punishment. The safest approach may well have been to leave well enough alone and turn a blind eye toward family regulation and punishment of a sexuality that threatened family interests.

The definition and regulation of sexuality, particularly female sexuality, in legal discourse was largely the province of the muftis, rather than the courts or the population. Insofar as the muftis elaborated views of sexuality and proper forms of regulation and punishment of sexual activities in virtual isolation from the social practices of the time, we are dealing here with a form of discourse that appears to differ somewhat from that on marital relations or parenting. The muftis approached the issues of a gendered sexuality in much the same way as they approached the regulation of family life: the received wisdom of their legal forebears was to be transmitted to succeeding generations subject to such cautious revisions as current social circumstances might dictate. Their concern for the stability and harmony of the community under their guidance figured largely in their discussions of sexuality, just as it had shaped their views on family relations. The discourse on sexuality, however, was *not* being refined and elaborated through a process of interaction with the qadis and the court's clients. On the contrary, most of the fatwas on sexuality appear to lie in the realm of juristic speculation on hypothetical or rumored situations: the virtual absence of court cases in which the definition and control of sexuality figured prominently suggests that the muftis were rarely consulted on such matters in relation to actual litigation.

The muftis' discussion of sexuality clearly reinforced male control of female sexuality, but also set certain limitations on that control: punishment for sexual transgressions, for example, was neither the right nor the responsibility of a woman's male relatives. There were set rules of evidence and procedure when illicit sexual relations were suspected, and no family had the right to take the law into its own hands. But contrary to legal discourse on other marital and family matters, it seems clear that the muftis' guidelines were virtually ignored by the population, and families controlled female sexuality, at least outside marriage, without recourse to the opinions of the muftis or the intervention of the court.

It is here, in the realm of sexuality and reproduction, that legal discourse exhibits a divide between the doctrines being developed by the muftis and the practices of the population. The muftis lacked the means, and perhaps more important the will, to encourage the interaction of doctrine and social forces that was so much at the center of other aspects of gendered law. When all was said and done, the family's monopoly over the sexuality and reproduction of its womenfolk lay too close to the heart of the kin-based social system for it to allow even a partial surrender to the courts.

Conclusion

The muftis, qadis, and urban populations of seventeenth- and eighteenth-century Syria and Palestine fashioned a discourse on Islamic law that spoke directly to the rights, social roles, and power of men and women and children in their society. The muftis, for their part, brought their knowledge of legal doctrine and past practices to bear on the concrete situations of members of their communities, in the course of issuing fatwas that might then be pressed into service, both inside and outside the court system, for the resolution of problems and disputes. The qadis in the local Islamic courts, issuing judgments that actualized the doctrines espoused by the muftis, ruled on various cases, many of which posed the issues of gendered rights and responsibilities. Members of the local populations, finally, through their decisions to bring certain disputes to court and settle other issues extrajuridically, helped define the areas in which Islamic legal doctrine would actually hold sway.

Legal doctrines on gendered roles and rights were applied and developed primarily in the context of relations within the family, particularly in deliberations about marriage, divorce, and parental responsibilities. The muftis and the courts agreed that the Muslim marital relationship was one of complementarity, not of equality. In fact, a net division of male and female roles within the household, the legitimation of the husband's authority, and the insistence on wifely obedience all worked to privilege male power. Such power, in the eyes of the muftis and courts, was not to be confused with license, however; women were not chattels. Certain rights accorded the woman, including the right to choose a marriage partner, to enter a marriage as a propertied person, to demand adequate support from her husband, and to seek protection from coercion, circumscribed her father's and husband's power and freedom of action. In elaborating and enforcing the law concerning these rights, the muftis and courts upheld a model of marriage in which the dichotomy of power was tempered by concepts of fairness and protection from abuse. Women, for their part, kept these issues on the legal agenda by coming to court to protest coerced marriage, for example, or to press claims for support payments.

The legal thought and practice of the day also upheld a strongly gendered system of divorce. Male dominance in this realm was enshrined in *talaq*, a procedure that starkly emphasized the primacy of male needs and desires. The muftis and courts did not question this male right of unilateral repudiation, but they were careful to insist that the related obligations of payment of dower and support to a repudiated wife be fully observed. These Hanafi thinkers and courts also proved willing to accommodate the doctrines of other legal schools on divorce when such flexibility appeared to provide a woman with more options and protections. In sanctioning female-initiated *faskh* (annulment), they accepted and even facilitated a woman's access to the more flexible Shafiʿi and Hanbali approaches to divorce. The manner in which the muftis elaborated the doctrine of *khulʿ*, the divorce negotiated at the wife's request, helps us understand the frequency with which women brought these divorce settlements to court. Legal thought and practice of the time did not, of course, gut the male privilege of divorce, which would have transformed the husband's ability to use this privilege as an instrument of control. In easing women's access to divorce, however, the muftis' fatwas and the qadis' judgments served to moderate male license in this area.

The rights and responsibilities of mothers and fathers were also clearly gendered in legal doctrine. A mother was defined principally as the nurturer of young children, whereas a father was the provider, protector, and bestower of lineage for his child. Neither the muftis nor the courts challenged this fundamentally patrilineal vision, one that highlighted the temporary nature of motherhood. They were careful, however, to define and implement legal doctrines that guaranteed the mother compensation for her task. They also allowed a mother to cross the line from caretaker to full guardian when the father's wishes and possibly the child's well-being required it. The elaboration of legal doctrines on parenting, as on marriage and divorce, exhibited considerable flexibility in the definition of gendered social roles.

The muftis discussed issues of sexuality in ways that appeared to minimize the potential for conflict and high-handed family intervention. Although they endorsed a certain level of sexual segregation in order to guard against unlawful sexual contact, they do not appear to have felt that female seclusion was either necessary or particularly desirable. Inherited legal doctrine on *zina'* (illicit sexual intercourse) prescribed draconian punishment for this crime, but the muftis preferred to follow a line of legal reasoning that converted the penalty to one of indemnification. They also proved flexible on the question of the legitimacy of children born of an illicit relationship, by allowing the parents to marry, a flexibility that accords with their broader "pro-legitimacy" position. Unlike their discussions of marriage and children, however, the muftis' opinions on these issues found little resonance in the courts; qadis rarely heard any case concerning problems of sexuality, perhaps because of problems of procedure, enforcement, or local custom that prevented such cases from reaching them.

As the muftis and courts discussed the issues of the day most concerned with gendered right, power, and social role, they did not eschew the Islamic legal doctrines they had inherited, which viewed male-female difference as a fundamental reality of all social life. Working with these doctrines, however, they seemed to opt, whenever possible, for the broader and more flexible interpretation of the law, for the interpretation that appeared to best serve the interests of justice as well as the needs and stability of their community. They were able to do so because of the nature of the law: there were certain incontrovertible principles and rules to be applied, but there were also a variety of textual sources and legal schools that offered possibilities both of selection and what amounted to interpretation. In general, the muftis and courts chose the approach that led away from confrontation and conflict and toward harmony in the community, as well as the protection of its weaker members. They softened the male/female dichotomy in marriage, they considered the paramount interest of the child in custody cases, they avoided the imposition of *hadd* penalities. Sometimes the need to champion the weak could lead the law into direct conflict with local custom, as in the issue of marital virginity and the rejection of brides. The muftis did not avoid conflicts of this sort: there was no accommodation of local practice if it flagrantly violated the law. Indeed, the muftis helped develop a "culture of law" that provided ideas about gendered right that might even encourage resistance to certain prevailing forms of social control.

This is not to suggest, however, that the muftis and courts stood above or apart from their society and community. The men who held the positions of mufti and qadi were very much members of the local power structure, and their overriding interests in stability and successful communal self-regulation were no doubt as much a product of their investment in the status quo as of their allegiance to abstract principles of justice. Theirs was a society where class and social position mattered very much: indeed, their ruminations on what women of various classes could expect in the form of marital support and their fulminations against (but apparent lack of control over) the loose living of their social inferiors suggest to us the many ways in which gendered right and gender definition were contingent on social context. Despite the law's claim to impartiality, neutrality, and universality, fatwas were delivered and courts ruled in specific and particular contexts where the society's structure of wealth and power could not but constitute a silent yet significant party to a case.[1]

This status quo was very much that of a kin-based society. Joint economic activities, networks of political patronage, and social relations of mutual support and obligation were structured by ties of blood. The family, and the ways in which the law defined the responsibilities and rights of individuals within the family, was thus inseparable from the larger society: our modern notions of public versus private or domestic life seem strikingly inappropriate here. The various rules elaborated for family membership, family obligations, and family rights must be seen, then, as central to relations of power. These rules determined to a large extent the ways in which property could be accumulated and transmitted and power could be consolidated and exercised. When the muftis and the courts handled matters pertaining to "family" law, they were mediating a set of social relations that shaped the distribution of wealth and power in the society at large.

The muftis and courts could thus be expected to act, in the main, as the guardians of the status quo. They protected male prerogatives, including the power of the patriarch, and buttressed a family institution in which females were subservient, by and large, to their male relations. They championed the affluent urban way of life and criticized the folkways of the rural poor. They were predictable pillars of their community. As we have seen, however, they also worked to prevent and correct the abuses that could occur if male privilege were permitted to slide toward male license. They drew on the considerable room for maneuver afforded by the law to balance male prerogative and female right in the specific contexts presented by members of their communities. Within certain limits, they were sensitive to local custom and ready to accommodate local practice. Their role as enforcers of gendered social control was thus modified, in part, by their own sense of responsibility for upholding justice for everyone under God's law.

What does the story of these muftis, these courts, and their clientele have to tell us of relevance to present debates about Islamic law and gender? Might the experience of the Muslim thinkers and Islamic courts of seventeenth- and eighteenth-century Syria and Palestine shed some light on the problem of identifying and comprehending a contemporary Islamic view of gender? Surely these men and institutions, as well as the general urban population, must take their place as part of a history of the development of Islamic thought and tradition in the context of lived experience. I have identified certain characteristics of the ways in which the law was mobilized and interpreted in this time and place. The muftis and courts responded to concrete situations presented by members of the general population with a flexibility and independence of judgment. They do not appear to have felt bound by state legal directives, and, indeed, ignored what the Ottoman state had to say about penal matters. Instead, they used a variety of scholarly texts from different legal schools in order to choose or even shape an interpretation that seemed to suit best the immediate situation. I do not mean to suggest that seventeenth- and eighteenth-century Syria and Palestine represent a lost paradise of equity and blind justice for women and men alike. The muftis and qadis of the period clearly formed part of an old boys' network whose interests lay in the preservation of a status quo that benefited them and other privileged males. Still, their ability to respond with flexibility, creativity, and even compassion to concrete legal problems in their communities remains a hallmark of their approach to the practice of law.

Islamic legal thought and practice inhabit a very different world today. The erosion of kin-based society and the emergence of interventionist states in the twentieth century—states that have arrogated to themselves the power to interpret and enforce Islamic law through a process of codification and court supervision—have transformed the ways in which the law operates. Codified law cannot, by definition, be flexible and fluid law. Legal codes no longer offer a variety of possible interpretations; rather, they work to standardize cases and minimize the element of judicial subjectivity. Today, one interpretation on any point of Islamic law is made the *only* interpretation that can be considered and applied by muftis and courts. Modern states have promulgated various codes of Islamic law in the interests of fairness and rationality, in the understanding that law should not be primarily a process of negotiation and judicial discretion, but rather should establish clear standards that apply equally to all. Whether or not such codification actually violates the Islamic legal tradition to such an extent as to rob it of fundamental coherence is a question, however important, that lies beyond the scope of the present study. But as far as the debate on Islamic law and gender is concerned, contemporary codifications raise some serious questions.

Islamic law, as we have seen, is a strongly gendered law, in the sense that many, though not all, legal rights and obligations are informed by the sexual identity of the individual. Men and women are constructed as different entities under the law, particularly in the sphere of family relations, where male privilege is undeniable. For as long as the law remained uncodified, the interpretations of the meaning of these differences retained some fluidity and flexibility. Gendered right and gendered duty could be modified, within certain limits, to fit the jurists' understanding of what would best serve the interests of justice as well as the well-being of their communities. But as soon as the law is codified, gendered right and gendered duty become incontrovertible points of law, brooking no adjustments or modifications except from on high. The prior history of Islamic legal practice in the area of gendered law—a practice in which the interpretive powers of the muftis, the discretion of the qadis, and the posing of legal questions by members of a community shaped the development of the law—comes to resemble, indeed, an artifact without much relevance to the new legal systems in the various states in which codified Islamic law governs family matters.

We may well ask whether Muslim women's interests have been served by this break in tradition. Certainly the ability of any individual woman to seek a legal judgment tailored to the specifics of her case is greatly reduced in the context, on the one hand, of impersonal codes and courts that are charged with strict and accurate application of the law, and, on the other hand, the obsolescence of the institution of the community-based mufti. At the same time, one might argue that fair and equal treatment under the law is surely more attainable when the rules are clear and the jurists are held accountable by a higher authority. And, in any case, the realities of modern life, where community identity and personal knowledge of all by all are largely relics of the past, would no longer accommodate such a system. Ultimately, however, the process of codifying Islamic law must entail the enshrinement of gendered right and privilege without the accompanying flexibility and judicial activism that had been the hallmarks of Islamic justice. The muftis and qadis of seventeenth- and eighteenth-century Syria and Palestine could modify gendered rights and privileges in specific cases in order to achieve an outcome they held to be fair and in the interests of community harmony. The legal system that permitted such flexibility is nowhere to be seen today, nor is it really conceivable in the context of contemporary society.

Do these muftis and qadis, then, those whose opinions we have so carefully attended, have no contribution to make to present debates about the Islamic vision of male and female, the gendering of Muslim society? Surely in the context of the present search for what is authentically Islamic through a revisiting of the Muslim past, the history of these thinkers and their communities acquires present meaning. The ways in which they studied their own heritage and adapted it to meet community needs help us grasp the richness of the law as a lived tradition. Their experience offers, as well, a caution in the search for authenticity: there is a long and varied history of Muslims reading, interpreting, and living out the implications of a large body of authoritative legal texts, and it is not so easy to agree on what part of this history represents an essentially Islamic gender system. This history also raises questions about process: how do we establish meaning in a fundamentally altered environment where the role of the state, for example, has changed so dramatically? Without studying Islamic law as history, moreover, we will be limited to the necessarily narrow perspectives offered by the concerns and agendas of our own small slice of time. The deliberations of the muftis, the decisions of the courts, and the activities of the population in seventeenth- and eighteenth-century Syria and Palestine enable us to trace how the best minds as well as the ordinary people of another time and place engaged basic questions of gendered right, power, and social roles under Islam. Their discussions and understandings cannot but enrich the debates of today.

NOTES

NOTES TO CHAPTER 1:
THE LAW, THE COURTS, AND THE MUFTIS

1. Khayr al-Din ibn Ahmad al-Ramli, *Kitab al-fatawa al-kubra li-nafʿ al-birriya*, Cairo, Bulaq: n.p., 1273 H./1856 A.D., vol. I, p. 26.

2. Fatima Mernissi, *The Veil and the Male Elite: A Feminist Interpretation of Women's Rights in Islam*, Reading, Mass.: Addison-Wesley, 1991, p. 24.

3. See Fadwa Malti-Douglas, *Woman's Body, Woman's Word: Gender and Discourse in Arabo-Islamic Writing*, Princeton, N.J.: Princeton University Press, 1991, for a pioneering examination of gender issues in Arabo-Islamic writing.

4. Barbara Stowasser, "Women's Issues in Modern Islamic Thought," in J. Tucker, ed., *Arab Women: Old Boundaries, New Frontiers*, Bloomington: University of Indiana Press, 1993, pp. 14–20.

5. Fazlur Rahman, "A Survey of Modernization of Muslim Family Law," *International Journal of Middle East Studies* 11 (1980), 452–453.

6. Haleh Esfandiari, "The Majles and Women's Issues in the Islamic Republic of Iran," in M. Afkhami and E. Friedl, eds., *In the Eye of the Storm: Women in Post-Revolutionary Iran*, Syracuse, N.Y.: Syracuse University Press, 1994, p. 66.

7. Charles H. Kennedy, "Islamic Legal Reform and the Status of Women in Pakistan," *Journal of Islamic Studies* 2, no. 1 (1991), 45–55.

8. Rudolf Peters, "The Islamization of Criminal Law: A Comparative Analysis," *Die Welt des Islams* 34 (1994), 246–274.

9. See Aziza Hussein, "Recent Amendments to Egypt's Personal Status Law," in E. W. Fernea, ed., *Women and the Family in the Middle East: New Voices of Change*, Austin: University of Texas Press, 1985, pp. 229–232.

10. See Joan Scott, *Gender and the Politics of History*, New York: Columbia University Press, 1988, chapter 2, for a useful working definition of gender as both a signifier of power and an element of social relationships.

11. See Joseph Schacht, *An Introduction to Islamic Law*, Oxford: Clarendon Press, 1964; and J. N. D. Anderson, *Law Reform in the Muslim World*, London: Athlone Press, 1976.

12. These comments owe much to the summary history of the field presented by Rudolph Peters in his Opening Speech, delivered at the Joseph Schacht Conference on Theory and Practice of Islamic Law, Leiden and Amsterdam, October 6–10, 1994.

13. Wael B. Hallaq, "Was the Gate of Ijtihad Closed?" *International Journal of Middle East Studies* 16 (1984), 3–41; Rudolph Peters, "Idjtihad and Taqlid in 18th and 19th Century Islam," *Die Welt des Islams* 20, nos. 3–4 (1980), 131–145.

14. Brinkley Messick, *The Calligraphic State: Textual Domination and History in a Muslim Society*, Berkeley: University of California Press, 1993, p. 16.

15. Baber Johansen, "Legal Literature and the Problem of Change: The Case of Land Rent," in Chibli Mallat, ed., *Islam and Public Law*, London: Graham and Trotman, 1993, pp. 29–47; see also Baber Johansen, *The Islamic Law on Land Tax and Rent*, London: Croom Helm, 1988, pp. 124–125.

16. Muhammad Khalid Masud, Brinkley Messick, and David S. Powers, "Muftis, Fatwas, and Islamic Legal Interpretation," in M. Masud, B. Messick, and D. Powers, eds., *Islamic Legal Interpretation: Muftis and Their Fatwas*, Cambridge, Mass.: Harvard University Press, 1996, pp. 18–19.

17. M. Khalid Masud, "Adab al-Mufti: The Muslim Understanding of Values, Characteristics, and Role of a Mufti," in Barbara D. Metcalf, ed., *Moral Conduct and Authority: The Place of Adab in South Asian Islam*, Berkeley: University of California Press, 1984, pp. 124–151.

18. Quoted in Wael Hallaq, "Murder in Cordoba: *Ijtihad Ifta'* and the Evolution of Substantive Law in Medieval Islam," *Acta Orientalia* 55 (1994), 76–77.

19. For a general discussion of the mufti and *ijtihad*, see Wael Hallaq, "Ifta' and Ijtihad in Sunni Legal Theory," in Masud, Messick, and Powers, *Islamic Legal Interpretation*, pp. 33–43.

20. We now have a few social histories of the period that make good use of the records of these transactions in the court to reconstruct the social and eco-

nomic life of parts of Ottoman Syria and Palestine. See, for example, Beshara Doumani, *Rediscovering Palestine: Merchants and Peasants in Jabal Nablus, 1700–1900*, Berkeley: University of California Press, 1995; and Abraham Marcus, *The Middle East on the Eve of Modernity: Aleppo in the Eighteenth Century*, New York: Columbia University Press, 1989.

21. Zouhair Ghazzal, "The Ethnography of Legal Discourses: A Textual Analysis of Two Shari'a Court Documents in Nineteenth-Century Beirut," an unpublished paper presented at the Joseph Schacht Conference on Theory and Practice of Islamic Law, Leiden and Amsterdam, October 6–10, 1994.

22. Haim Gerber, *State, Society and Law in Islam: Ottoman Law in Comparative Perspective*, Albany: State University of New York Press, 1994, chap. 3.

23. John Voll, "Old 'Ulama' Families and Ottoman Influence in Eighteenth-Century Damascus," *American Journal of Arabic Studies*, 3 (1975), 48–59.

24. In the seventeenth and eighteenth centuries, almost every chief judge in Damascus, for example, was not a local man but rather a member of Ottoman officialdom sent to the city for a brief period. Although a chief judge might remain in place for anywhere from one to four years in the seventeenth century, all eighteenth-century judges served for just one year. See Abdul-Karim Rafeq, *The Province of Damascus, 1723–1783*, Beirut: Khayats, 1966, p. 44.

25. The *sanjaq* of Gaza and Ramla was detached, at least in theory, from the province of Damascus in 1742. It would appear, however, that the governor of Damascus was able to assert his authority in the *sanjaq* more often than not throughout the eighteenth century. Amnon Cohen, *Palestine in the 18th Century: Patterns of Government and Administration*, Jerusalem: Magnes Press, 1973, pp. 147–150.

26. For details of provincial administration in the eighteenth century, see Cohen, *Palestine in the 18th Century*, pp. 144–172.

27. Rafeq, *The Province of Damascus*, p. 52.

28. Antoine Abdel Nour, *Introduction à l'histoire urbaine de la Syrie Ottomane XVIe–XVIIIe siècle*, Beyrouth: Librairie Orientale, 1982, pp. 341, 342; see also Karl Barbir, *Ottoman Rule in Damascus, 1708–1758*, Princeton, N.J.: Princeton University Press, 1980, pp. 44–56.

29. Abdel Nour, *Introduction à l'histoire urbaine*, pp. 338–340, 365; Rafeq, *The Province of Damascus*, p. 76.

30. Abdel Nour, *Introduction à l'histoire urbaine*, pp. 35–41, 72–74.

31. Rafeq, *The Province of Damascus*, pp. 42–48; Linda Schilcher, *Families in Politics*, Stuttgart: Franz Steiner, 1985, pp. 30–33.

32. Abdel Nour, *Introduction à l'histoire urbaine*, pp. 338–339.

33. See Barbir, *Ottoman Rule in Damascus*, pp. 152–153.

34. Ibid., pp. 163–167.

35. See Doumani, *Rediscovering Palestine*, chap. 1.

36. Cohen, *Palestine in the 18th Century*, pp. 169–172.

37. Amnon Cohen, *Economic Life in Ottoman Jerusalem*, Cambridge: Cambridge University Press, 1989, pp. 2–6. See Wolf-Dieter Hütteroth and Kamal Abdulfattah, *Historical Geography of Palestine, Transjordan, and Southern Syria in the Late 16th Century*, Erlangen: Selbstverlag der Frankischen Geographischen Gesellschaft in Kommission bei Palm & Enke, 1977, map 4, Regional Waqf-Links.

38. Hütteroth and Abdulfattah, *Historical Geography*, p. 83; Cohen, *Economic Life in Ottoman Jerusalem*, p. 86.

39. Hütteroth and Abdulfattah, *Historical Geography*, map 1, Settlements and Population 1005 H./1586 A.D.

40. Rafeq, *The Province of Damascus*, p. 203.

41. See Rafeq, *The Province of Damascus*, pp. 70–72.

42. See, for example, Abdel Nour, *Introduction à l'histoire urbaine*; and Doumani, *Rediscovering Palestine*.

43. al-Muhibbi, *Khulasat al-athar fi a'yan al-qarn al-hadi 'ashr*, Bulaq, Cairo: 1284 H./1867–68 A.D., vol. 2, pp. 134–139. See also the very helpful article on Khayr al-Din's life and fatwas by Ihsan 'Abbas, "Hair ad-din ar-Ramli's *Fatawa: A New Light on Life in Palestine in the Eleventh/Seventeenth Century*," in *Die Islamische Welt zwischen Mittelalter und Neuzeit: Festschrift für Hans Robert Roemer*, Beirut and Wiesbaden: Franz Steiner, 1979, pp. 1–19.

44. al-Muhibbi, *Khulasat*, p. 139.

45. The biographical information on al-'Imadi is taken from Muhammad Khalil Muradi, *Silk al-durar fi a'yan al-qarn al-thamin 'ashr*, Cairo, Bulaq: 1201 H./1786–87 A.D., vol. 2, pp. 11–17.

46. Muradi, *Silk al-durar*, vol. 2, pp. 41–42. For more information on 'Abd al-Fattah, see Mustafa Murad al-Dabbagh, *Biladna Filistin*, Hebron: University Graduates Union, 3d ed., 1985, vol. 2, 2, pp. 165–166.

NOTES TO CHAPTER 2:
WITH HER CONSENT: MARRIAGE

1. Khayr al-Din ibn Ahmad al-Ramli, *Kitab al-fatawa al-kubra li-naf' al-birriya*, Cairo, Bulaq: n.p., 1273 H./1856 A.D., vol. 1, p. 23.

2. Khayr al-Din, vol. 1, pp. 47, 50. None of the several hundred marriage contracts I have seen in the records of the Jerusalem, Nablus, and Damascus courts in the eighteenth century included such conditions.

3. In extant court records for the town of Nablus between 1720 and 1858, for example, only 107 marriage contracts have survived.

4. Mahkamat Nablus (Nablus Islamic Court), s. 4, p. 269.

5. al-ʿImadi as edited by Ibn ʿAbidin, *al-ʿUqud al-durriya*, Cairo, Bulaq: n.p., 1300 H./1882–83 A.D., vol. 1, p. 19.

6. al-ʿImadi, vol. 1, p. 19.

7. Ibid., p. 21

8. Ibid., p. 19.

9. Ibid., p. 22.

10. Ibid., p. 22.

11. Khayr al-Din, vol. 1, pp. 21–22. In applying the rules of *kafaʾa*, the jurists recognized most aspects of suitability mentioned in the legal sources reviewed by Ziadeh—lineage, free/slave status, piety, wealth, and occupation. They did not, however, allude directly to the length of time a family had been Muslim, an aspect with little relevance in their highly stable Muslim communities. See Farhat J. Ziadeh, "Equality (*kafaʾah*) in the Muslim Law of Marriage," *American Journal of Comparative Law* 6 (1957), 503–517.

12. Khayr al-Din, vol. 1, pp. 21–22.

13. Ibid., pp. 63–64.

14. al-ʿImadi, vol. 1, pp. 69, 74.

15. Khayr al-Din, vol. 1, p. 69.

16. Ibid., p. 13.

17. The muftis' discussion of the quantity, quality, and method of payment of marital *nafaqa* is a clear instance of the legal flexibility and change possible in response to changing social situations. See Yaʿakov Maron, *L'obligation alimentaire entre époux en droit Musulman Hanéfite*, Paris: Bibliothèque de droit privée, 1971, for a thorough study of the evolution of the concept of marital *nafaqa* in fatwa literature from early Islam up to the nineteenth century.

18. al-ʿImadi, citing Khayr al-Din al-Ramli, vol. 1, p. 28; ʿAbd al-Fattah al-Tamimi, *Fatawa*, ms. copy from Maktabat Masjid al-Hajj Nimr al-Nabulsi, Nablus: n.p., n.d., p. 9.

19. al-ʿImadi, vol. 1, pp. 24–25.

20. al-Tamimi, p. 7.

21. al-ʿImadi, vol. 1, p. 77.

22. Ibid., p. 79.

23. al-Tamimi, p. 8.

24. al-'Imadi, vol. 1, p. 33.

25. Ibid., p. 22.

26. Ibid., p. 32.

27. Khayr al-Din, vol. 1, pp. 22, 24; al-'Imadi, vol. 1, p. 17.

28. Khayr al-Din, vol. 1, pp. 22–23.

29. Ibid., p. 23.

30. al-'Imadi, vol. 1, p. 31; Khayr al-Din, vol. 1, p. 21.

31. al-'Imadi, vol. 1, p. 17.

32. Ibid., p. 28.

33. Ibid., p. 30.

34. If, however, a woman was no longer a virgin, she had to give express consent to a marriage. See G. H. Bousquet and L. Bercher, *Le statut personnel en droit Musulman Hanéfite: Texte et traduction annotée du Muhtasar d'al-Quduri,* Tunis: Institut des hautes études de Tunis, n.d., pp. 18–19.

35. al-'Imadi, vol. 1, pp. 18–19; Khayr al-Din, vol. 1, p. 24.

36. al-'Imadi, vol. 1, p. 31; al-Tamimi, p. 7.

37. Khayr al-Din, vol. 1, p. 23.

38. This was by no means an empty privilege: the majority of marriage contracts examined in the Damascus, Jerusalem, and Nablus records recorded the marriages of brides in their legal majority. The marrying of girls in their minority, while not unusual, was not the dominant marriage pattern. See Judith Tucker, "Marriage and Family in Nablus, 1720–1856: Toward a History of Arab Marriage," *Journal of Family History* 13, no. 2 (1988), 165–179, for a discussion of age at marriage.

39. See Tucker, "Marriage and Family," for a discussion of the typical amounts of *mahr.*

40. al-'Imadi, vol. 1, pp. 24, 26, 31.

41. Ibid., pp. 24–25.

42. Ibid., pp. 25–26; Khayr al-Din, vol. 1, p. 28.

43. Khayr al-Din, vol. 1, p. 27.

44. Ibid., p. 26.

45. Ibid., p. 30.

46. Ibid., p. 26.

47. al-'Imadi, vol. 1, pp. 24, 25, 30.

48. Khayr al-Din, vol. 1, p. 25.

49. al-ʿImadi, vol. 1, p. 28.

50. Ibid., pp. 27, 28.

51. Ibid., pp. 27, 28.

52. Ibid., pp. 27–28.

53. See Tucker, "Marriage and Family," pp. 168–171.

54. al-ʿImadi, vol. 1, pp. 73, 76.

55. Ibid., p. 74.

56. Ibid., p. 75.

57. Khayr al-Din, vol. 1, pp. 71–72.

58. Ibid., p. 63.

59. al-ʿImadi, vol. 1, p. 306.

60. Khayr al-Din, vol. 1, pp. 62–63; al-ʿImadi, vol. 1, p. 69.

61. Khayr al-Din, vol. 1, pp. 66–67, 69, 72.

62. al-ʿImadi, vol. 1, pp. 71, 75–76, 79.

63. Khayr al-Din, vol. 1, pp. 66, 73; al-ʿImadi, vol. 1, pp. 70–71.

64. al-ʿImadi, vol. 1, pp. 23, 30.

65. Khayr al-Din, vol. 1, p. 66; al-ʿImadi, vol. 1, p. 70.

66. al-ʿImadi, vol. 1, p. 71.

67. Ibid., p. 71.

68. Ibid., pp. 71, 82.

69. Ibid., pp. 23, 32.

70. Khayr al-Din, vol. 1, p. 27.

71. al-Tamimi, p. 7.

72. Khayr al-Din, vol. 1, p. 63; al-ʿImadi, vol. 1, p. 73; al-Tamimi, p. 7.

73. Khayr al-Din, vol. 1, p. 70.

74. al-ʿImadi, vol. 1, p. 77.

75. Ibid., p. 71.

76. Khayr al-Din, vol. 1, p. 38.

77. Ibid., p. 63.

78. Khayr al-Din, vol. 2, p. 179.

79. al-ʿImadi, vol. 2, pp. 143–145.

80. Khayr al-Din, vol. 1, pp. 26–27; al-ʿImadi, vol. 1, p. 31; al-Tamimi, p. 7.

81. Khayr al-Din, vol. 1, p. 26.

82. Khayr al-Din, vol. 1, p. 83.

83. A village shaykh might even act as abductor. Khayr al-Din, vol. 1, p. 23.

84. Khayr al-Din, vol. 1, pp. 29, 30; al-'Imadi, vol. 1, p. 18.

85. For examples of different marriage contracts and analysis of their contents by socioeconomic class, see Tucker, "Marriage and Family."

86. Mahkamat al-Quds (Jerusalem Islamic Court), s. 226, p. 29, 10 Dhu al-qa'da 1145 H./1732 A.D.

87. Mahkamat al-Quds, s. 230, p. 286, 15 Dhu al-qa'da 1153 H./1741 A.D.

88. Mahkamat Nablus, s. 4, p. 295, end Rabi' I 1138 H./1725 A.D.

89. Mahkamat Dimashq (Damascus Islamic Court), s. 106, p. 37, Rabi' II 1154 H./1741 A.D.

90. Mahkamat Dimashq, s. 106, pp. 230–231, 19 Dhu al-qa'da 1154 H./1742 A.D.; s. 106, pp. 293–294, 17 Muharram 1155 H./1742 A.D.

91. Mahkamat Dimashq, s. 106, p. 314, 18 Muharram 1155 H./1742 A.D.; Mahkamat al-Quds, s. 226, p. 54, 17 Dhu al-hijjah 1145 H./1732 A.D.

92. Mahkmat Nablus, s. 4, p. 299, beginning of Rabi' I 1138 H./1725 A.D.

93. Mahkamat al-Quds, s. 226, p. 185 (17 Rajab 1146 H./1733 A.D.). See also Mahkamat Dimashq, s. 106, p. 215 (17 Dhu al-qa'da 1154 H./1742 A.D.); Mahkamat Nablus, s. 4, p. 34 (18 Safar 1136 H./1723 A.D.), s. 4, p. 237 (27 Shawwal 1137 H./1724 A.D.), s. 4, p. 299 (beginning of Rajab 1138 H./1725 A.D.), s. 4, p. 254 (13 Dhu al-hijjah 1138 H./1726 A.D.), s. 4, p. 307 (2 Muharram 1138 H./1725 A.D.); and Mahkamat al-Quds, s. 226, p. 41 (12 Dhu al-qa'da 1145 H./1732 A.D.).

94. See Mahkamat Dimashq, s. 106, p. 82 (20 Jumada II 1154 H./1741 A.D.), s. 106, p. 88 (11 Rajab 1154 H./1741 A.D.), s. 106, p. 172 (18 Jumada I 1154 H./1741 A.D.); Mahkamat Nablus, s. 5, p. 140 (end of Safr 1142 H./1729 A.D.); Mahkamat al-Quds, s. 226, p. 160 (14 Jumada II 1146 H./1733 A.D.), s. 230, p. 59 (15 Ramadan 1152 H./1739 A.D.), s. 230, p. 141 (3 Rajab 1153 H./1740 A.D.), s. 231, p. 11 (17 Safr 1154 H./1741 A.D.).

NOTES TO CHAPTER 3:
RELEASE HER WITH KINDNESS: DIVORCE

1. Khayr al-Din ibn Ahmad al-Ramli, *Kitab al-fatawa al-kubra li-naf' al-birriya*, Cairo, Bulaq: n.p., 1273 H./1856–57 A.D., vol. 1, p. 67.

2. Khayr al-Din, vol. 1, p. 34; al-'Imadi, as edited by Ibn 'Abidin, *al-'Uqud al-durriya*, Cairo, Bulaq: n.p., 1300 H./1882–83 A.D., vol. 1, p. 30.

3. See Linant de Bellefonds, *Traité de droit musulman comparé*, Paris: Mouton, 1965, vol. 2, pp. 310, 451, 465–467.

4. al-'Imadi, vol. 1, pp. 56–57.

5. Khayr al-Din, vol. 1, p. 23; al-'Imadi, vol. 1, p. 19.

6. Khayr al-Din, vol. 1, pp. 22–23; al-'Imadi, vol. 1, pp. 17, 32.

7. Khayr al-Din, vol. 1, p. 49.

8. 'Abd al-Fattah al-Tamimi, *Fatawa*, ms. copy from Maktabat Masjid al-Hajj Nimr al-Nabulsi: n.p., n.d., p. 8; al-'Imadi, vol. 1, p. 32.

9. Khayr al-Din, vol. 1, pp. 20, 67; al-'Imadi, vol. 1, pp. 29–30, 31, 55.

10. There are examples of this kind of *faskh* in the Mahkamat Dimashq (Damascus Islamic Court), s. 106, on pp. 9, 43, 105–106, 124, 165, 188, 259, 260, 275, 300, 317, 322, 323–324; in the Mahkamat al-Quds (Jerusalem Islamic Court) s. 230, on pp. 50 and 90; in the Mahkamat Nablus (Nablus Islamic Court), s. 4, on pp. 67, 95, 98, 127, 209, 218, and #5, on pp. 11, 19, 103, 142.

11. Mahkamat Dimashq, s. 106, p. 124.

12. Mahkamat al-Quds, s. 230, p. 90.

13. Mahkamat Nablus, s. 5, p. 105.

14. al-'Imadi, vol. 1, pp. 44–45.

15. Khayr al-Din, vol. 1, p. 34. For an expanded discussion of the legal interdiction of the insane under Islamic law, see Michael W. Dols, *Majnun: The Madman in Medieval Islamic Society*, Oxford: Clarendon Press, 1992, 434–455.

16. al-'Imadi, vol. 1, p. 42.

17. Ibid., p. 39.

18. Mahkamat Nablus, s. 4, p. 256.

19. al-'Imadi, vol. 1, p. 36.

20. Ibid., p. 32.

21. Khayr al-Din, vol. 1, pp. 69–70,

22. See, for example, al-'Imadi, vol. 1, p. 55.

23. Mahkamat al-Quds, s. 226, p. 156.

24. See chapter 2 for a discussion of *mahr.*

25. al-'Imadi, vol. 1, pp. 25, 44.

26. Ibid., pp. 23, 26.

27. Khayr al-Din, vol. 1, p. 36; al-'Imadi, vol. 1, p. 305.

28. Khayr al-Din, vol. 1, p. 65; al-'Imadi, vol. 1, p. 57.

29. Mahkamat Dimashq, s. 106, p. 68.

30. Typical registrations of *talaq* and the payment of connected obligations include Mahkamat Dimashq, s. 106, pp. 68, 71, 100, 101, 199, 314. Mahkamat al-Quds, s. 226, p. 71, records the *talaq* of a Jewish woman by her Jewish husband, and her receipt of the balance of her dower.

31. Mahkamat Dimashq, s. 106, p. 287; ibid., p. 37, records a similar case.

32. Ibid., pp. 262, 263; Mahkamat al-Quds, s. 230, p. 4.

33. Mahkamat Dimashq, s. 106, pp. 93–94, 230–231, 293–294; Mahkamat al-Quds, s. 230, p. 85.

34. Mahkamat Dimashq, s. 106, pp. 200–201.

35. al-ʿImadi, vol. 1, p. 53.

36. Ibid., p. 52.

37. Ibid., p. 54. See Susan A. Spectorsky, *Chapters on Marriage and Divorce: Responses of Ibn Hanbal and Ibn Rahwayh*, Austin: University of Texas Press, 1993, pp. 50–51, for discussion of the somewhat different Hanbali view of *khulʿ* and *faskh*.

38. Khayr al-Din, vol. 1, p. 54.

39. al-ʿImadi, vol. 1, p. 52.

40. Ibid., p. 30.

41. Ibid., pp. 53–54.

42. Mahkamat al-Quds, s. 230, p. 48.

43. This kind of identification procedure appears to be distinct from the normal process of identification of witnesses and testimony to their character. The special identification of veiled women was a common practice in the Jerusalem court, where many of the women present were veiled and needed testimony to their identities. Such was not the practice in the Damascus and Nablus courts, where most women in court appear to have been identified by sight alone. It may well be that the less-affluent women, who were the ones who came to court in person in any case, did not veil in the courts of Damascus and Nablus, unlike those who sought rulings in the more conservative Jerusalem.

44. Examples of such agreements include: Mahkamat Dimashq, s. 106, pp. 30, 239, 299; Mahkamat Nablus, s. 4, p. 65.

45. Examples of this kind of agreement include Mahkamat Dimashq, s. 106, pp. 18, 53, 63–64, 89, 142, 174, 180, 186, 240; and Mahkamat Nablus, s. 4, pp. 14, 85.

46. Mahkamat Dimashq, s. 106, pp. 180, 249, 285.

47. Mahkamat Nablus, s. 5, pp. 132, 141, 160.

48. Mahkamat Dimashq, s. 106, p. 19.

49. Ibid., p. 235.

50. Ibid., pp. 236–237.

51. Ibid., pp. 130–131.

52. al-ʿImadi, vol. 1, p. 47.

53. Khayr al-Din, vol. 1, pp. 77–78; al-ʿImadi, vol. 1, p. 38.

54. al-ʿImadi, vol. 1, p. 40.

55. Khayr al-Din, vol. 1, pp. 76, 78

56. Mahkamat Dimashq, s. 106, pp. 161, 184.

57. Khayr al-Din, vol. 1, pp. 41–42.

58. Ibid., pp. 46, 42. al-Tamimi discussed a similar case in which the husband took an oath of divorce to take effect if he failed to move his wife from her father's house into a marital domicile: al-Tamimi, p. 12.

59. Khayr al-Din, vol. 1, p. 36; al-ʿImadi, vol. 1, pp. 37, 38, 46.

60. Khayr al-Din, vol. 1, p. 42.

61. Mahkamat Dimashq, s. 106, p. 203.

62. There are many examples of this kind of oath: Khayr al-Din, vol. 1, pp. 75–80; al-ʿImadi, vol. 1, pp. 36–43; al-Tamimi, pp. 10–13.

63. Khayr al-Din, vol. 1, p. 39. This fatwa refers to the practices of the soap industry in eighteenth-century Palestine. Oil merchants would place their oil with soap manufacturers for "cooking" into soap, and would pay for this service. See Beshara Doumani, *Rediscovering Palestine: Merchants and Peasants in Jabal Nablus, 1700–1900*, Berkeley: University of California Press, 1995, chap. 5.

64. al-ʿImadi, vol. 1, pp. 36, 40, 43.

65. Khayr al-Din, vol. 1, pp. 45–46.

66. Ibid., p. 134. There is a second fatwa in response to a very similar case in Khayr al-Din, vol. 2, p. 134.

NOTES TO CHAPTER 4:
THE FULLNESS OF AFFECTION:
MOTHERING AND FATHERING

1. al-ʿImadi, as edited by Ibn ʿAbidin, *al-ʿUqud al-durriya*, Cairo, Bulaq: n.p., 1300 H./1882–83 A.D., vol. 1, p. 61.

2. It is, of course, important to remember that as "natural" as some of the roles of mother and father may appear to us, they are by no means universal. Motherhood and fatherhood, just like woman and man, have been very differently constructed in different cultures. See a good summary discussion on this point in Henrietta L. Moore, *Feminism and Anthropology*, Minneapolis: University of Minnesota Press, 1988, pp. 25–30.

3. In this context, Western feminist theory on mothering in capitalist society, in which the public/private split and the location of motherhood and its

related power in a private sphere are central, may serve better as a framework for comparison than as a theoretical guide. See Elizabeth Fox-Genovese, *Feminism without Illusions: A Critique of Individualism*, Chapel Hill: University of North Carolina Press, 1991, pp. 26–28, for a summary discussion of Western feminist approaches to mothering.

4. al-ʿImadi, vol. 2, p. 300.

5. Khayr al-Din ibn Ahmad al-Ramli, *Kitab al-fatawa al-kubra li-nafʿ al-birriya*, Cairo, Bulaq: n.p., 1273 H./1856–57 A.D., vol. 2, p. 179; al-ʿImadi, vol. 2, pp. 249, 253.

6. Khayr al-Din, vol. 1, p. 13.

7. Ibid., p. 61.

8. Ibid., p. 61; al-ʿImadi, vol. 1, p. 63.

9. al-ʿImadi, vol. 1, p. 61; al-Tamimi, *Fatawa*, ms. copy from Maktabat Masjid al-Hajj Nimr al-Nabulsi: n.p., n.d., p. 9.

10. Khayr al-Din, vol. 1, pp. 60–61.

11. Ibid., pp. 29–30.

12. Ibid., p. 61.

13. See chapter 2 for a discussion of the parameters of this choice.

14. Khayr al-Din, vol. 1, p. 62.

15. Ibid., p. 59.

16. Ibid., pp. 59–60; al-ʿImadi, vol. 1, p. 65. This distinction between physical and mental maturity sounds very much like the concept of *rushd*, the state of mental maturity discussed by Shafiʿi jurists: see Brinkley Messick, *The Calligraphic State: Textual Domination and History in a Muslim Society*, Berkeley: University of California Press, 1993, pp. 77–79. The Hanafi muftis under discussion here did not use this term, although the conceptual distinction they make between physical and mental maturity appears to be quite similar.

17. Khayr al-Din, vol. 1, p. 60.

18. Ibid., pp. 60–61.

19. Khayr al-Din, vol. 2, p. 176; al-ʿImadi, vol. 2, p. 253.

20. Mahkamat Dimashq (Damascus Islamic Court), s. 106, p. 42. Other cases of miscarriage claims include: Mahkamat Dimashq, s. 106, pp. 19, 110; Mahkamat al-Quds (Jerusalem Islamic Court), s. 226, pp. 71, 143, 228.

21. al-ʿImadi, vol. 2, p. 242.

22. al-ʿImadi, vol. 1, p. 332.

23. Khayr al-Din, vol. 1, pp. 33, 62.

24. Mahkamat Dimashq, s. 106, p. 169.

25. Khayr al-Din, vol. 1, pp. 59, 61. It is interesting to note that fatwas from Ibn 'Abidin's edition of al-'Imadi's collection were still being cited in Sudanese courts as recently as 1980, in support of a mother's custody; see Carolyn Fleur-Lobban, "Issues in the *Shari'a* Child Custody Law of the Sudan," *Northeast African Studies* 4, no. 2 (1982), 5.

26. Khayr al-Din, vol. 1, p. 61.

27. al-'Imadi, vol. 1, pp. 60–61.

28. Ibid., p. 63.

29. Khayr al-Din, vol. 1, pp. 59–60; al-'Imadi, vol. 1, p. 60.

30. Khayr al-Din, vol. 1, pp. 59, 60; al-'Imadi, vol. 1, pp. 58–59, 60, 63.

31. Khayr al-Din, vol. 1, p. 59.

32. al-'Imadi, vol. 1, p. 332.

33. Khayr al-Din, vol. 1, pp. 54–55.

34. al-'Imadi, vol. 1, p. 52.

35. Khayr al-Din, vol. 2, pp. 177–178.

36. al-'Imadi, vol. 1, p. 63.

37. Ibid., pp. 60, 63–64; al-Tamimi, p. 7.

38. Khayr al-Din, vol. 1, p. 59.

39. al-'Imadi, vol. 1, p. 61.

40. Ibid., p. 58.

41. Ibid., p. 61.

42. Ibid., p. 61.

43. Ibid., p. 58.

44. Mahkamat Dimashq, s. 106, p. 247; ibid., p. 33.

45. Ibid., p. 112.

46. Mahkamat al-Quds, s. 230, p. 12.

47. Examples of support-assignment cases, in which women requested and received support from ex-husbands, include: Mahkamat Dimashq, s. 106, pp. 27, 49, 56, 106, 169, 193, 234, 288, 323; Mahkamat Nablus (Nablus Islamic Court), s. 4, p. 82; Mahkamat al-Quds, s. 230, pp. 12, 224.

48. Mahkamat Dimashq, s. 106, pp. 126–127.

49. Ibid., p. 120.

50. Ibid., p. 66.

51. Mahkamat al-Quds, s. 230, p. 224.

52. Examples of support awards to children in a widow's care include: Mahkamat Dimashq, s. 106, p. 49; Mahkamat Nablus, s. 4, p. 291, s. 5, pp. 29, 93; Mahkamat al-Quds, s. 230, pp. 40, 64, 203, 220, 224, 285.

53. Mahkamat Nablus, s. 5, pp. 62–63.

54. Mahkamat al-Quds, s. 230, p. 205.

55. al-'Imadi, vol. 1, p. 60.

56. Ibid., p. 79.

57. Ibid., pp. 58–59.

58. Ibid., pp. 69, 72, 77.

59. Ibid., p. 65.

60. Khayr al-Din, vol. 1, p. 66; al-'Imadi, vol. 1, pp. 66, 81.

61. al-'Imadi, vol. 1, p. 69.

62. Ibid., p. 70.

63. Khayr al-Din, vol. 1, pp. 65, 66; al-'Imadi, vol. 1, pp. 66–70.

64. The muftis usually employed the term *wali* when discussing guardianship for the purposes of marriage arrangements; *wasi* was the term most often employed in the context of guardianship for all the other affairs of a minor. Sometimes, however, the terms seem to have been used interchangeably.

65. Khayr al-Din, vol. 2, p. 304; al-'Imadi, vol. 2, pp. 290, 294, 295, 299.

66. al-'Imadi, vol. 2, p. 289.

67. Ibid., p. 304.

68. Khayr al-Din, vol. 1, p. 61; al-'Imadi makes a similar point about how boys need to be "civilized" and "educated" by men.

69. Khayr al-Din, vol. 1, pp. 60–61; al-'Imadi, vol. 1, p. 65.

70. al-'Imadi, vol. 1, p. 64.

71. Khayr al-Din, vol. 1, pp. 59–60; al-'Imadi, vol. 1, p. 65.

72. Khayr al-Din, vol. 1, p. 62.

73. Examples of male paternal guardians seeking support awards include: Mahkamat al-Quds, s. 226, pp. 17, 41, 209, and s. 230, p. 247; Mahkamat Nablus, s. 4, p. 99, and s. 5, p. 171.

74. al-'Imadi, vol. 2, pp. 292, 294.

75. Khayr al-Din, vol. 1, p. 23.

76. al-'Imadi, vol. 2, pp. 289–291.

77. Ibid., p. 305.

78. Ibid., p. 305.

79. Ibid., p. 308.

80. Ibid., p. 305.

81. Ibid., pp. 292–293.

82. Mahkamat al-Quds, s. 226, p. 95. In her study of the Aleppo Islamic court in the late eighteenth and early nineteenth centuries, Margaret Meriwether also

encountered the phenomenon of the mother-guardian. Indeed, Meriwether asserts that in the event of the death of a father, the mother was chosen as often as not to be her child's legal guardian. Margaret L. Meriwether, "The Rights of Children and the Responsibilities of Women: Women as *Wasis* in Ottoman Aleppo," in A. Sonbol, ed., *Women, the Family and Divorce Laws in Islamic History*, Syracuse, N.Y.: Syracuse University Press, 1996, pp. 219–235.

83. Other examples of mother-guardian cases include: Mahkamat al-Quds, s. 226, p. 127, and s. 230, pp. 205, 245.

NOTES TO CHAPTER 5:
IF SHE WERE READY FOR MEN:
SEXUALITY AND REPRODUCTION

1. Khayr al-Din ibn Ahmad al-Ramli, *Kitab al-fatawa al-kubra li-naf* ʿ *al-birriya*, Cairo, Bulaq: n.p., 1273 H./1856–57 A.D., vol. 1, pp. 29–30.

2. Gayle S. Rubin, "Thinking Sex: Notes for a Radical Theory of the Politics of Sexuality," in L. Kauffman, ed., *American Feminist Thought at Century's End: A Reader*, Cambridge, Mass.: Blackwell, 1993, p. 12.

3. Michel Foucault, *The History of Sexuality*, New York: Pantheon, 1978.

4. Jeffrey Weeks, *Sexuality and Its Discontents*, London: Routledge and Kegan Paul, 1985, p. 6; for expanded investigations of these arguments, see Weeks, *Coming Out: Homosexual Politics in Britain from the Nineteenth Century to the Present*, London: Quartet Books, 1977, and Weeks, *Sex, Politics and Society: The Regulation of Homosexuality Since 1800*, London: Longman, 1981.

5. From a legal point of view, a child born outside the bounds of legal marriage or licit concubinage would lack a *nasab*, or lineage, the key to social identity as well as all the rights and obligations of membership in a family. Coulson noted that such a person would be born, and live, as an outlaw; their very presence would undermine the foundations of the Islamic legal view of family as the basis of social relations. See Noel Coulson, "Regulation of Sexual Behavior under Traditional Islamic Law," in Afaf Lutfi al-Sayyid-Marsot, ed., *Society and the Sexes in Medieval Islam*, Malibu, Calif.: Undena, 1979, pp. 67–68.

6. al-ʿImadi, as edited by Ibn ʿAbidin, *al-ʿUqud al-durriya*, Cairo, Bulaq: n.p., 1300H./1882–83 A.D., vol. 1, p. 16.

7. Indeed, polygyny was reserved, by and large, for an economic elite who could afford the expenses of multiple wives. For a discussion of polygyny as a class phenomenon in eighteenth- and nineteenth-century Nablus, see Judith

Tucker, "Marriage and Family in Nablus, 1720–1856: Toward a History of Arab Marriage," *Journal of Family History* 13, no. 2 (1988), 165–179.

8. al-'Imadi, vol. 2, pp. 321–322.

9. al-'Imadi, vol. 1, pp. 84, 342; vol. 2, p. 288.

10. Ahmad al-Husari, *al-Nikah wa al-qadaya al-muta'alliqa bih*, Beirut: Dar Ibn Zaydun, 1986, p. 71. The *mahram* relations are, for a man, his "female ascendants and descendants, the (former) wives of one's ascendants and descendants, one's sister and the female descendants of one's sister and brother, one's paternal and maternal aunts and the sisters and aunts of the ascendants, one's mother-in-law and the other female ascendants of one's wife, and one's stepdaughter and the other female descendants of one's wife," as summarized in Joseph Schacht, *An Introduction to Islamic Law*, Oxford: Clarendon Press, 1964, p. 162.

11. al-'Imadi, vol. 1, p. 56.

12. Ibid., p. 25.

13. Khayr al-Din, vol. 1, p. 60.

14. Everett K. Rowson, "The Categorization of Gender and Sexual Irregularity in Medieval Arabic Vice Lists," in J. Epstein and K. Straub, eds., *Body Guards: The Cultural Politics of Gender Ambiguity*, New York: Routledge, 1991, pp. 61–62. See Rowson for valuable information on medieval literature and sexuality in general.

15. Khayr al-Din, vol. 1, pp. 50–51.

16. Of the some 60 marriage contracts registered in the extant court records of eighteenth-century Nablus, for example, not one names a groom in his legal minority, that is, prepubescent. Mahkamat Nablus (Nablus Islamic Court), s. 3 and s. 4.

17. Khayr al-Din, vol. 1, p. 30.

18. al-'Imadi, vol. 1, p. 63.

19. Khayr al-Din, vol. 1, pp. 29–30; similar approaches to the assessment of a girl's readiness for intercourse were used in other fatwas, including Khayr al-Din, vol. 1, pp. 29, 31; and al-'Imadi, vol. 1, p. 28.

20. al-'Imadi, vol. 2, p. 321.

21. Khayr al-Din, vol. 1, p. 84.

22. al-'Imadi, vol. 1, p. 65.

23. Khayr al-Din, vol. 1, p. 35.

24. al-'Imadi, vol. 1, pp. 317, 338.

25. Khayr al-Din, vol. 1, pp. 13–14.

26. See Schacht, *Introduction*, pp. 173–178.

27. Khayr al-Din, vol. 1, p. 80.

28. Amira Sonbol notes that, in addition to *hudud* punishments, compensation was also commonly required in rape cases in seventeenth- and eighteenth-century Egypt. Amira El Azhary Sonbol, "Law and Gender Violence in Ottoman and Modern Egypt," in Sonbol, ed., *Women, the Family and Divorce Laws in Islamic History*, pp. 286–287.

29. See Colin Imber, *"Zina'* in Ottoman Law," in Jean-Louis Bacque-Grammont and Paul Dumont, eds., *Contributions à l'histoire économique et sociale de l'Empire ottoman*, Paris: Editions Peeters, 1983, pp. 61–62.

30. Khayr al-Din, vol. 1, p. 80 (three cases of this kind); al-'Imadi, vol. 1, p. 26.

31. Uriel Heyd, *Studies in Old Ottoman Criminal Law*, ed. V. L. Menage, Oxford: Clarendon Press, 1973, p. 151.

32. Heyd, *Studies*, p. 155.

33. Khayr al-Din, vol. 1, p. 83.

34. See Schacht, *Introduction*, pp. 191–192.

35. Mahkamat al-Dimashq (Damascus Islamic Court), s. 106, p. 28.

36. Heyd, *Studies*, p. 96.

37. 'Abd al-Fattah al-Tamimi, *Fatawa*, ms. copy from Maktabat Masjid al-Hajj Nimr al-Nabulsi, Nablus: n.p.; n.d., p. 16.

38. Khayr al-Din, vol. 1, p. 80.

39. al-Tamimi, pp. 15–16.

40. Khayr al-Din, vol. 1, pp. 26–27. There is a similar case on p. 26.

41. al-'Imadi, vol. 1, p. 31; al-Tamimi, p. 7.

42. al-Tamimi, p. 15.

43. Abdelwahab Bouhdiba cites the inability to recognize as legitimate any child born of illicit intercourse and the ban on the adoption of this or any other child as underscoring the seriousness of *zina'* as an offense striking at the heart of the Muslim view of social relations. See Abdelwahab Bouhdiba, *Sexuality in Islam*, translated from the French by A. Sheridan, London: Routledge & Kegan Paul, 1985, p. 17.

44. al-'Imadi, vol. 1, p. 83.

45. Ibid., pp. 57–58.

46. Ibid., p. 57.

47. Ibid., pp. 83–84.

48. Ibid., p. 31.

49. Ibid., p. 57.

50. Ibid., p. 84.

51. Ibid., pp. 33, 58.

52. Khayr al-Din, vol. 1, p. 58.

53. al-Tamimi, pp. 14, 16.

54. Ibid., p. 16.

55. al-'Imadi, vol. 1, pp. 83–84.

56. Ibid., p. 83.

57. al-Tamimi, p. 16.

58. Ibid., p. 16.

59. al-'Imadi, vol. 1, p. 83.

60. Abdul-Karim Rafeq, "Public Morality in 18th Century Ottoman Damascus, *Revue du Monde Musulman et de la Méditerranée* 55/56 (1990), 181–183.

NOTE TO CONCLUSION

1. For critical discussions of law and gender issues that deal with questions of the autonomy of the law, the absence of determinant meaning, and embeddedness of law in social structure, see Martha Minow, "Partial Justice: Law and Minorities," in A. Serat and T. Kearns, eds., *The Fate of Law*, Ann Arbor: University of Michigan Press, 1991, pp. 15–77; and Ursula Vogel, "Under Permanent Guardianship: Women's Condition under Modern Civil Law," in K. Jones and A. Jonesdottir, *The Political Interests of Gender: Developing Theory and Research with a Feminist Face*, London: Sage, 1988, pp. 135–159.

GLOSSARY OF THE MOST
FREQUENTLY USED ARABIC WORDS

Afandi: a title of respect.

'Aqil(m.), *'aqila*(f.): rational; in full possession of the mental faculties.

'Aqila: agnatic relatives; the relatives of a murderer who are liable for blood money (*diya*).

'Aura: lit. pudendum, genitals; that which is sexually stimulating.

Baligh: see *bulugh*.

Batil: null and void, said of a marriage.

Bin (abbrev. *b.*): son

Bint (abbrev. *bt.*): girl; daughter.

Bulugh (n.), *baligh* (adj.): the state of sexual maturity that in Hanafi law also marks legal majority.

Damm: tutelage.

Dhahab bunduqi: Venetian sequin.

Dhimmi: a free non-Muslim subject living in a Muslim country.

Dirham: dirhem, a coin.

Diya: financial compensation for wounds or loss of life; blood money for voluntary or involuntary homicide, which the perpetrator can be required to pay to the relative of the victim as satisfaction.

Faqih, pl. *fuqaha'*: a jurisprudent or legal thinker.

Faskh (n.), *fasakha* (v.): annulment of the marriage contract.

Fatwa, Arabic pl. *fatawa*; anglicized pl. (as used in this book) *fatwas*: a legal opinion, usually delivered by a mufti, that pronounces on specific points, but not necessarily a specific situation, often as a result of a petition or inquiry; cf. *shuruh*.

Fiqh: Islamic jurisprudence; a system or body of law.

Fuqaha': see *faqih*.

Gharra: financial compensation paid for inflicting injury that results in the death of a fetus through miscarriage.

Ghulam: boy, youth.

Ghurush: a unit of money; piaster.

H.: see *hijri*.

Hadd, pl. *hudud*: a fixed penalty, prescribed Islamic punishment; cf. *ta'zir*.

Hadith: the traditions of the Prophet Muhammad; cf. *sunna*.

Hajj: the pilgrimage to Mecca; a male who has made the pilgrimage.

Hajja: a female who has made the pilgrimage.

Hidana: the care and custody of children.

Hijri (abbrev. *H.*): denoting the Muslim era (calendar) when used after a date.

Hudud: see *hadd*.

Hurma: a title for a lower-class woman; cf. *khatun*, *sitt*.

'Idda: a legally prescribed period of waiting during which a woman may not remarry after being widowed or divorced, and during which her former husband or his estate must continue to support her.

Ijtihad: interpretation of the law; independent scholarly reasoning on legal issues on the basis of the Qur'an and the *sunna*.

Iltizam: a tax farm.

Jihaz: the bride's trousseau, given her (not her husband) by her family.

Kafa'a: the legal concept of the mutual suitability of spouses.

Kanun (Ottoman Turkish): the Ottoman legal codes, collectively.

Khalwa: a period of privacy, perhaps quite brief, shared by a man and a woman, usually assumed to include intercourse.

Khatun: a title for an upper-class woman; cf. *hurma, sitt.*

Khulʿ: divorce at the instance of the wife, who must pay a compensation or otherwise negotiate an agreement acceptable to her husband.

Madhhab: a school of Islamic law.

Mahkama: an Islamic court or tribunal.

Mahr: the dower; the gift or collection of gifts given to the bride by the husband, without which the marriage is not valid; cf. *mu'akhkhar, muqaddam.*

Mahram: unmarriageable; being in a degree of consanguinity precluding marriage.

Mu'akhkhar: that part of the *mahr* (dower) to be paid at the time of termination of the marriage; the deferred dower; cf. *muqaddam.*

Mufti: a jurisconsult; a learned man empowered to deliver formal legal opinions (*fatwas*).

Muhsan: a person who has already consummated a marriage and then has unlawful sexual intercourse with someone else; a free person who has never been found guilty of unlawful intercourse.

Muqaddam: that part of the *mahr* (dower) to be paid at the time of the signing of a marriage contract; the prompt dower; cf. *mu'akhkhar.*

Murahiq: adolescent; a child on the verge of puberty.

Mutasallim: the Ottoman governor's deputy.

Mutun: the textbooks that sum up the doctrine of a legal school.

Nafaqa: legally required material maintenance and support based on bonds of kinship.

Nahiya: a subdistrict of a *sanjaq.*

Na'ib: deputy; assistant.

Nasab: lineage.

Nashiza: recalcitrant or disobedient, used to characterize such behavior on the part of a wife.

Nushuz: the state of disobedience of a wife, following which the husband is not bound to maintain her.

Qadhf: calumny; false accusation of fornication.

Qadi: a judge in an Islamic court.

Qadi al-qudah: the judge of judges; the chief *qadi* of a district.

Qadi ʿaskar: the highest-ranking judge in the Ottoman Empire.

Qitaʿ misriyya: unit of currency; Egyptian coins.

Ratl: rotl, a unit of weight.

Sabih: a pretty, comely male youth.

Sanjaq: an administrative district in the Ottoman Empire.

Sayyid (m.), *sayyida* (f.): title of one of Muhammad's direct descendants, used most often for middle-class people.

Shariʿa: the revealed or canonical law of Islam.

Shaykh: an honorific title denoting any of several possible roles in society.

Shubha: judicial doubt.

Shuruh: a legal commentary related to a specific situation or problem; cf. *fatwa*.

Sijill: a bound record of court transactions.

Sitt: a title for an upper-class woman; cf. *hurma*, *khatun*.

Sunna: the sayings and doings of the Prophet Muhammad, later established as legally binding precedents (in addition to the law established by the Qur'an); cf. *hadith*.

Talaq (n.), *tallaqa* (v.): divorce of a wife by "repudiation"; the pronouncing of a formula of divorce by a husband resulting in a legally binding dissolution of a marriage.

Taqlid: imitation; the acceptance and application (by, for example, a *qadi*) of the doctrines of established schools and jurists.

Taʿzir: discretionary punishment, in contrast to *hadd* (fixed punishment).

Timar (Ottoman Turkish): a land grant.

Ujra: the wage paid to the caretaker of a young child.

'*Ulama*': the jurist-theologians of Islam, collectively.

Umm walad: literally, the mother of a child; a slave woman who has become pregnant with a child recognized by her master.

Usul al-fiqh: the roots or basic principles of Islamic law.

Wakil: legal agent for another person.

Wali: the legal guardian of a minor, particularly for the purposes of marriage arrangement; cf. *wilaya.*

Waqf: a religious endowment; private property entailed for religious or charitable purposes.

Wasi: the executor or guardian of a minor's property following the death of his or her natural guardian.

Wasi mukhtar: a guardian who has been chosen by the natural guardian, usually the father, to replace him if and when he should die.

Wilaya: guardianship; cf. *wali.*

Zina': unlawful sexual intercourse; fornication; adultery.

BIBLIOGRAPHY

All works cited in the text and the notes, as well as several others, are given here.

COURT RECORDS

Mahkamat Dimashq (Damascus Islamic Court), sijill #106, 1154–55 H./1741–43 A.D.; #220, 1201–02 H./1786–88 A.D.

Mahkamat Nablus (Nablus Islamic Court), sijill #4, 1134–38 H./1722–26 A.D.; #5, 1139–1141 H./1728–29 A.D.

Mahkamat al-Quds (Jerusalem Islamic Court), sijill #226, 1145–46 H./1732–34 A.D.; #230, 1151–52 H./1738–40 A.D.

FATWA COLLECTIONS

al-'Imadi as edited by Ibn 'Abidin. *al-'Uqud al-durriya*, Cairo, Bulaq: n.p., 1300 H./1882–83 A.D.

Khayr al-Din ibn Ahmad al-Ramli. *Kitab al-fatawa al-kubra li naf ' al-birriya* (2 vols. in 1), Cairo, Bulaq: n.p., 1273 H./1856–57 A.D.

al-Tamimi, 'Abd al-Fattah. *Fatawa*, ms. copy from Maktabat Masjid al-Hajj Nimr al-Nabulsi, Nablus: n.p., n.d.

SECONDARY LITERATURE

'Abbas, Ihsan. "Hair ad-Din ar-Ramli's *Fatawa*: A New Light on Life in Palestine in the Eleventh/Seventeenth Century," in *Die Islamische Welt zwischen Mittelalter und Neuzeit: Festschrift für Hans Robert Roemer,* Beirut and Wiesbaden: Franz Steiner, 1979, pp. 1–19.

Abdel Nour, Antoine. *Introduction à l'histoire urbaine de la Syrie Ottomane XVIe–XVIIIe siècle,* Beyrouth: Librairie Orientale, 1982.

Ahmed, Leila. *Women and Gender in Islam: Historical Roots of a Modern Debate,* New Haven, Conn.: Yale University Press, 1992.

Anderson, J. N. D. *Law Reform in the Muslim World,* London: Athlone Press, 1976.

Baer, Gabriel. "Woman and Waqf: An Analysis of the Istanbul Tahrir of 1546," *Asian and African Studies* (Jerusalem) 17, nos. 1–3 (1983), 9–28.

Barbir, Karl. *Ottoman Rule in Damascus, 1708–1758,* Princeton, N.J.: Princeton University Press, 1980.

de Bellefonds, Linant. *Traité de droit musulman comparé,* Paris: Mouton, 1965.

Bouhdiba, Abdelwahab. *Sexuality in Islam* (translated from the French by Alan Sheridan), London: Routledge & Kegan Paul, 1985.

Bousquet, G. H., and Bercher, L. *Le statut personnel en droit musulman Hanéfite: Texte et traduction annotée du Muhtasar d'al-Quduri,* Tunis: Institut des hautes études de Tunis, n.d.

Cohen, Amnon. *Economic Life in Ottoman Jerusalem,* Cambridge: Cambridge University Press, 1989.

———. *Palestine in the 18th Century: Patterns of Government and Administration,* Jerusalem: Magnes Press, 1973.

Coulson, Noel. "Regulation of Sexual Behavior under Traditional Islamic Law," in A. L. al-Sayyid-Marsot, ed., *Society and the Sexes in Medieval Islam,* Malibu, Calif.: Undena, 1979, pp. 63–68.

al-Dabbagh, Mustafa Murad. *Biladna Filistin,* 3d ed., Hebron, West Bank: University Graduates Union, 1985.

Dols, Michael W. *Majnun: The Madman in Medieval Islamic Society,* Oxford: Clarendon Press, 1992.

Doumani, Beshara. *Rediscovering Palestine: Merchants and Peasants in Jabal Nablus, 1700–1900,* Berkeley: University of California Press, 1995.

Esfandiari, Haleh. "The Majles and Women's Issues in the Islamic Republic of Iran," in M. Afkhami and E. Friedl, eds., *In the Eye of the Storm: Women in Post-Revolutionary Iran*, Syracuse, N.Y.: Syracuse University Press, 1994, pp. 61–79.

Fay, Mary Ann. "Women and Households: Gender, Power and Culture in Eighteenth-Century Egypt," Ph.D. dissertation, Georgetown University, 1993.

Fleur-Lobban, Carolyn. "Issues in the *Sharia* Child Custody Law of the Sudan," *Northeast African Studies* 4, no. 2 (1982), 1–9.

Foucault, Michel. *The History of Sexuality*, New York: Pantheon, 1978.

Fox-Genovese, Elizabeth. *Feminism without Illusions: A Critique of Individualism*, Chapel Hill: University of North Carolina Press, 1991.

Gerber, Haim. *State, Society, and Law in Islam: Ottoman Law in Comparative Perspective*, Albany: State University of New York Press, 1994.

Ghazzal, Zouhair. "The Ethnology of Legal Discourses: A Textual Analysis of Two Shari'a Court Documents in Nineteenth-Century Beirut," an unpublished paper presented at the Joseph Schacht Conference on Theory and Practice of Islamic Law, Leiden and Amsterdam, October 6–10, 1994.

Hallaq, Wael B. "Ifta' and Ijtihad in Sunni Legal Theory," in M. Masud, B. Messick, and D. Powers, eds., *Islamic Legal Interpretation: Muftis and Their Fatwas*, Cambridge, Mass.: Harvard University Press, 1996, pp. 33–43.

———. "Murder in Cordoba: *Ijtihad, Ifta'* and the Evolution of Substantive Law in Medieval Islam," *Acta Orientalia* 55 (1994), 55–83.

———. "Was the Gate of Ijtihad Closed?" *International Journal of Middle East Studies* 16 (1984), 3–41.

Heyd, Uriel. *Studies in Old Ottoman Criminal Law* (ed. V. L. Menage), Oxford: Clarendon Press, 1973.

al-Husari, Ahmad. *al-Nikah wa al-qadaya al-muta'alliqa bih*, Beirut: Dar Ibn Zaydun, 1986.

Hussein, Aziza. "Recent Amendments to Egypt's Personal Status Law," in E. W. Fernea, ed., *Women and the Family in the Middle East: New Voices of Change*, Austin: University of Texas Press, 1985, pp. 229–232.

Hütteroth, Wolf-Dieter, and Abdulfattah Kamal. *Historical Geography of Palestine, Transjordan, and Southern Syria in the Late 16th Century*, Erlangen: Selbstverlag der Frankischen Geographischen Gesellschaft in Kommission bei Palm and Enke, 1977.

Imber, Colin. "*Zina*' in Ottoman Law," in J. L. Bacque and P. Dumont, eds., *Contributions à l'histoire économique et sociale de l'Empire ottoman*, Paris: Editions Peeters, 1985, pp. 59–92.

Jennings, Ronald C. "Women in the Early Seventeenth Century Ottoman Judicial Records: The Sharia Court of Anatolian Kayseri," *Journal of the Economic and Social History of the Orient* 18 (1975), 53–114.

Johansen, Baber. *The Islamic Law on Land Tax and Rent*, London: Croom, Helm, 1988.

———. "Legal Literature and the Problem of Change: The Case of Land Rent," in C. Mallat, ed., *Islam and Public Law*, London: Graham and Trotman, 1993, pp. 29–47.

Kennedy, Charles H. "Islamic Legal Reform and the Status of Women in Pakistan," *Journal of Islamic Studies* 2, no. 1 (1991), 44–55.

Malti-Douglas, Fadwa. *Woman's Body, Woman's Word: Gender and Discourse in Arabo-Islamic Writing*, Princeton, N.J.: Princeton University Press, 1991.

Marcus, Abraham. "Men, Women and Property: Dealers in Real Estate in 18th Century Aleppo," *Journal of the Economic and Social History of the Orient* 26, no. 2 (1983), 137–173.

———. *The Middle East on the Eve of Modernity: Aleppo in the Eighteenth Century*, New York: Columbia University Press, 1989.

Maron, Ya'akov. *L'obligation alimentaire entre époux en droit Musulman Hanéfite*, Paris: Bibliothèque de droit privée, 1971.

Masud, Khalid Masud. "Adab al-Mufti: The Muslim Understanding of Values, Characteristics, and Role of a Mufti," in B. Metcalf, ed., *Moral Conduct and Authority: The Place of Adab in South Asian Islam*, Berkeley: University of California Press, 1984, pp. 124–151.

Masud, Muhammad Khalid, Brinkley Messick, and David S. Powers. "Muftis, Fatwas, and Islamic Legal Interpretation," in M. Masud, B. Messick, and D. Powers, eds., *Islamic Legal Interpretation: Muftis and Their Fatwas*, Cambridge, Mass.: Harvard University Press, 1996, pp. 124–125.

Meriwether, Margaret. "The Rights of Children and the Responsibilities of Women: Women as *Wasis* in Ottoman Aleppo, 1770–1840," in A. Sonbol, ed., *Women, the Family and Divorce Laws in Islamic History*, Syracuse, N.Y.: Syracuse University Press, 1996, pp. 219–235.

———. "Women and Economic Change in Nineteenth-Century Syria: The Case of Aleppo," in J. Tucker, ed., *Arab Women: Old Boundaries, New Frontiers*, Bloomington: Indiana University Press, 1993, pp. 65–83.

Mernissi, Fatima. *The Veil and the Male Elite: A Feminist Interpretation of Women's Rights in Islam*, Reading, Mass.: Addison-Wesley, 1991.

Messick, Brinkley. *The Calligraphic State: Textual Domination and History in a Muslim Society*, Berkeley: University of California Press, 1993.

Minow, Martha. "Partial Justice: Law and Minorities," in A. Serat and T. Kearns, eds., *The Fate of Law*, Ann Arbor: University of Michigan Press, 1991, pp. 15–77.

Moore, Henrietta L. *Feminism and Anthropology*, Minneapolis: University of Minnesota Press, 1988.

al-Muhibbi. *Khulasat al-athar fi a'yan al-qarn al-hadi 'ashr*, Cairo: n.p., 1284 H./1867–68 A.D., 4 vols.

Muradi, Khalil Muhammad. *Silk al-durar fi a'yan al-qarn al-thamin 'ashr*, Cairo, Bulaq, 1201 H./1786–87A.D.

Peirce, Leslie P. *The Imperial Harem: Women and Sovereignty in the Ottoman Empire*, New York: Oxford University Press, 1993.

Peters, Rudolph. "Idjtihad and Taqlid in 18th and 19th Century Islam," *Die Welt des Islams* 20, nos. 3–4 (1980), 131–145.

———. "The Islamization of Criminal Law: A Comparative Analysis," *Die Welt des Islams* 34 (1994), 246–274.

Rafeq, Abdul-Karim. *The Province of Damascus, 1723–1783*, Beirut: Khayats, 1966.

———. "Public Morality in 18th Century Ottoman Damascus," *Revue du Monde Musulman et de la Méditerranée* 55/56 (1990), 180–196.

Rahman, Fazlur. "A Survey of Modernization of Muslim Family Law," *International Journal of Middle East Studies* 11 (1980), 451–465.

Rowson, Everett K. "The Categorization of Gender and Sexual Irregularity in Medieval Arabic Vice Lists," in J. Epstein and K. Straub, eds., *Body Guards: The Cultural Politics of Gender Ambiguity*, New York: Routledge, 1991, pp. 50–79.

Rubin, Gayle S. "Thinking Sex: Notes for a Radical Theory of the Politics of Sexuality," in L. Kauffman, ed., *American Feminist Thought at Century's End: A Reader*, Cambridge, Mass.: Blackwell, 1993, pp. 3–64.

Schacht, Joseph. *An Introduction to Islamic Law*, Oxford: Clarendon Press, 1964.

Schilcher, Linda. *Families in Politics*, Stuttgart: Franz Steiner, 1985.

Scott, Joan. *Gender and the Politics of History*, New York: Columbia University Press, 1988.

Sonbol, Amira El Azhary. "Law and Gender Violence in Ottoman and Modern Egypt," in A. Sonbol, ed., *Women, the Family and Divorce Laws in Islamic History*, Syracuse, N.Y.: Syracuse University Press, 1996, pp. 277–289.

Spectorsky, Susan, A. *Chapters on Marriage and Divorce: Responses of Ibn Hanbal and Ibn Rahwayh*, Austin: University of Texas Press, 1993.

Stowasser, Barbara. "Women's Issues in Modern Islamic Thought," in J. Tucker, ed., *Arab Women: Old Boundaries, New Frontiers*, Bloomington: University of Indiana Press, 1993, pp. 14–20.

Tucker, Judith. "Marriage and Family in Nablus, 1720–1856: Toward a History of Arab Marriage," *Journal of Family History* 13, no. 2 (1988), 165–179.

Vogel, Ursula. "Under Permanent Guardianship: Women's Condition under Modern Civil Law," in K. Jones and A. Jonesdottir, eds., *The Political Interests of Gender: Developing Theory and Research with a Feminist Face*, London: Sage, 1988, pp. 135–159.

Voll, John. "Old 'Ulama Families and Ottoman Influence in Eighteenth-Century Damascus," *American Journal of Arabic Studies* 3 (1975), 48–59.

Weeks, Jeffrey. *Coming Out: Homosexual Politics in Britain from the Nineteenth Century to the Present*, London: Quartet Books, 1977.

———. *Sex, Politics and Society: The Regulation of Homosexuality Since 1800*, London: Longman, 1981.

———. *Sexuality and Its Discontents*, London: Routledge and Kegan Paul, 1985.

Ziadeh, Farhat J. "Equality (*kafa'ah*) in the Muslim Law of Marriage," *American Journal of Comparative Law* 6 (1957), 503–517.

INDEX

obedience of wives, 59, 63–65, 101–2
orphans, 40, 48, 125, 141
Ottoman criminal codes (kanun): concerning zina', 162–63, 164

parenthood: mothering, 121–135, 142–45, 145–47; fathering, 135–41, 145–47
paternity, and the regulation of reproduction, 150–51, 152, 167–75, 181
Peters, Rudolph, 12
polygyny, 151, 152. *See also* co-wives
prostitution, 175
Province of Damascus, 22–29

qadis (judges), 23, 25, 30; authorized to grant faskh (annulment), 79, 81, 82–86; can assign nafaqa (support), 42, 59–60; and elaboration of gender, 10; relationship with the muftis (jurisconsults), 20–22, 36, 76; role of, 17–19, 71; and sexuality issues, 156; 181. *See also* Islamic courts
Qur'anic punishment. *See* hadd

Rafeq, Abdul-Karim, 175
Rahman, Fazlur, 6
Ramla, 22–24, 28–29
al-Ramli, Khayr al-Din, 16; condemns domestic violence, 65–66; condemns outside interference in marriage, 203n66; condemns the practice of marriage by abduction, 68–69; on damm (tutelage) of youths, 121, 204n7; on divorce by oath, 103, 203n63; on establishing paternity, 210n52; on faskh (annulment), 47, 79, 82, 83–84, 85, 196n1, 200n1; on hidana (custody), 125, 127–28; on homosexuality, 153–55; on kafa'a (suitability), 42, 196n1; life of, 31–33; on marriage contracts, 38; on nafaqa (support), 43, 59–60, 61, 64, 78, 83–84, 85, 90; on pre-wedding gifts, 55; on rape, 160–61, 163;

on the religious identity of the fetus, 116–17; on the role of male guardians for boys, 119; on the sexual maturity of girls, 207n1; on sexual segregation, 157, 158–59; style and concerns of his fatwas, 16–17, 30; on talaq (divorce), 88–89, 90, 203n65; on an unmarried woman's right to choose her place of residence, 140; upholds women's rights to mahr (dower), 53–54; on virginity, 1–2, 67–68; on wifely obedience, 64; on the wife's waiving of ujra (child support) in khul' (divorce at the instance of the wife), 205n33; on wilaya (guardianship), 47, 48
rape, 44, 160–64
reproduction. *See* paternity

Schacht, Joseph, 11
seclusion (of women), 158, 181
segregation of the sexes, 156–59, 181
sexuality, 177–78; of children, 44, 118, 139, 148, 149, 155–56; concubinage, 151–2; in the courts, 175–77; female sexual desire, 151, 152–53, 155–56; homosexuality, 120–21, 149, 153–55, 159; impotence, 45, 81, 82; male sexual desire, 151–55; and marriage, 44–46, 81, 148–49; polygyny, 151, 152; prostitution, 175; and the regulation of reproduction (*see also under* paternity); sexual segregation and seclusion, 156–59, 181; zina' (unlawful sexual intercourse), 1, 159–67, 168, 172, 173–77, 181. *See also* rape; virginity
Shafi'i legal school, 31–32, 33; permits faskh, 78, 83–84, 86, 87, 103, 111, 180
shubha (judicial doubt), 160–62, 164, 167
sijills (court registers). *See under* Islamic courts

Designer: Barbara Jellow
Compositor: BookMasters, Inc.
Text: 10/15 Janson
Display: Janson